AF885574

Essential tables

INCOME TAX RATES

(*ITA 2007, Pt 2, Ch 2*)

Taxable income £	Rate %	Tax £	Cumulative £
2019/20			
Savings: 0–5,000	0	Nil	Nil
0–37,500	20	7,500.00	7,500.00
37,501–150,000	40	45,000.00	52,500.00
Over 150,000	45	–	–
2018/19			
Savings: 0–5,000	0	Nil	Nil
0–34,500	20	6,900.00	6,900.00
34,501–150,000	40	46,200.00	53,100.00
Over 150,000	45	–	–
2017/18			
Savings: 0–5,000	0	Nil	Nil
0–33,500	20	6,700.00	6,700.00
33,501–150,000	40	46,600.00	53,300.00
Over 150,000	45	–	–
2016/17			
Savings: 0–5,000	0	Nil	Nil
0–32,000	20	6,400.00	6,400.00
32,001–150,000	40	47,200.00	53,600.00
Over 150,000	45	–	–
2015/16			
Savings: 0–5,000	0	Nil	Nil
0–31,785	20	6,357.00	6,357.00
31,786–150,000	40	47,286.00	53,643.00
Over 150,000	45	–	–
2014/15			
Savings: 0–2,880	10	288.00	288.00
0–31,865	20	6,373.00	6,373.00
31,866–150,000	40	47,254.00	53,627.00
Over 150,000	45	–	–

continued

Taxable income £	Rate %	Tax £	Cumulative £
2013/14			
Savings: 0–2,790	10	279.00	279.00
0–32,010	20	6402.00	6,402.00
32,011–150,000	40	47,196.00	53,598.00
Over 150,000	45	–	–

See further **Personal Taxation**, p 1 and **Scottish Taxes** p 220.

PERSONAL ALLOWANCES AND RELIEFS

(*ITA 2007, Pt 3*)

	2019/20 £	2018/19 £	2017/18 £	2016/17 £	2015/16 £
Personal allowance					
Born after 5 April 1948	12,500	11,850	11,500	11,000	10,600
Income limit for personal allowance	100,000	100,000	100,000	100,000	100,000
Age-related allowances					
Born between 5 April 1938 and 6 April 1948	–	–	–	–	10,600
Born before 6 April 1938	–	–	–	–	10,660
Income limit for age-related allowances	29,600	28,900	28,000	27,700	27,700
Married allowances					
Marriage (born on/after 6 April 1935)	1,250	1,190	1,150	1,100	1,060
Minimum (born before 6 April 1935)	3,450	3,360	3,260	3,220	3,220
Maximum (born before 6 April 1935)	8,915	8,695	8,455	8,355	8,355
Blind person's allowance	2,450	2,390	2,320	2,290	2,290
Rent-a-room relief	7,500	7,500	7,500	7,500	4,250
Trading income	1,000	1,000	1,000	–	–
Property income	1,000	1,000	1,000	–	–
Savings allowance – basic rate	1,000	1,000	1,000	1,000	–
Savings allowance – higher rate	500	500	500	500	–

See further **Personal Taxation**, p 4.

CORPORATION TAX RATES

(*CTA 2010, Pt 2, Ch 2, 3*; *Pt 3*)

Year from 1 April	2020	2019	2018	2017	2016
Main rate	17%	19%	19%	19%	20%
Year from 1 April	**2015**	**2014**	**2013**	**2012**	**2011**
Main rate	20%	21%	23%	24%	26%
Small Profits Rate	–	20%	20%	20%	20%
Small Profits Rate can be claimed by qualifying companies with profits not exceeding	–	£300,000	£300,000	£300,000	£300,000
Marginal Relief Lower Limit	–	£300,000	£300,000	£300,000	£300,000
Marginal Relief Upper Limit	–	£1,500,000	£1,500,000	£1,500,000	£1,500,000
Standard fraction	–	1/400	3/400	2/200	3/200

See further **Taxation of Companies**, p 80.

CGT RATES AND ANNUAL EXEMPTIONS

(*TCGA 1992, ss 3, 4, Sch 1*)

Tax Year	Annual exempt amount		Tax rate paid by		
	Individuals, personal representatives (PRs) and trusts for disabled	General trusts	Individuals within:		Trustees and PRs
			Basic rate band	Higher tax bands	
	£	£	%	%	%
2019/20	12,000	6,000	10	20	20
residential property & carried interest			18	28	28
2018/19	11,700	5,850	10	20	20
residential property & carried interest			18	28	28
2017/18	11,300	5,650	10	20	20
residential property & carried interest			18	28	28
2016/17	11,100	5,550	10	20	20
residential property & carried interest			18	28	28
2015/16	11,100	5,550	18	28	28
2014/15	11,000	5,500	18	28	28
2013/14	10,900	5,450	18	28	28

See further **Capital Gains Tax**, p 94.

NIC RATES AND THRESHOLDS

NIC: Class 1 monthly thresholds

(SSCBA 1992, ss 5(1), 8, 19(4); SI 2001/1004, regs 10, 131; Pension Schemes Act 1993, ss 41, 42A; SI 2006/1009, art 3)

Employee (primary)	2019/20 £	2018/19 £	2017/18 £	2016/17 £	2015/16 £	2014/15 £
Lower earnings limit (LEL)	512	503	490	486	486	481
Primary threshold (PT)	720	702	680	672	672	663
Upper accrual point (UAP)	N/A	N/A	N/A	N/A	3,337	3,337
Upper earnings limit (UEL) and Upper secondary threshold (UST)	4,167	3,863	3,750	3,583	3,532	3,489
Employer (secondary threshold)	720	702	680	676	676	663

See further **National Insurance Contributions**, p 170.

NIC: Class 2 rates and exception

(SSCBA 1992, ss 11(1), (4), 117(1); SI 2001/1004, regs 46(a), 125(c), 152(b))

Tax year	Flat rate per week	Share fishermen per week	Volunteer development workers per week	Small earnings exception/profit threshold
	£	£	£	£
2019/20	3.00	3.65	5.90	6,365
2018/19	2.95	3.60	5.80	6,205
2017/18	2.85	3.50	5.65	6,025
2016/17	2.80	3.45	5.60	5,965
2015/16	2.80	3.45	5.60	5,965
2014/15	2.75	3.40	5.55	5,885
2013/14	2.70	3.35	5.45	5,725

See further **National Insurance Contributions**, p 176.

NIC: Class 3 rates

(*SSCBA 1992, s 13*)

Tax Year	Weekly Rate £
2019/20	15.00
2018/19	14.65
2017/18	14.25
2016/17	14.10
2015/16	14.10
2014/15	13.90
2013/14	13.55

See further **National Insurance Contributions**, p 177.

NIC: Class 4 rates and thresholds

(*SSCBA 1992, s 15(3), (3ZA)*)

Tax Year	Main rate	Additional rate	Lower profits limit	Upper profits limit
	%	%	£	£
2019/20	9	2	8,632	50,000
2018/19	9	2	8,424	46,350
2017/18	9	2	8,164	45,000
2016/17	9	2	8,060	43,000
2015/16	9	2	8,060	42,385
2014/15	9	2	7,956	41,865
2013/14	9	2	7,755	41,450

See further **National Insurance Contributions**, p 177.

Key Tax Dates

Monthly

- 19th – Non-electronic payments of PAYE, Class 1 NIC and CIS deductions for tax month to 5th should reach HMRC's Accounts Office (*SI 2003/2682, reg 69(1)(b); SI 2005/2045, reg 7(1)(b); SI 2001/1004, Sch 4, reg 10(1)*).
- 22nd – Electronic payments of PAYE, Class 1 NIC and CIS deductions for tax month ended 5th should clear into HMRC's bank account (*SI 2003/2682, reg 69(1)(a); SI 2001/1004, Sch 4, reg 10(1); SI 2005/2045, reg 7(1)(a)*).

30 December 2018

- Last day for person to submit an electronic self-assessment return for 2017/18 if they wish HMRC to collect the tax due through their future PAYE code where possible (*ITEPA 2003, s 684(3A); SI 2003/2682, reg 186(4)*).

20 January 2019

- VAT-MOSS return for quarter to 31 December 2018 must be submitted online.

31 January 2019

- Electronic income tax self-assessment returns, and any paper returns or self-assessment returns which are excluded from online filing, for 2017/18 must be filed by this date (*TMA 1970, ss 8(1D)(b), (1G), 8A(1B)(b), (1E), 12AA(4B), 12AA(4E)*).
- Any balancing payment of self-assessment income tax (and Class 4 NIC, if applicable) for 2017/18 plus any capital gains tax for that year. Where notice to file was issued after 31 October 2018, the payable date is extended to three months after the date on which the notice to file was issued (*TMA 1970, s 59B(3), (4)*).
- If a first payment on account is required for the tax year 2019/20, the payment of tax (and Class 4 NIC, if applicable) must reach HMRC (*TMA 1970, s 59A(2)(a)*).
- Deadline to file an outstanding 2014/15 self-assessment return to displace a determination.
- Last day to provide final income figures for tax credits claim for 2017/18, if renewal done by 31 July 2018 used an estimated figure.

1 February 2019

- Individual taxpayers who have not paid their remaining tax and NI liabilities for 2016/17 by this date face a further 5% penalty, in addition to the 5% penalties suffered on amounts outstanding at 1 March 2018 and 1 August 2018 (*FA 2009, Sch 56, para 3; SI 2011/702, art 3*).

2 February 2019

- Employers must submit Form P46 (Car) to report new cars provided during the quarter to 5 January 2019.

2 March 2019

- Individual taxpayers who have not paid their tax and NI liabilities for 2017/18 by this date face a 5% penalty (*FA 2009, Sch 56, para 3; SI 2011/702, art 3*).

1 April 2019

- Those VAT registered taxpayers with annual turnover in excess of £85,000, who are not subject to the deferral, must enter the MTD for VAT regime for VAT periods starting on and after this date (*SI 2019/ 261*) – see **Chapter 6**.

5 April 2019

- Last opportunity to utilise income tax personal allowances, annual ISA allowances and exemptions for CGT and IHT for 2018/19.
- Last day to pay Class 2 or Class 3 NIC for 2012/13.
- Final day for claims for 2014/15 relating to: personal allowances, remittance basis, terminal loss relief, overlap relief carry-forward of trading losses and capital losses (see **Chapter 6**).
- Deadline to claim that asset became negligible value or loan became unrecoverable in 2016/17 (*TCGA 1992, ss 24(2), 253*).

6 April 2019

- Minimum contributions for workplace pensions increase to 8% of pensionable pay in total; at least 3% from the employer and the balance from the employee.

19 April 2019

- Employers must make final payroll report for 2018/19 using FPS or EPS.

20 April 2019

- VAT-MOSS return for quarter to 31 March 2019 must be submitted online.

30 April 2019

- Payment of IHT on lifetime transfers between 6 April and 30 September 2018 is due by this date (*IHTA 1984, s 226(1)*).
- ATED returns and ATED charge must be paid for 2019/20. Deadline for amending ATED returns for 2018/19.

1 May 2019

- Daily £10 penalties commence if 2017/18 self-assessment return has not been submitted.

3 May 2019

- Employers must submit Form P46 (Car) to report new cars provided during the quarter to 5 April 2019.

5 May 2019

- Last day for a 2019/20 tax credits claim to be back dated to 6 April 2019

19 May 2019

- Deadline for earlier year update (EYU) for 2018/19.

31 May 2019

- Employers must provide a 2018/19 form P60 to employees who they employed at 5 April 2019 (*SI 2003/2682, reg 67*).
- FATCA returns due for year to 31 December 2018.

5 July 2019

- PAYE Settlement Agreements (PSAs) for 2018/19 must be agreed with HMRC (*SI 2003/2682, reg 112*).

6 July 2019

- Employers to submit forms P11D and returns of Class 1A NICs (forms P11D(b)) to HMRC for 2018/19 (*SI 2003/2682, reg 85; SI 2001/1004, reg 80*).
- Employers must supply relevant employees with P11D(b) and P11D information for 2018/19 (*SI 2003/2682, reg 94*).
- Annual returns for reporting events relating to employee share schemes in 2018/19 must be submitted through ERS (*ITEPA 2003, s 421J*).

19 July 2019

- Employer non-electronic payments of Class 1A NICs for 2018/19 on benefits returned on a declaration of expenses and benefits (form P11D(b)) must reach HMRC. The due date is 22 July for payments made by an approved electronic payment method (*SI 2001/1004, reg 71*).

20 July 2019

- VAT-MOSS return for quarter to 30 June 2019 must be submitted online.

31 July 2019

- The second payment on account of self-assessment income tax (and Class 4 NIC) by individuals for 2017/18 must reach HMRC to avoid late payment interest charges (*TMA 1970, s 59A(2)*).
- Tax credit claims for 2018/19 must be confirmed and renewed for 2019/20 if required.

1 August 2019

- Individual taxpayers who have not paid their remaining tax liabilities for 2017/18 face a further 5% penalty, in addition to the 5% penalty suffered on amounts outstanding at 1 March 2019 (*FA 2009, Sch 56, para 3; SI 2011/702, art 3*).

2 August 2019

- Employers must submit Form P46 (Car) if appropriate to report new cars provided during the quarter to 5 July 2019.

31 August 2019

- If HMRC have not issued a notice to file a 2018/19 income tax self-assessment return by now, the normal submission deadline of 31 October 2019 is extended to two months after the date on which the notice to file the tax return is issued (*TMA 1970, s 9(2)(b)*).

30 September 2019

- If the UK has not left the EU this is the last day to submit claim for VAT on business expenses incurred in other EU countries during 2018.

1 October 2019

- Those VAT-registered taxpayers with annual turnover in excess of £85,000, who are subject to the deferral, must enter the MTD for VAT regime for VAT periods starting on and after this date (*SI 2019/ 261*) – see **Chapter 6**.

5 October 2019

- Any person chargeable to income tax or CGT for 2018/19 who has not received a notice to file a self-assessment return must notify HMRC by this date that they are so chargeable (*TMA 1970, s 7(1)*).

19 October 2019

- Deadline for non-electronic payments of tax and NI due under PAYE settlement agreements (PSAs) for 2016/17 to reach HMRC Accounts Office (*SI 2003/2682, reg 109(2); SI 2001/1004, Sch 4, reg 13(1)*). The due date is extended to 22 October 2019 for payments made by an approved electronic payment method.

20 October 2019

- VAT-MOSS return for quarter to 30 September 2019 must be submitted online.

31 October 2019

- Paper income tax self-assessment returns for 2018/19 must be filed for individuals (*TMA 1970, s 8(1D)–(1F)*), trustees (*TMA 1970, s 8A(1B)–(1D)*) and partnerships which include one or more individuals, if the taxpayer's circumstances do not fall within one of the exclusions (*TMA 1970, s 12AA(4A)–(4D)*).
- If HMRC have not already issued a notice to file a 2018/19 self-assessment income tax return, the return must be filed within three months from the date of the notice, whether the return is electronic or paper (*TMA 1970, ss 8(1G), 8A(1E), 12AA(4E)*).
- An individual who submits a paper self-assessment return for 2018/19 must do so by 31 October 2019 if they wish HMRC to collect the tax due through their future PAYE code (*ITEPA 2003, s 684(3A); SI 2003/2682, reg 186(4)*).

2 November 2019

- Employers must submit Form P46 (Car) to report cars first provided during the quarter to 5 October 2019.

30 December 2019

- Last day for person to submit an electronic self-assessment return for 2018/19 if they wish HMRC to collect the tax due through their future PAYE code where possible (*ITEPA 2003, s 684(3A); SI 2003/2682, reg 186(4)*).

Note

The above list is for general information purposes only, and is not exhaustive.

Bloomsbury's Tax Rates and Tables 2019/20

Budget Edition

Compiled by:

Rebecca Cave FCA CTA MBA

Welcome to *Tax Rates and Tables 2019/20 (Budget Edition)*, published by Bloomsbury Professional.

This edition of *Tax Rates and Tables 2019/20* been updated to reflect measures introduced or amended by the 2018 Budget on 29 October 2018.

I have also included the measures and rates announced by the Scottish and Welsh Parliaments with regard to taxes devolved to those countries (see **Chapter 18**). The section on Making Tax Digital (MTD) in **Chapter 6** has been amended to reflect the revised commencement dates for MTD for VAT.

The proposed new capital allowance for structures and buildings (SBA) came into effect on 29 October 2018, but the Government has not published the detailed definitions required for the operation of this allowance. I have included the outline rules of the SBA in **Chapter 10**, and I'm grateful to Steven Bone for reviewing that chapter.

Finally a big 'thank you' to the editorial team at Bloomsbury Professional, particularly Jane Bradford for her patience and considerable skill in bringing all the material together.

I hope that you find *Tax Rates and Tables 2019/20 (Budget Edition)* useful and practical. I would welcome your constructive comments or suggestions for future editions.

Rebecca Cave FCA CTA
Rebecca@taxwriter.co.uk
December 2018

Bloomsbury Professional
LONDON • DUBLIN • EDINBURGH • NEW YORK • NEW DELHI • SYDNEY

BLOOMSBURY PROFESSIONAL
Bloomsbury Publishing Plc
41–43 Boltro Road, Haywards Heath, RH16 1BJ, UK

BLOOMSBURY and the Diana logo are trademarks of Bloomsbury Publishing Plc

First published in Great Britain 2019

British Library Cataloguing-in-Publication Data

A catalogue record for this book is available from the British Library.

ISBN: PB: 978 1 52650 938 3
ePDF: 978 1 52650 940 6
ePub: 978 1 52650 939 0

Typeset by Compuscript Ltd, Shannon
Printed and bound by CPI Group (UK) Ltd, Croydon, CR0 4YY

1

Personal taxation

RATES OF INCOME TAX

(*ITA 2007, Pt 2, Ch 2*)

Taxable income £	Rate %	Tax £	Cumulative £
2019/20			
Savings: 0–5,000	0	Nil	Nil
0–37,500	20	7,500.00	7,500.00
37,501–150,000	40	45,000.00	52,500.00
Over 150,000	45	–	–
2018/19			
Savings: 0–5,000	0	Nil	Nil
0–34,500	20	6,900.00	6,900.00
34,501–150,000	40	46,200.00	53,100.00
Over 150,000	45	–	–
2017/18			
Savings: 0–5,000	0	Nil	Nil
0–33,500	20	6,700.00	6,700.00
33,501–150,000	40	46,600.00	53,300.00
Over 150,000	45	–	–
2016/17			
Savings: 0–5,000	0	Nil	Nil
0–32,000	20	6,400.00	6,400.00
32,001–150,000	40	47,200.00	53,600.00
Over 150,000	45	–	–
2015/16			
Savings: 0–5,000	0	Nil	Nil
0–31,785	20	6,357.00	6,357.00
31,786–150,000	40	47,286.00	53,643.00
Over 150,000	45	–	–
2014/15			
Savings: 0–2,880	10	288.00	288.00
0–31,865	20	6,373.00	6,373.00
31,866–150,000	40	47,254.00	53,627.00
Over 150,000	45	–	–

continued

Taxable income £	Rate %	Tax £	Cumulative £
2013/14			
Savings: 0–2,790	10	279.00	279.00
0–32,010	20	6402.00	6,402.00
32,011–150,000	40	47,196.00	53,598.00
Over 150,000	45	–	–

Notes

(1) *Scottish tax bands* – From 6 April 2017 the above tax bands do not apply to income which is not savings or dividend income, received by Scottish taxpayers see **Chapter 18**.

(2) *Scottish Income Tax* – From 6 April 2017 Scottish taxpayers pay the SIT at Scottish rates, see **Chapter 18**.

(3) *Order of taxation* – Income is deemed to be taxed in this order (*ITA 2007, s 16*):

- Non-savings income: net rent, profits and earned income
- Savings income
- Dividend income

(4) *Savings rate band* – Where non-savings income exceeds this band, the savings rate band does not apply (*FA 2014, s 3*). 'Non-savings income' does not include dividend income.

(5) *Savings rates* – See Tax rates for savings income.

(6) *Dividend rates* – See Tax rates for dividend income

(7) *Non-residents* – Pay savings rates on savings income, dividend rates on dividend income, and the default rates on all other income (*ITA 2007, s 9A*).

TAX RATES FOR SAVINGS INCOME

(*ITA 2007, ss 7–18*)

Savings within:	2019/20	2018/19	2017/18	2016/17	2015/16	2014/15
Savings rate band	0%	0%	0%	0%	0%	10%
Basic rate band	20%	20%	20%	20%	20%	20%
PSA: £1,000 (note 1)	0%	0%	0%	0%	N/A	N/A
Higher rate band	40%	40%	40%	40%	40%	40%
PSA: £500 (note 1)	0%	0%	0%	0%	N/A	N/A
Additional rate band	45%	45%	45%	45%	45%	45%

Notes

(1) *Personal savings allowance (PSA)* – Applies to all individual taxpayers, including Scottish taxpayers, on the same basis as taxpayers in the rest of the UK. Those with any income in the additional rate band have a PSA of nil. Taxpayers with income

in the higher-rate band, but not in the additional rate band, have a PSA worth £500, all other taxpayers have a PSA worth £1,000 (*ITA 2007, s 12B(2), (3)*).

(2) *Net income* – The income measured for the PSA determination is the result of step 3 of *ITA 2007, s 23*; total income less reliefs.

(3) *Thresholds* – The higher and additional rate band thresholds can be expanded by making personal pension contributions or gift aid donations. These thresholds also apply to Scottish taxpayers for the purpose of deciding the level of PSA.

(4) *Tax rate* – Savings income (defined in *ITA 2007, s 18*) not within the savings rate band which is covered by the PSA is taxed at the savings nil rate (*ITA 2007, ss 12A, 12B*). Savings income in excess of the savings allowance is taxed at the income tax rate for the tax band, if it is not covered by the personal allowance.

(5) *Interest received* – From 6 April 2016 deposit takers (banks, building societies and other institutions including NS&I) are not required to deduct income tax from yearly interest paid in respect of relevant investments (*ITA 2007, Pt 15, Ch 2*).

(6) *Reclaim tax* – Companies which are not deposit takers, who pay yearly interest are required to deduct 20% tax from the interest paid. Where tax has been deducted, but the interest is taxed at the nil rate, the taxpayer can reclaim the tax deducted at source (*ITA 2007, s 17*).

TAX RATES FOR DIVIDEND INCOME

(*ITA 2007, ss 10–19*)

Dividends within:	2019/20	2018/19	2017/18	2016/17	2015/16	2014/15
Basic rate band	7.5%	7.5%	7.5%	7.5%	10%	10%
Dividend allowance	£2,000	£2,000	£5,000	£5,000	N/A	N/A
Higher rate band	32.5%	32.5%	32.5%	32.5%	32.5%	32.5%
Dividend allowance	£2,000	£2,000	£5,000	£5,000	N/A	N/A
Additional rate band	38.1%	38.1%	38.1%	38.1%	37.5%	37.5%
Dividend allowance	£2,000	£2,000	£5,000	£5,000	N/A	N/A

Notes

(1) *Dividend allowance (DA)* – Dividend income covered by this allowance is taxed at 0%, but it does use up the tax band it falls into. Only applicable for UK-resident individual taxpayers, not trustees or PRs (*ITA 2007, s 13A*).

(2) *Tax credit* – The 10% non-repayable dividend tax credit was abolished on 6 April 2016. Before that date dividend income received was grossed-up by applying a fraction of 1/9th to the net amount (*ITTOIA 2005, ss 397–397C*).

(3) *Dividend income* – Before 6 April 2016 where gross dividend income did not exceed the basic rate threshold, the income tax was charged at 10%, and the tax due was covered by the dividend tax credit.

(4) *Requirement to notify* – The taxpayer doesn't have to notify HMRC of receipt of dividend income if there is no lability to tax on that income (*TMA 1970, s 7*).

TRUST RATES

(*ITA 2007, s 9*)

Income within:	2019/20	2018/19	2017/18	2016/17	2015/16	2014/15
Standard rate band: up to £1,000 (note 1)	default basic rates apply see note 2					
Dividend income	38.1%	38.1%	38.1%	38.1%	37.5%	37.5%
Other income	45%	45%	45%	45%	45%	45%

Notes

(1) *Standard rate band* – In the case of trusts made by the same settlor, the standard rate band is divided by the number of such trusts, subject to a minimum starting rate band of £200 (*ITA 2007, ss 491, 492*).

(2) *Default rates* – Income within the standard rate band is generally taxable at the (non-trust) rates applicable to the particular source of income (see tables above). From 6 April 2016 dividends within this band are taxed at the dividend ordinary rate (7.5%), savings and other income is taxed at the default basic rate (20%) (*ITA 2007, s 9A*).

(3) *No allowances* – Trustees and estates of deceased persons are not entitled to the personal savings allowance or dividend allowance.

(4) *Notification* – For 2016/17 to 2018/19, where the only income of a trust, or estate in administration, is savings interest and the tax liability is below £100, the trustees and personal representatives are not required to notify HMRC (*HMRC Trusts & Estates newsletter* December 2017).

(5) *Discretionary trusts* – The above trust rates broadly apply to accumulated or discretionary trust income (*ITA 2007, s 479*).

(6) *Interest in possession trusts* – These trusts are generally liable to income tax at the rates applicable within the basic rate band for individuals (see **Tax rates for savings income** and **Tax rates for dividend income**), although certain capital receipts for trust law purposes are liable at the above trust rates (*ITA 2007, ss 481, 482*).

PERSONAL ALLOWANCES AND RELIEFS

(*ITA 2007, Pt 3; ITTOIA 2005, Pt 7, Ch1*)

	2019/20 £	2018/19 £	2017/18 £	2016/17 £	2015/16 £	2014/15 £
Personal allowance	12,500	11,850	11,500	11,000		
Born after 5 April 1948	N/A	N/A	N/A	N/A	10,600	10,000
Income limit for personal allowance	100,000	100,000	100,000	100,000	100,000	100,000

	2019/20 £	2018/19 £	2017/18 £	2016/17 £	2015/16 £	2014/15 £
Age-related allowances						
Born between 5 April 1938 and 6 April 1948	N/A	N/A	N/A	N/A	10,600	10,500
Born before 6 April 1938	N/A	N/A	N/A	N/A	10,660	10,660
Income limit for age-related and married allowances	29,600	28,900	28,000	27,700	27,700	27,000
Allowances for couples						
Marriage Allowance (notes 4 & 5)	1,250	1,190	1,150	1,100	1,060	
Married couple's: min	3,450	3,360	3,260	3,220	3,220	3,140
Married couple's: max (note 3)	8,695	8,695	8,445	8,355	8,355	8,165
Blind person's allowance	2,450	2,390	2,320	2,290	2,290	2,230
Rent-a-room relief (note 6)	7,500	7,500	7,500	7,500	4,250	4,250
Trading allowance (note 7)	1,000	1,000	1,000	N/A	N/A	N/A
Property allowance (note 8)	1,000	1,000	1,000	N/A	N/A	N/A

Notes

(1) *Abatement of personal allowance* – Personal and age allowances are reduced by £1 for every £2 above the £100,000 threshold, where the taxpayer's adjusted net income (see *ITA 2007, s 58*) exceeds £100,000 (*ITA 2007, s 35*).

(2) *Age-related allowances* – Age-related personal and married couple's allowances are reduced, by £1 for every £2 of income above the limit shown in the table above. The aged-related personal allowance was withdrawn from 6 April 2016.

(3) *Married couple's allowance* – The rate of tax relief for the married couple's allowance is 10%. At least one party to the marriage or civil partnership must have been born before 6 April 1935 (*ITA 2007, s 45*).

(4) *Marriage allowance election* – Married couples and civil partners can elect to transfer 10% of their personal allowance (rounded up to the nearest £10) to their spouse or civil partner, if the conditions in note (5) apply. From 29 November 2017 this election can be made on behalf of a deceased spouse or civil partner (*ITA 2007, Pt 3, Ch 3A*).

(5) *Recipient of marriage allowance* – Must be taxed at no more than the basic rate (20%) or the Scottish intermediate rate (21%). The recipient is given a tax reduction of 20% × marriage allowance (£250 for 2019/20), whatever their marginal tax rate actually is for the year (*ITA 2007, s 55B(2)*).

(6) *Rent-a-room* – Where more than one person is receiving rent from the property the relief per person is half the total (*ITTOIA 2005, s 789*).

(7) *Trading allowance* – Applies to treat income as nil within the limit for miscellaneous trading income, as well as income from providing assets and services. It cannot apply to income from a partnership or property (*ITTOIA 2005, s 783A*).

(8) *Property allowance* – Applies to treat as nil, income from property that does not qualify for rent-a-room relief, and is within the limit (*ITTOIA 2005, s 783B*).

HIGH INCOME CHILD BENEFIT CHARGE (HICBC)

(*ITEPA 2003, ss 681B–681H*)

The amount of the high income child benefit charge is the appropriate percentage of child benefit. The 'appropriate percentage' is the lower of:

(a) 100%; or

(b) $\frac{ANI - L\ \%}{X}$

Where: ANI = adjusted net income;

L = £50,000;

X = £100.

Notes

(1) *Applies where* – The taxpayer or their partner receives child benefit on or after 7 January 2013, and the taxpayer's 'adjusted net income' exceeds £50,000. If both partners have adjusted net income over £50,000, the charge is levied on the partner with the highest income (*ITEPA 2003, s 681D*).

(2) *Effect* – The HICBC is 1% of child benefit for every £100 of adjusted net income above £50,000. The HICBC claws back 100% of child benefit where adjusted net income exceeds £60,000. The amounts and percentages used in the formula are rounded down if not whole numbers.

(3) *Election* – A taxpayer may elect to stop receiving child benefit payments to avoid the HICBC. This election can be revoked with retrospective effect for up to two years (*SSAA 1992, s 13A; SSA(NI)A 1992, s 11*).

(4) *Declaration* – Taxpayers who are subject to the HICBC must declare the child benefit received by themselves or their partner on their self-assessment tax return for the relevant tax year.

(5) *Claim benefit* – Parents should claim child benefit at the earliest opportunity to protect their rights to NI credits, and to ensure their child is allocated an NI number just before they reach age 16.

(6) *Further information* – For rates of child benefit see **Chapter 15: State Benefits**. For HMRC guidance see: https://www.gov.uk/child-benefit-tax-charge

STATUTORY RESIDENCE TEST (SRT)

(*FA 2013, Sch 45, paras 3–15*)

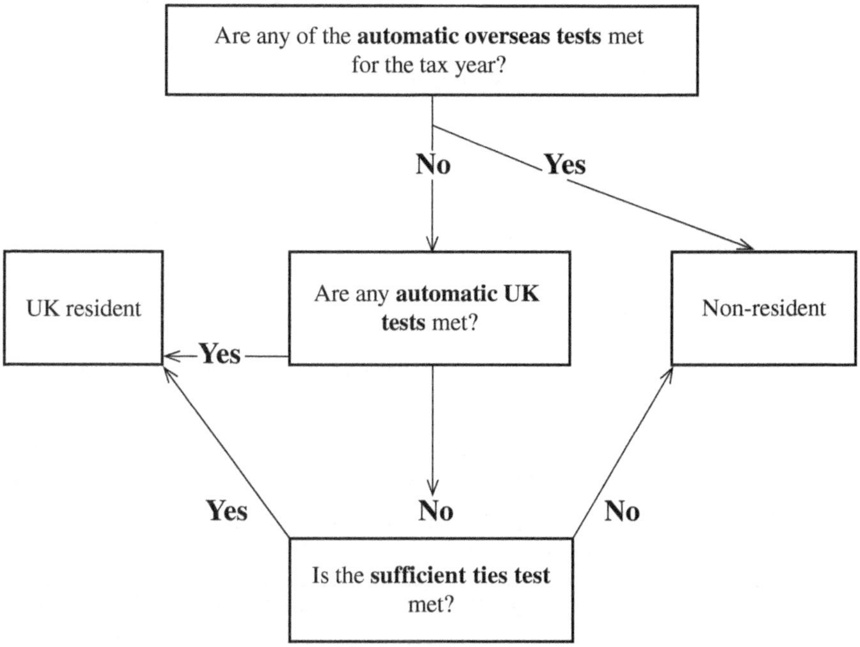

Notes

(1) *Order of tests* – To establish whether an individual is resident in the UK or not in a tax year, follow the diagram above. Start with the **automatic overseas tests**. If any of these tests are met the individual will be automatically non-UK resident for the tax year, and no further tests are required.

(2) *Automatic overseas tests* – The automatic overseas tests for living taxpayers are summarised as:

(a) fewer than16 days in the UK – for those individuals resident in the UK for one or more of the three preceding tax years;

(b) fewer than 46 days in the UK – for those individuals resident in the UK for none of the three preceding tax years;

(c) fewer than 91 days in the UK – for individuals who work full-time overseas with no significant breaks.

(3) *Automatic UK tests* – The automatic UK tests for living taxpayers are summarised as:

(a) 183 days or more in the UK;

(b) has a home in the UK and spends sufficient time there;

(c) works full-time in the UK.

Sufficient ties test

(*FA 2013, Sch 45, paras 17–20, 31–38*)

Notes

(1) *Scope* – If the individual has 'sufficient UK ties' for that tax year he will be UK resident.

(2) *UK* ties – these are summarised as:

(a) family tie;

(b) accommodation tie;

(c) work tie;

(d) 90-day tie; and

(e) country tie (only be considered if the individual was UK resident in one or more of the preceding three tax years).

(3) *Sufficient UK ties* – The number of UK ties needed for an individual to be UK resident is based on the number of days spent in the UK, in accordance with the tables below:

(a) If individual was UK resident for one or more of the three tax years before the tax year under consideration:

Days in the UK in tax year	Number of UK ties sufficient for residence
16–45	At least 4
46–90	At least 3
91–120	At least 2
Over 120	At least 1

(b) If individual was UK resident for none of the three tax years before the tax year under consideration:

Days in the UK in the tax year	Number of UK ties sufficient for residence
46–90	All 4
91–120	At least 3
Over 120	At least 2

SRT – General points

(*FA 2013, s 218, Sch 45*)

Notes

(1) *Commencement* – The SRT has effect from 6 April 2013 (*FA 2013, Sch 45, para 153*).

(2) *Scope* – The SRT applies to individuals for income tax, CGT and IHT purposes to the extent that an individual's residence status is relevant to those taxes.

(3) *Temporary non-residence* – There are separate rules for temporary non-residence, which apply for departures from the UK on and after 6 April 2013, in respect of distributions to participators in close companies (*ITTOIA 2005, s 401C*), and for CGT purposes (*TCGA 1992, s 10A*).

(4) *Days in the UK* – An individual is present in the UK if he is there at midnight at the end of a day, with limited exceptions. However, the taxpayer may be deemed to be in the UK, when he was not physically present, if certain conditions are satisfied (*FA 2013, Sch 45, paras 22, 23*).

(5) *Deceased persons* – There are different automatic tests where the individual dies in the tax year. The 'sufficient UK ties' tests also apply to individuals who die during the tax year, but subject to specified modifications in some cases (*FA 2013, Sch 45, para 20*).

(6) *Split year treatment* – An individual is generally either UK resident or non-UK resident for a full tax year. However, the tax year may be split into two parts (ie a UK part and an overseas part) in eight specified circumstances (*FA 2013, Sch 45, Pt 3*).

(7) *Transitional provisions* – These apply if an individual is considering residence status for any of the tax years 2013/14 to 2017/18, or the application of the split-year rules to those years, and it is necessary for to determine the individual's residence status for a tax year before 2013/14 (*FA 2013, Sch 45, para 154*).

(8) *Further guidance* – See HMRC guides: RDR1, RDR3, and RDR4. For detailed guidance, see *Booth and Schwarz: Residence, Domicile and UK Taxation* (19th edition, Bloomsbury Professional).

REMITTANCE BASIS CHARGE (RBC)

(*ITA 2007, s 809H*)

Resident in the UK in at least:	**2019/20 £**	**2018/19 £**	**2017/18 £**	**2016/17 £**	**2015/16 £**
7 of last 9 tax years	30,000	30,000	30,000	30,000	30,000
12 of last 14 tax years	60,000	60,000	60,000	60,000	60,000
17 of last 20 tax years (note 3)	N/A	N/A	N/A	90,000	90,000

Notes

(1) *Payable by* – Individuals who are not domiciled in the UK, but who are tax resident in the UK and who make a claim to use the remittance basis. The charge is in addition to any tax payable in the UK on remitted income or gains (*ITA 2007, Pt 14, Ch A1*).

(2) *Nominated income* – The taxpayer must nominate a source of offshore income or gains against which the RBC is levied and must be very careful not to remit that income or gains to the UK.

(3) *Deemed domicile* – From 6 April 2017 non-domiciled individuals who have been resident in the UK for at least 15 out of the preceding 20 tax years are deemed to be domiciled in the UK for income tax and CGT purposes. Individuals with UK domicile of origin are not eligible to claim non-domiciled status while resident in the UK (*F(No 2)A 2017, s 29, Sch 8*)

CAP ON INCOME TAX RELIEFS

(*FA 2013, s 16, Sch 3*)

Title and description of relief	Legislation
Trade loss relief against general income (aka 'sideways loss relief')	*ITA 2007, s 64*
Early years trade losses relief – available in the first four years of the trade, profession or vocation	*ITA 2007, s 72*
Post-cessation trade relief – for qualifying payments/events within seven years of the permanent cessation of the trade.	*ITA 2007, s 96*
Property loss relief against general income – property business losses arising from capital allowances or agricultural expenses	*ITA 2007, s 120*
Post-cessation property relief – for qualifying payments/events within seven years of the permanent cessation of the UK property business	*ITA 2007, s 125*
Employment loss relief	*ITA 2007, s 128*
Former employees deduction for liabilities	*ITEPA 2003, s 555*
Share loss relief (see note 3)	*ITA 2007, s 131*
Losses on deeply discounted securities – only for losses on gilt strips and listed securities held since 26 March 2003	*ITTOIA 2005, ss 446–488, 453–456*
Qualifying loan interest – on loans to buy an interest in certain types of company, or in a partnership	*ITA 2007, Pt 8, Ch 1*

Notes

(1) *Commencement* – The cap is applied in respect of the above income tax reliefs claimed by individuals for 2013/14 and subsequent years.

(2) *Application* – Where the individual seeks to claim more than £50,000 in reliefs, the cap is set at the greater of £50,000 and 25% of adjusted total income (*ITA 2007, s 24A*).

(3) *Exclusions for venture capital* – The cap does not apply to share loss relief where the shares are qualifying EIS, SEIS or SITR shares (*ITA 2007, s 24A(7)(d)*).

(4) *Overlap relief* – The cap does not apply to overlap relief allowed under *ITTOIA 2005, s 205* or *220.*

(5) *Business premises renovation* – The cap does not apply to business premises renovation allowance under *CAA 2001, Pt 3A.*

(6) *Same trade* – The cap does not apply to deductions for trade or property loss relief or post-cessation trade or property relief made from profits of the same trade or property business (*ITA 2007, s 24A(7)(b)*).

SELF-ASSESSMENT TAX RETURNS

Filing dates: individuals and trustees

(*TMA 1970, ss 8, 8A*)

Type of tax return	Filing date
Paper returns (non-electronic)	31 October following the end of the tax year unless an exclusion applies (*TMA 1970, ss 8(1D)(a), 8A(1B)(a)*).
Electronic returns	31 January following the end of the tax year (*TMA 1970, ss 8(1D)(b), 8A(1B)(b)*).
Return (or notice to file) issued after 31 July but before 31 October following the end of the tax year	3 months from the date of the return/notice for paper returns, or 31 January for electronic returns (*TMA 1970, ss 8(1F), 8A(1D)*).
Return (or notice to file) issued after 31 October following the end of the tax year	3 months from the date of the return/notice (whether paper or electronic) (*TMA 1970, ss 8(1G), 8A(1E)*).

Notes

(1) *PAYE coding* – Individuals who wish to have their tax coded-out through their PAYE code for the following year must file their tax return by 30 December at the latest, instead of 31 January.

(2) *Partnerships* – The above filing dates also apply to partnerships with individual members (*TMA 1970, s 12AA(4)–(4E)*). Separate provisions apply in the case of partnerships involving one or more companies (*TMA 1970, s 12AA(5)–(5E)*).

(3) *Must be paper* – The following tax returns cannot be submitted online and must be submitted in paper form by 31 January following the tax year end:

- SA970 – Trustees of Registered Pension Schemes
- SA200 – Short tax return
- Where the taxpayer's circumstances fall into one of the self-assessment individual exclusions for online filing.

(4) *Needs commercial software* – The following types of tax return and supplementary pages to the SA100 are not supported by the HMRC free software so require commercial software for submission:

- SA800 – Partnership tax return
- SA900 – Trust and estate return
- SA102M – Ministers of religion
- SA102MP – Members of Westminster Parliament
- SA102MLA – Members of Northern Ireland Assembly
- SA102MSP – Members of Scottish Parliament
- SA102WAM – Members of the National Assembly for Wales

- SA103L – Lloyds underwriters
- SA107 – Trust income
- SA109 – Residence, remittance basis etc.

Due dates for payment of tax

(*TMA 1970, ss 59A, 59B*)

Due date	What is payable:
31 January in the tax year	1st payment on account
31 July following tax year end	2nd payment on account
31 January following tax year end	Balancing payment and any CGT due

Notes

(1) *No payments on account* – These are not required where:

- More than 80% of the previous year's tax liability was covered by tax deducted at source and dividend tax credits; or
- the previous year's liability (net of tax deducted at source) was less than £1,000 (*SI 1996/1654, SI 2008/838*).

(2) *Late notice* – If a return (or a notice to file) was not issued until after 31 October following the end of the tax year, and the taxpayer notified HMRC of chargeability by 5 October, the due date for the final payment (including any CGT) is three months from the issue of the return/notice (*TMA 1970, s 59B(3), (4)*).

(3) *Penalties* – For penalties and interest that may apply to late payments see **Chapter 17**.

ASSESSMENTS, CLAIMS AND ELECTIONS

Normal time limits

(*TMA 1970, ss 34, 43; FA 2008, s 118, Sch 39*)

Tax year	Claim by
2019/20	5 April 2024
2018/19	5 April 2023
2017/18	5 April 2022
2016/17	5 April 2021
2015/16	5 April 2020
2014/15	5 April 2019

Notes

(1) *Timing of claim* – Except where otherwise specified, a relief claim for income tax and capital gains purposes must be made within four years after the end of the tax year. A self-assessment must be made within four years of the tax year it relates to (*TMA 1970, ss 8, 8A*).

(2) *Form of claim* – Claims or elections should generally be made on the tax return or on a form specifically provided for the claim, such as form P87, or by an amendment to the tax return.

(3) *Claims by phone* – HMRC will accept claims for relief on employment expenses if:

- a P87 form has not been sent to the taxpayer to complete;
- the claim is for less than £1,000, or £2,500 for professional subscriptions; and
- the taxpayer made a similar claim for an earlier tax year which was accepted by HMRC.

2

Expenses and benefits

COMPANY CAR BENEFIT CHARGES

(ITEPA 2003, ss 139–142)

Appropriate percentages from 6 April 2017 to 5 April 2020

CO_2 emissions (g/km)	2019/2020		2018/2019		2017/2018	
(see Note 1 below)	**Petrol and electric %**	**Diesel %**	**Petrol and electric %**	**Diesel %**	**Petrol & electric %**	**Diesel %**
0–50	16	20	13	17	9	12
51–75	19	23	16	20	13	16
76–94	22	26	19	23	17	20
95–99	23	27	20	24	18	21
100–104	24	28	21	25	19	22
105–109	25	29	22	26	20	23
110–114	26	30	23	27	21	24
115–119	27	31	24	28	22	25
120–124	28	32	25	29	23	26
125–129	29	33	26	30	24	27
130–134	30	34	27	31	25	28
135–139	31	35	28	32	26	29
140–144	32	36	29	33	27	30
145–149	33	37	30	34	28	31
150–154	34	37	31	35	29	32
155–159	35	37	32	36	30	33
160–164	36	37	33	37	31	34
165–169	37	37	34	37	32	35
170–174	37	37	35	37	33	36
175–179	37	37	36	37	34	37
180–184	37	37	37	37	35	37
185–189	37	37	37	37	36	37
190 and above	37	37	37	37	37	37

Appropriate percentages from 6 April 2014 to 5 April 2017

CO_2 emissions (g/km)	2016/17		2015/16		2014/15	
(see Note 1 below)	**Petrol & electric %**	**Diesel %**	**Petrol & electric %**	**Diesel %**	**Petrol & electric %**	**Diesel %**
0	7	10	5	8	0	0
1–50	7	10	5	8	5	8
51–75	11	14	9	12	5	8
76–94	15	18	13	16	11	14
95–99	16	19	14	17	12	15
100–104	17	20	15	18	13	16
105–109	18	21	16	19	14	17
110–114	19	22	17	20	15	18
115–119	20	23	18	21	16	19
120–124	21	24	19	22	17	20
125–129	22	25	20	23	18	21
130–134	23	26	21	24	19	22
135–139	24	27	22	25	20	23
140–144	25	28	23	26	21	24
145–149	26	29	24	27	22	25
150–154	27	30	25	28	23	26
155–159	28	31	26	29	24	27
160–164	29	32	27	30	25	28
165–169	30	33	28	31	26	29
170–174	31	34	29	32	27	30
175–179	32	35	30	33	28	31
180–184	33	36	31	34	29	32
185–189	34	37	32	35	30	33
190–194	35	37	33	36	31	34
195–199	36	37	34	37	32	35
200–204	37	37	35	37	33	36
205–209	37	37	36	37	34	37
210–214	37	37	37	37	35	37
215–219	37	37	37	37	36	37
220 and above	37	37	37	37	37	37

Appropriate percentages from 6 April 2012 to 5 April 2014

CO_2 emissions (g/km)	2013/14		2012/13	
(see Note 1 below)	Petrol %	Diesel %	Petrol %	Diesel %
0	0	0	0	0
1–75	5	8	5	8
76–94	10	13	10	13
95–99	11	14	10	13
100–104	12	15	11	14
105–109	13	16	12	15
110–114	14	17	13	16
115–119	15	18	14	17
120–124	16	19	15	18
125–129	17	20	16	19
130–134	18	21	17	20
135–139	19	22	18	21
140–144	20	23	19	22
145–149	21	24	20	23
150–154	22	25	21	24
155–159	23	26	22	25
160–164	24	27	23	26
165–169	25	28	24	27
170–174	26	29	25	28
175–179	27	30	26	29
180–184	28	31	27	30
185–189	29	32	28	31
190–194	30	33	29	32
195–199	31	34	30	33
200–204	32	35	31	34
205–209	33	35	32	35
210–214	34	35	33	35
215–219	35	35	34	35
220 and above	35	35	35	35

Notes

(1) *Zero percentage* – This applies to cars which cannot produce CO_2 emissions under any circumstances when driven, for tax years 2010/11 to 2014/15 inclusive (*ITEPA 2003, s 140(3A)*).

(2) *Rounding* – The income tax charge is based on a percentage of the car's list price graduated according to the level of CO_2 emissions measured in grams per

kilometre (g/km) and rounded down to the nearest 5g/km. Rounding does not apply to cars with emissions below 75g/km in 2014/15 or below 95g/km in 2013/14.

(3) *Ultra-low emissions* – From 6 April 2010 to 5 April 2015, a reduced appropriate percentage of 5% (8% for diesels) applied for company cars with an approved CO_2 emissions figure not exceeding 75g/km (*ITEPA 2003, s 139(1B)*).

(4) *Car not available* – The car benefit is proportionately reduced if the company car is only available for part of the year, where the benefit ceases part way through a tax year (and is not reinstated in that year), or where the benefit of the company car is shared (*ITEPA 2003, ss 143, 148*).

(5) *Payment for use* – From 6 April 2017 where an employee makes a payment for private use of the car or fuel to reduce the chargeable benefit, that payment must be made by 6 July after the end of the tax year in which the benefit was provided (*ITEPA 2003, s 144(1)*).

(6) *Diesel cars* – The higher percentages for diesel in the tables above apply to all diesel cars first registered on or after 1 January 1998 and before 1 September 2017, and to diesel cars first registered on or after 1 September 2017 which do not meet Euro 6d emission standards (*FA 2018, s 9*).

(7) *OpRA vehicles* – Where a car or van is provided under an optional remuneration arrangement (salary sacrifice) the amount foregone includes all costs connected with the vehicle which are regarded as part of the benefit in kind (*F(No 3)B 2017–19, cl 7*).

Cars registered with no CO_2 emission figures

(*ITEPA 2003, ss 140–142;* see also EIM24950, EIM24975)

Registered at any time	2019/20 %	2018/19 %	2017/18 %	2016/17 %	2015/16 %
1,400 cc or less	23	20	18	16	15
Over 1,400 cc to 2,000 cc (note 2)	34	31	29	27	25
Over 2,000 cc (note 2)	37	37	37	37	37

Notes

(1) *Diesel cars* – A 3% supplement (4% from 6 April 2018) applies to diesel cars up to a maximum of 37%, see note 6: **diesel cars** above.

(2) *2015/16 and earlier* – If the vehicle was registered before 1998 the appropriate percentage was 22 for engines 1400cc to 2000 cc, and 32 for engines over 2000 cc.

Appropriate percentages: 2020/21

CO_2 emissions g/km	Hybrid miles on zero emissions	Petrol and electric %	Diesel %
0	N/A	2	N/A
1–50	Up to 30	14	18
1–50	30–39	12	16
1–50	40–69	8	12
1–50	70–129	5	9
1–50	130 or more	2	6
51–54	N/A	15	19
54–59	N/A	16	20
60–64	N/A	17	21
65–69	N/A	18	22
70–74	N/A	19	23
75–79	N/A	20	24
80–84	N/A	21	25
85–89	N/A	22	26
90–94	N/A	23	27
95–99	N/A	24	28
100–104	N/A	25	29
105–109	N/A	26	30
110–114	N/A	27	31
115–119	N/A	28	32
120–124	N/A	29	33
125–129	N/A	30	34
130–134	N/A	31	35
135–139	N/A	32	36
140–144	N/A	33	37
145–149	N/A	34	37
150–154	N/A	35	37
155–159	N/A	36	37
160 and above	N/A	37	37

Fuel benefit charges

(*ITEPA 2003, ss 149–153; SI 2018/1176*)

Car fuel benefit multiplier

Tax year	£	Tax year	£
2019/20	24,100	2016/17	22,200
2018/19	23,400	2015/16	22,100
2017/18	22,600	2014/15	21,700

Notes

(1) *Nil fuel benefit* – This applies in the following circumstances:

- if the employee is required to make good the full cost of all fuel provided for private use, and actually does so by 6 July following the tax year for 2017/18 and later years;
- if fuel is made available only for business travel (*ITEPA 2003, s 151*); or
- where the employer provides free charging for the electric vehicle.

(2) *Reductions* – The fuel benefit is proportionately reduced if the company car is only available for part of the year, where the benefit ceases part way through a tax year (and is not reinstated in that year), or where the benefit of the company car is shared (*ITEPA 2003, ss 152–153*).

(3) *Cash equivalent* – The benefit charge for fuel provided for private motoring is calculated by applying the appropriate percentage to the relevant multiplier in the table above. The 'appropriate percentage' is broadly that used to calculate the car benefit (*ITEPA 2003, s 150*).

(4) *Further information* – The HMRC company car and car fuel calculator can be used to compute the benefit charge for tax years from 2013/14 to 2018/19 see: www.gov.uk/calculate-tax-on-company-cars.

Fuel benefit charges from 6 April 2015 to 5 April 2020

(*ITEPA 2003, s 150*)

Petrol engines

CO_2 emissions (g/km)	2019/20 £	2018/19 £	2017/18 £	2016/17 £	2015/16 £
0–50	3856	3,042	2,034	1,554	1,105
51–75	4579	3,744	2,938	2,442	1,989
76–94	5302	4,446	3,842	3,330	2,873
95–99	5543	4,680	4,068	3,552	3,094
100–104	5784	4,914	4,294	3,774	3,315
105–109	6025	5,148	4,520	3,996	3,536
110–114	6266	5,382	4,746	4,218	3,757
115–119	6507	5,616	4,972	4,440	3,978
120–124	6748	5,850	5,198	4,662	4,199
125–129	6989	6,084	5,424	4,884	4,420
130–134	7230	6,318	5,650	5,106	4,641
135–139	7471	6,552	5,876	5,328	4,862
140–144	7712	6,786	6,102	5,550	5,083
145–149	7953	7,020	6,328	5,772	5,304
150–154	8194	7,254	6,554	5,994	5,525

continued

CO_2 emissions (g/km)	2019/20	2018/19	2017/18	2016/17	2015/16
	£	£	£	£	£
155–159	8435	7,488	6,780	6,216	5,746
160–164	8676	7,722	7,006	6,438	5,967
165–169	8917	7,956	7,232	6,660	6,188
170–174	8917	8,190	7,458	6,882	6,409
175–179	8917	8,424	7,684	7,104	6,630
180–184	8917	8,658	7,910	7,326	6,851
185–189	8917	8,658	8,136	7,548	7,072
190–194	8917	8,658	8,362	7,770	7,293
195–199	8917	8,658	8,362	7,992	7,514
200–204	8917	8,658	8,362	8,214	7,735
205–209	8917	8,658	8,362	8,214	7,956
210 and over	8917	8,658	8,362	8,214	8,177

Diesel engines

CO_2 emissions (g/km)	2019/20	2018/19	2017/18	2016/17	2015/16
	£	£	£	£	£
0–50	4820	3,978	2,712	2,220	1,768
51–75	5543	4,680	3,616	3,108	2,652
76–94	6266	5,382	4,520	3,996	3,536
95–99	6507	5,616	4,746	4,218	3,757
100–104	6748	5,850	4,972	4,440	3,978
105–109	6989	6,084	5,198	4,662	4,199
110–114	7230	6,318	5,424	4,884	4,420
115–119	7471	6,552	5,650	5,106	4,641
120–124	7712	6,786	5,876	5,328	4,862
125–129	7953	7,020	6,102	5,550	5,083
130–134	8194	7,254	6,328	5,772	5,304
135–139	8435	7,488	6,554	5,994	5,525
140–144	8676	7,722	6,780	6,216	5,746
145–149	8917	7,956	7,006	6,438	5,967
150–154	8917	8,190	7,232	6,660	6,188
155–159	8917	8,424	7,458	6,882	6,409
160–164	8917	8,658	7,684	7,104	6,630
165–169	8917	8,658	7,910	7,326	6,851
170–174	8917	8,658	8,136	7,548	7,072
175–179	8917	8,658	8,362	7,770	7,293
180–184	8917	8,658	8,362	7,992	7,514
185–189	8917	8,658	8,362	8,214	7,735
190–194	8917	8,658	8,362	8,214	7,956
195 and over	8917	8,658	8,362	8,214	8,177

Notes

(1) *Electric vehicles* – No fuel benefit arises where employees are provided with free electricity for their company-owned vehicles (*ITEPA 2003, s 149(4)*).

(2) *Employer provided power* – Before 6 April 2018 where employees were provided with free electricity at work to charge their own vehicles, or through a charge card, or where the employer pays for a charging point at the employee's home, those employees should be taxed on the cost of the electricity or service provided (EIM23900).

(3) *Charging at work* – From 6 April 2018 there is no chargeable benefit where an employee is permitted to charge a privately owned vehicle at or near their place of work (*ITEPA 2003, s 237A*).

Mileage allowances

Advisory fuel rates for company cars

(www.gov.uk/government/publications/advisory-fuel-rates)

Engine size	Rate per Mile		
	Petrol	Diesel	LPG
From 1 December 2018		Electric cars: 4p/ mile	
Up to 1,400 cc	12p		8p
1,401–2,000 cc	15p		10p
Over 2,000 cc	22p		15p
Up to 1,600 cc		10p	
1,601–2,000 cc		12p	
Over 2,000 cc		14p	
From 1 September 2018		Electric cars: 4p/ mile	
Up to 1,400 cc	12p		7p
1,401–2,000 cc	15p		9p
Over 2,000 cc	22p		13p
Up to 1,600 cc		10p	
1,601–2,000 cc		12p	
Over 2,000 cc		13p	
From 1 June 2018			
Up to 1,400 cc	11p		7p
1,401–2,000 cc	14p		9p
Over 2,000 cc	22p		14p
Up to 1,600 cc		10p	
1,601–2,000 cc		11p	
Over 2,000 cc		13p	
From 1 March 2018			
Up to 1,400 cc	11p		7p
1,401–2,000 cc	14p		8p
Over 2,000 cc	22p		13p

continued

Engine size	Rate per Mile		
	Petrol	**Diesel**	**LPG**
Up to 1,600 cc		9p	
1,601–2,000 cc		11p	
Over 2,000 cc		13p	
From 1 December 2017			
Up to 1,400 cc	11p		7p
1,401–2,000 cc	14p		9p
Over 2,000 cc	21p		14p
Up to 1,600 cc		9p	
1,601–2,000 cc		11p	
Over 2,000 cc		13p	
From 1 September 2017			
Up to 1,400 cc	11p		7p
1,401–2,000 cc	13p		8p
Over 2,000 cc	21p		13p
Up to 1,600 cc		9p	
1,601–2,000 cc		11p	
Over 2,000 cc		12p	
From 1 June 2017			
Up to 1,400 cc	11p		7p
1,401–2,000 cc	14p		9p
Over 2,000 cc	21p		14p
Up to 1,600 cc		9p	
1,601–2,000 cc		11p	
Over 2,000 cc		13p	
From 1 March 2017			
Up to 1,400 cc	11p		7p
1,401–2,000 cc	14p		9p
Over 2,000 cc	22p		14p
Up to 1,600 cc		9p	
1,601–2,000 cc		11p	
Over 2,000 cc		13p	
From 1 December 2016			
Up to 1,400 cc	11p		7p
1,401–2,000 cc	14p		9p
Over 2,000 cc	21p		13p
Up to 1,600 cc		9p	
1,601–2,000 cc		11p	
Over 2,000 cc		13p	
From 1 September 2016			
Up to 1,400 cc	11p		7p
1,401–2,000 cc	13p		9p
Over 2,000 cc	20p		13p

Engine size	Rate per Mile		
	Petrol	Diesel	LPG
Up to 1,600 cc		9p	
1,601–2,000 cc		11p	
Over 2,000 cc		13p	
From 1 June 2016			
Up to 1,400 cc	10p		7p
1,401–2,000 cc	13p		9p
Over 2,000 cc	20p		13p
Up to 1,600 cc		9p	
1,601–2,000 cc		10p	
Over 2,000 cc		12p	

Notes

(1) *Quarterly updates* – The advisory fuel rates are reviewed quarterly and updated as necessary to be effective from 1 March, 1 June, 1 September and 1 December.

(2) *Hybrids* – Petrol hybrid cars are treated as either petrol or diesel cars for this purpose.

(3) *VAT* – HMRC accept these figures for VAT purposes, ie a business can reclaim the VAT element on the amount attributable to fuel or mileage allowances paid to employees or subcontractors.

(4) *Earlier periods* – Advisory fuel rates for periods from 1 December 2013: http://tinyurl.com/afr12-16.

Approved mileage allowance payments (AMAPs) rates for private vehicles

(*ITEPA 2003, ss 229–232, 235, 236*)

	Rate per business mile			
	From 2011/12		2002/03 to 2010/11	
	First 10,000 miles	Over 10,000 miles	First 10,000 miles	Over 10,000 miles
Cars	45p	25p	40p	25p
For each passenger making the same business journey	5p	5p	5p	5p
Motorcycles	24p	24p	24p	24p
Bicycles	20p	20p	20p	20p

Notes

(1) *Additional claims* – Where the employer pays less than the authorised rate, the employee may claim tax relief (mileage allowance relief) on the difference.

(2) *Passengers* – The additional rate which applies when carrying passengers was extended to volunteers with effect from 6 April 2011.

Company vans

(*ITEPA 2003, ss 154–164; SI 2018/1176*)

Tax Year	Cash equivalent of private use		
	Ordinary van £	Fuel £	Zero emissions £
2019/20	3,430	655	2,058
2018/19	3,350	633	1,340
2017/18	3,230	610	646
2016/17	3,170	598	634
2015/16	3,150	594	630
2014/15	3,090	581	Nil
2013/14	3,000	564	Nil

Notes

(1) *Zero emissions* – The cash equivalent for private use of zero emission vans is calculated as a percentage of the benefit of an ordinary van: 60% for 2019/20, 80% for 2020/21 and 90% for 2021/22 (*ITEPA 2003, s 155(1C)*).

(2) *No benefit* – No charge arises if the restricted private use condition is satisfied (see *ITEPA 2003, s 155(4)*).

Buses

(*ITEPA 2003, ss 242, 243*)

(1) *Works buses* – No income tax charge arises on the provision for employees of a works transport service, if the following conditions are satisfied:

- (a) the service is available generally to employees of the employer (or each employer) concerned;
- (b) the main use of the service is for qualifying journeys by those employees; and
- (c) the service:
  - (i) is used only by the employees for whom it is provided or their children, or
  - (ii) is substantially used only by those employees or children.

(2) *Local buses* – No charge to tax arises in respect of financial or other support provided for local bus services, if the following conditions are satisfied:

- (a) the service is available to employees generally;
- (b) it is used for qualifying journeys by employees of one or more employers; and
- (c) either:
  - (i) it is a local bus service, discounts for regional or zonal tickets are not permitted; or

(ii) the bus must be provided to other passengers on terms that are as favourable as the terms on which the bus is provided to employees.

(3) *Further information* – See EIM21850.

Bicycles

(*ITEPA 2003, s 244*)

(1) *Loan of bicycle* – No income tax charge arises on the provision for employees of cycles and/or cyclists' safety equipment, if the following conditions are satisfied:

(a) the cycles are available to all employees generally; and

(b) the cycles are used mainly for qualifying journeys, but other use of the cycle pleasure use does not disqualify the exemption.

(2) *Transfer of ownership* – No charge to tax arises if the cycle is transferred to an employee after a period of use in return for the market value of the cycle at the time of transfer, see **Valuation of used cycles**.

(3) *Further information* – See HMRC's Employment Income Manual at EIM21665-21668

Valuation of used cycles

Age of cycle (years)	**Original price of the cycle**	
	less than £500	**£500+**
1	18%	25%
1.5	16%	21%
2	13%	17%
3	8%	12%
4	3%	7%
5	Negligible	2%
6 or over	Negligible	Negligible

TRAVEL AND SUBSISTENCE

(*SI 2015/1948*)

Meal allowance while travelling

Duration of travel in the day	**Rate per day (maximum) £**	**Additional claim if travel ongoing at 8pm £**
5 hours or more	5	10
10 hours or more	10	10
15 hours or more and travel is ongoing at 8pm	15	–

Notes

(1) *What it applies to* – For payments made from 6 April 2016 to reimburse an employee for meals taken while in the course of qualifying travel (*ITEPA 2003, s 289A*).

(2) *Tax free* – The amounts paid within these limits are exempt from income tax.

Daily subsistence rate

Description	Rate per day (maximum) £	Detail
Breakfast pre 6am	5	Irregular early starters
One meal (5 hour)	5	Away for at least 5 hours
Two meals (10 hour)	10	Away for at least 10 hours
Late evening meal	15	Irregular late finishers after 8pm

Notes

(1) *What it applies to* – For periods before 6 April 2016, when travel is to a temporary place of work. The employee should be absent from his/her normal place of work for a continuous period exceeding 5 or 10 hours and make a purchase of food or drink.

(2) *How to use* – The employer must opt to use these rates on their P11D dispensation application. Lower rates can be paid.

(3) *Further information* – See HMRC's Employment Income Manual at EIM05231.

Personal incidental expenses

(*ITEPA 2003, ss 240, 241*)

From	Permitted amount per night	
	In UK £	Overseas £
6 April 1995	5	10

Notes

(1) *What it applies to* – Employees' minor personal expenditure, incurred whilst on business-related activities away from home. If the permitted amount is exceeded, the whole sum provided is taxable, unless it is refunded to the employer within a reasonable time.

(2) *Further information* – See HMRC's Employment Income Manual at EIM02730.

Lorry drivers' overnight subsistence allowance

(*ITEPA 2003, ss 289A, 289B*)

Period:	Permitted expense claim per night	
	No sleeper cab £	Sleeper cab £
2013 to 2017	34.90	26.20
Year 2012	33.85	25.39

Notes

(1) *Approval needed* – From 6 April 2017 the employer must apply for approval from HMRC to pay or reimburse employees at the above rates agreed to apply to overnight allowances for lorry drivers.

(2) *Evidence* – From 6 April 2017 HMRC require employers to carry out random checks to ensure that drivers are incurring an expense for food or accommodation, so the drivers need to retain at least some receipts.

(3) *Bespoke agreements* – Payments in excess of the above rates can be paid tax free if the employer has agreed a bespoke rate with HMRC.

(4) *Further information* – See HMRC's Employment Income Manual: EIM30255, EIM30200, EIM30260, EIM66110.

MOBILE PHONES

(*ITEPA 2003, s 319*)

(1) *One phone policy* – From 6 April 2006 no chargeable benefit arises where the employer provides one mobile phone per employee. There is no tax exemption for mobile phones provided for family members.

(2) *Top-up vouchers* – There is no tax charge on the provision of top-up payments for use of a mobile phone which is owned by the employer and provided to the employee.

(3) *What is a mobile phone?* – Includes a SIM card provided independently of a phone. Does not include devices that are solely PDAs, tablets or laptop computers (EIM21779).

CHILDCARE

Employer provided childcare vouchers

(*ITEPA 2003, ss 270A, 318A; SI 2013/513*)

Year	Weekly tax-free limit:		
Taxpayer's marginal rate	Basic rate £	Higher rate £	Additional rate £
2013/14 and later years	55	28	25
2012/13	55	28	22

Notes

(1) *Pre-April 2011* – Employees who joined the employer-provided childcare voucher scheme before 6 April 2011, and who are still employed by that employer, can continue to receive a tax-free benefit of £55 per week, whatever their marginal rate of tax.

(2) *Leaving the employer's scheme* – Within three months of opening a tax-free childcare account (see below) the parents must notify their employer that they are no longer eligible for employer-supported childcare.

(3) *Stay in employer's scheme* – Members of an employer-provided childcare voucher scheme can stay in that scheme or opt to open a tax-free childcare account (see below).

(4) *Closure of voucher scheme* – No new employees can join the employer-provided childcare voucher scheme from 4 October 2018. This date was extended by six months from 6 April 2018 (*SI 2018/462*).

Tax-free childcare accounts

(*SI 2015/488; SI 2015/522; Childcare Payments Act 2014*)

	Maximum contribution:		
	Parent contributes £	**Government matches £**	**Total per year £**
Child aged up to 12	8,000	2,000	10,000
Disabled child under 17	16,000	4,000	20,000

Notes

(1) *Savings account* – Parents can apply for an online savings account, into which the government will contribute funds as indicated above. The funds from the tax-free childcare account can only be spent with registered childcare providers who are signed-up to the scheme.

(2) *Earnings limits* – To qualify for the matching funds both partners must be employed or self-employed earning at least the National Minimum Wage for 16 hours per week, with neither having an income of over £100,000. The self-employed are not required to earn the minimum amount in the first 12 months of their business. Claimants of tax credits or universal credit do not qualify for the tax-free childcare account.

(3) *Further information* – See www.gov.uk/tax-free-childcare.

HEALTH RELATED BENEFITS

(ITEPA 2003, Pt 4)

Benefit	Limit of tax & NI exemption
Recommend medical treatment (see Note 1)	£500 per employee per year *(ITEPA 2003, s 320C)*
Eye test and spectacles or lenses	Required solely for VDU use *(ITEPA 2003, s 320A)*
Health screening or medical check-up	One screening per tax year *(ITEPA 2003, s 320B)*
Overseas medical treatment	Only when working abroad *(ITEPA 2003, s 325)*

Notes

(1) *Recommend treatment* – From 1 January 2015 the health-related intervention must be recommended by occupational health services and must be provided to help the employee return to work *(SI 2014/3226)*

(2) *Further information* – See HMRC's Employment Income Manual at EIM21765-21766.

RELOCATION EXPENSES

(ITEPA 2003, ss 271–289)

(1) *Exemption* – Up to £8,000 of reimbursed expenses for qualifying removal costs incurred on a change of the employee's residence.

(2) *Conditions* – The change of residence must be connected with starting a new employment or change of place of work or duties with an existing employer. The old residence must not be within reasonable commuting distance of the new work location.

(3) *Further information* – See HMRC's Employment Income Manual EIM03100-EIM03139.

TERMINATION PAYMENTS

(ITEPA 2003, Pt 6, Ch 3)

Tax year	Maximum tax free amount
From 1998/99 onwards	£30,000

Notes

(1) *Commencement* – All of the conditions described below apply where the employment ended, and the relevant termination benefits or payments were received, on or after

6 April 2018. Please refer to an earlier edition of *Bloomsbury's Tax Rates and Tables* for the conditions which applied to termination payments made before that date.

(2) *Relevant termination award* – This must be split between amount treated as employment income (PENP) and any residue which may be covered by the tax free amount.

(3) *Tax free amount* – No tax or National Insurance (employers' or employees') is payable to the extent that the residue of the 'relevant termination award' above the 'post-employment notice pay' (PENP) is sheltered by the available tax free amount. Payments taxed as earnings can't be sheltered by the tax free amount and are liable to NIC (*ITEPA 2003, s 402C*).

(4) *Post-employment notice pay* – PENP = ((BP × D) ÷ P) – T) where:

BP = employee's basic pay for last pay period before trigger date

D = number of days in post-employment period

P = number of calendar days in last pay period

T = payment or benefit received in connection with termination of employment which is taxable earnings

(5) *Exemptions* – Statutory redundancy pay and approved contractual payments, to the extent that they are exempt under *ITEPA 2003, s 309*, don't form part of the 'relevant termination award' but count towards the tax free amount.

(6) *Foreign service relief* – This no longer applies to employees who are resident in the UK at the time of the termination, except for seafarers (*FA 2018, s 10*).

(7) *Further information* – HMRC's Employment Income Manual EIM138744+.

(8) *Proposal* – Class 1A NIC will apply to taxable termination payments in excess of £30,000 from 6 April 2020.

SCHOLARSHIPS

(*ITTOIA 2005, s 776(1); SP 4/86*)

Period	**Specified amount**
From 1 September 2007	£15,480
From 1 September 2005–31 August 2007	£15,000
From 6 April 1992–31 August 2005	£7,000

Notes

(1) *Exemption* – No liability to income tax arises in respect of scholarship income, but only for the holder of the scholarship.

(2) *Benefit charge* – A scholarship will give rise to a chargeable benefit where it is provided to a member of the family or household of a director or employee, by reason of the employment of that director or employee (*ITEPA 2003, ss 211–215*).

EMPLOYMENT RELATED LOANS

Actual official rates of interest

(*ITEPA 2003, s 181; SI 2017/305*)

Period	Rate %
From 6 April 2017	2.50
6 April 2015–5 April 2017	3.00
6 April 2014–5 April 2015	3.25
6 April 2010–5 April 2014	4.00

Average official rates of interest

(*ITEPA 2003, s 182*)

Year	Average official rate %
2018/19	2.50
2017/18	2.50
2016/17	3.00
2015/16	3.00
2014/15	3.25
2013/14	4.00
2012/13	4.00

Notes

(1) *Maximum value* – No liability to tax or NIC arises where the combined value of all loans made by the employer to the employee in the year do not exceed £10,000 (£5,000 before 6 April 2014).

(2) *Interest charged* – No tax or NIC liability arises where the interest charged to the employee is equal to or higher than the official rate of interest at the time the loan was taken out.

(3) *Average rate* – The average official rates of interest are used if the loan was outstanding throughout the year and the normal averaging method of calculation is being used. The employer can use the alternative precise method to calculate the benefit.

(4) *Close company* – Where the loan is made by a close company to the directors or shareholders of that company, a corporation tax charge may also be due, see **Chapter 7**.

FLAT RATE ALLOWANCES

(*ITEPA 2003, s 367;* EIM32712)

Occupation			Deduction from 2013/14 onwards £	Deduction for 2008/09 to 2012/13 £
Agriculture		All workers	100	100
Airlines		Uniformed flight deck crew not cabin staff	1,022	850
Aluminium	A	Continual casting operators, process operators, de-dimplers, driers, drill punchers, dross unloaders, firemen (see Note 3), furnace operators and their helpers, leaders, mouldmen, pourers, remelt department labourers, roll flatteners	140	140
	B	Cable hands, case makers, labourers, mates, truck drivers and measurers, storekeepers	80	80
	C	Apprentices	60	60
	D	All other workers	120	120
Armed forces		For ranks below Officer:		
	A	Royal Navy	80	80
	B	Army	100	100
	C	Royal Marines	100	100
	D	Royal Air Force	100	100
Banks and Building societies		Uniformed doormen and messengers	60	60
Brass and copper		Braziers, coppersmiths, finishers, fitters, moulders, turners and all other workers.	120	120
Building	A	Joiners and carpenters	140	140
	B	Cement works and roofing felt and asphalt labourers	80	80
	C	Labourers and navvies	60	60
	D	All other workers	120	120
Building materials	A	Stone-masons	120	120
	B	Tilemakers and labourers	60	60
	C	All other workers	80	80

Occupation			**Deduction from 2013/14 onwards £**	**Deduction for 2008/09 to 2012/13 £**
Clothing	A	Lacemakers, hosiery bleachers, dyers, scourers and knitters, knitwear bleachers and dyers	60	60
	B	All other workers	60	60
Constructional engineering (see Note 4)	A	Blacksmiths and their strikers, burners, caulkers, chippers, drillers, erectors, fitters, holders up, markers off, platers, riggers, riveters, rivet heaters, scaffolders, sheeters, template workers, turners, welders	140	140
	B	Banksmen labourers, shop-helpers, slewers, straighteners	80	80
	C	Apprentices and storekeepers	60	60
	D	All other workers	100	100
Electrical and electricity supply	A	Those workers incurring laundry costs only	60	60
	B	All other workers	120	120
Trades ancillary to Engineering	A	Pattern makers	140	140
	B	Labourers, supervisory and unskilled workers	80	80
	C	Apprentices and storekeepers	60	60
	D	Motor mechanics in garage repair shop	120	120
	E	All other workers	120	120
Fire service		Uniformed firefighters and fire officers	80	80
Food		All workers	60	60
Forestry		All workers	100	100
Glass		All workers	80	80
Healthcare	A	Ambulance staff on active service (ie excluding staff who take telephone calls or provide clerical support)	140	140
	B	Nurses and midwives, chiropodists, dental nurses, occupational speech physios and therapists, phlebotomists, radiographers. For shoes, stocking and socks where style/ colour is obligatory	100 18	100 18

continued

Occupation			Deduction from 2013/14 onwards £	Deduction for 2008/09 to 2012/13 £
	C	Plaster room orderlies, hospital porters, ward clerks, sterile supply workers, hospital domestics, hospital catering staff	100	100
	D	Laboratory staff, pharmacists, pharmacy assistants	60	60
	E	Uniformed ancillary staff – maintenance workers, grounds staff, drivers, parking attendants and security guards, receptionists and other uniformed staff	60	60
Heating	A	Pipe fitters and plumbers	120	120
	B	Coverers, laggers, domestic glaziers, heating engineers and all their mates	120	120
	C	All gas workers and all other workers	100	100
Iron Mining	A	Fillers, miners and underground workers	120	120
	B	All other workers	100	100
Iron and steel	A	Day labourers, general labourers, stockmen, time-keepers, warehouse staff and weighmen	80	80
	B	Apprentices	60	60
	C	All other workers	140	140
Leather	A	Curriers (wet workers), fellmongering workers, tanning operatives (wet)	80	80
	B	All other workers	60	60
Particular engineering (see Note 5)	A	Pattern makers	140	140
	B	Chainmakers; cleaners, galvanisers, tinners and wire drawers in the wire drawing industry; tool-makers in the lock making industry	120	120
	C	Apprentices and storekeepers	60	60
	D	All other workers	80	80

Occupation			**Deduction from 2013/14 onwards £**	**Deduction for 2008/09 to 2012/13 £**
Police force	A	Police officers (ranks up to and including Chief Inspector)	140	140
	B	Community support officers and	140	140
	C	Other uniformed police employees	60	60
Precious metals		All workers	100	100
Printing	A	Letterpress Section – Electrical engineers (rotary presses), electrotypers, ink and roller makers, machine minders (rotary), maintenance engineers (rotary) and stereotypers	140	140
	B	Bench hands (periodical and bookbinding), compositors and readers (letterpress section) telecommunications and electronic section wireroom operators, warehousemen (paper box making section)	60	60
	C	All other workers	100	100
Prisons		Uniformed prison officers	80	80
Public service: docks and inland waterways	A	Dockers, dredger drivers, hopper steerers	80	80
	B	All other workers	60	60
Public service: public transport	A	Garage hands (including cleaners and mechanics)	80	80
	B	Conductor and drivers	60	60
Quarrying		All workers	100	100
Railways	A	See the appropriate category for craftsmen, eg engineers, vehicle builders etc.		
	B	All other workers	100	100
Seamen	A	Carpenters on passenger liners	165	165
	B	Carpenters on cargo vessels, tankers, coasters and ferries	140	140

continued

Occupation			**Deduction from 2013/14 onwards £**	**Deduction for 2008/09 to 2012/13 £**
Shipyards	A	Blacksmiths and their strikers, boilermakers, burners, carpenters, caulkers, drillers, furnacemen (platers), holders up, fitters, platers, plumbers, riveters, sheet iron workers, shipwrights, tubers, welders	140	140
	B	Labourers	80	80
	C	Apprentices and storekeepers	60	60
	D	All other workers	100	100
Textiles and textile printing	A	Carders, carding engineers, overlookers and technicians in spinning mills	120	120
	B	All other workers	80	80
Vehicles	A	Builders, railway wagon etc. repairers and railway wagon lifters	140	140
	B	Railway vehicle painters and letterers, railway wagon etc. builders' and repairers' assistants	80	80
	C	All other workers	60	60
Wood and furniture	A	Carpenters, cabinet makers, joiners, wood carvers and woodcutting machinists	140	140
	B	Artificial limb makers (other than in wood), organ builders and packaging case makers	120	120
	C	Coopers not providing own tools, labourers, polishers and upholsterers	60	60
	D	All other workers	100	100

Notes

(1) *Flat rate allowance* – For most classes of industry a tax deduction is given for certain amounts 'representing the average annual expenses incurred by employees of the class to which the employee belongs in respect of the repair and maintenance of work equipment'.

(2) *'Workers' and 'all other workers'* – These are references to manual workers or to workers who have to pay for the upkeep of tools and special clothing.

(3) *'Firemen'* – Means persons engaged to light and maintain furnaces.

(4) *'Constructional engineering'* – Means engineering undertaken on a construction site, including buildings, shipyards, bridges, roads and other similar operations.

(5) *'Particular engineering'* – Means engineering undertaken on a commercial basis in a factory or workshop for the purposes of producing components such as wire, springs, nails and locks.

(6) *Other occupations* – If the occupation is not listed in the table, a standard amount of £60 can be claimed for the laundry costs of uniforms or protective clothing (tinyurl.com/flatra).

Payroll matters

REAL TIME INFORMATION (RTI)

RTI procedures

(*SI 2003/2682, regs 67B–67H*)

PAYE procedure	**Under RTI**
Application of PAYE to employees' pay.	The amounts of PAYE deductions and payments must be reported online, generally on or before the contractual payment date (note 3).
Payment of PAYE must be made by: • 19th of the month if paying by cheque; or • 22nd of the month, for electronic payments.	Nil payments must be reported monthly on EPS, unless the scheme is registered as an annual scheme (see below). Where employees are paid quarterly, a nil EPS must be submitted for months in which no payment is made. HMRC match the employer's liability for PAYE to the payments made by the employer each month or quarter. Any apparent underpayments will be chased promptly.
End of year	Last FPS for the tax year marked as 'final' to be submitted by the last payment date in the year, or EPS can be used as the final submission by 19 April following the year end. Forms P60 to given to those employed on 5 April, by 31 May following the tax year end.
Starters	New worker's details are sent to HMRC in the FPS that includes the first payment to that person.
Leavers	Date the worker left employment should be included on the FPS when making the final payment to that employee, or include the leaving date on next FPS with zero amounts for pay. Leavers are given a P45 or leaver statement, but the P45 is not sent to HMRC.
Annual PAYE scheme: all employees are paid once per year in the same tax month	The PAYE scheme must be registered as 'annual' with HMRC, in which case one FPS should be submitted for the month of payment. Nil EPS are not required for the months when no payments are made.
Expenses and benefits reporting	Forms P11D, and P11D(b) must be submitted to HMRC and given to employees by 6 July after the tax year end.

PAYE procedure	Under RTI
Construction Industry Scheme (CIS)	CIS reports are submitted monthly outside RTI. Companies (not unincorporated businesses) can set off CIS tax against their own PAYE liabilities by reporting CIS deductions on the EPS each month.
Statutory payments (see **Chapter 16**)	Payments of statutory pay are recorded on the FPS. Any recovery of statutory pay must be claimed on the EPS each month and once a recovery has been made in a tax year the YTD figure must continue to be reported for that year.

Notes

(1) *Commencement* – All employers must report under RTI from 6 April 2014. However, employers who can't use a computer due to a disability or a religious objection can ask HMRC for permission to submit paper forms.

(2) *Universal Credit* – RTI is required in order to implement Universal Credit (see **Chapter 15**) and to improve fraud detection for Tax Credits.

(3) *Payment date* – If this falls at a weekend or bank holiday and payment to the employees is brought forward to the first banking day before the weekend/bank holiday the contractual payment date must still be used to report for RTI not the actual date when the employee was paid; see RTI reports below.

(4) *Further information* – See tinyurl.com/RTrunpay, tinyurl.com/RTIestaff, and tinyurl.com/RTIwtdwed.

Data items for RTI

(*SI 2003/2682, reg 67CA, Sch A1, paras 21, 38*)

Data	What and why
Hours worked	To compare to Tax Credits claims: record the number of hours the employee is contracted to work within these bands: A Up to 15.99 hours B 16 to 23.99 hours C 24 to 29.99 hours D 30 hours or more E Other
Passport number	Not a requirement, but record where it is collected as part of checks for whether the person is entitled to work in the UK.
BACS hash code	Where employees are paid by BACS a four-character hash code must be added into the BACS payment file.
Late reporting reason	For each employee include a late reporting reason, eg: G reasonable excuse.

RTI Reports

(*SI 2003/2682, regs 67B–67H*)

Reports	Function and submission period
Full Payment Submission (FPS)	Must be submitted on or before the 'payment date', when the employees are due to be paid, see notes below for exceptions.
Employer Payment Summary (EPS)	To report nil payments to employees or to claim set-off of statutory payments or CIS deductions against PAYE due. To correct EPS figures send a new EPS using the appropriate EPS for the year affected.
Earlier Year Update (EYU)	Ideally submit before 19 May following tax year end, to correct any of the year-to-date totals submitted in the final FPS for the previous tax year, but can be submitted at any time post year end.
NI Number Verification Request (NVR)	To verify or obtain a National Insurance number for new employees. Can only be submitted after an EAS or the first FPS has been submitted.

Notes

(1) *Cash payments to casuals* – Where the employee is paid in cash for work done on the day, at a time when it would be impractical to make an RTI report, the FPS can be submitted on the earliest of the next regular RTI report date, or seven days after the payment date.

(2) *Notional payments* – Where there is no transfer of money from the employer to the employee, such as an award of shares, the RTI report can be made at the earliest of the time the employer operates PAYE on the notional payment or 14 days after the end of the tax month.

(3) *Error code* – When the FPS is late the employer should include the appropriate code in the late reporting reason field on the FPS.

(4) *Late reporting* – Situations for which an FPS can be submitted after the date of payment see: tinyurl.com/RTIfpsaPay, and note the codes for late reporting reasons: tinyurl.com/RTIltrp.

Other PAYE returns

(*SI 2003/2682, regs 85, 90*)

Forms	Due Date
P11D, P11D(b)	6 July following the end of the tax year
P46 (Car)	When a car is first provided report by: ● 2 May for q/e 5 April; ● 2 August for q/e 5 July; ● 3 November for q/e 5 October; and ● 2 February for q/e 5 January.

PAYE thresholds

(*SI 2003/2682, reg 9*)

	2019/20 £	2018/19 £	2017/18 £	2016/17 £	2015/16 £	2014/15 £
LEL weekly	118	116	113	112	112	111
Weekly	240	228	221	212	204	192
Monthly	1042	988	958	917	883	833
Annual	12,500	11,850	11,500	11,000	10,600	10,000

Notes

(1) *Tax thresholds* – The above thresholds are the level of earnings at which income tax becomes payable, but NICs will be due at lower thresholds (see **Chapter 14**).

(2) *PAYE requirement* – The employer must operate a PAYE scheme and report under RTI once an employee earns over the lower earnings limit (LEL).

PAYE codes

(*SI 2003/2682, reg 7*)

PAYE code	Application
Suffix	
L	For those eligible for the personal allowance. Also used for 'emergency' tax codes (note 3).
M	For those who have received the marriage allowance.
N	For those who have surrendered the marriage allowance.
T	Used where HMRC are reviewing other items in tax code (eg the income-related reduction in the personal allowance). Also used if allowances have been used up or reduced to nil (0T).
BR	Deduct tax at 20% from all pay.
D0	Deduct tax at 40% on all pay.
D1	Deduct tax at 45% from all pay.
SD0	Deduct tax at 21% on all pay (note 4).
SD1	Deduct tax at 41% from all pay (note 4).
SD2	Deduct tax at 46% from all pay (note 4).
NT	No tax should be deducted from the pay or pension.
OT	Used as default PAYE tax code to deduct tax at the basic, higher and additional rates where new employees have no form P45 or starter information, and for pension income of a person still in receipt of employment income.

continued

PAYE code	Application
Prefix:	
K	Used where total coding 'deductions' (eg other income) exceed allowances.
S	For Scottish taxpayer
C	For Welsh taxpayer

Notes

(1) *Use of codes* – PAYE codes are used by employers or pension providers to calculate the amount of tax, if any, to be deducted from an individual's pay or pension.

(2) *Maximum deduction* – The maximum which can be deducted using any PAYE code is 50% of gross pay.

(3) *Emergency code* – The emergency tax codes for 2019/20 are:

- 1250L W1(week 1);
- 1250L M1(month 1).

(4) *Scottish tax codes* – Apply from 2018/19 although SDO applied in 2017/18 to take tax at 40% (see **Chapter 18**)

(5) *Welsh tax codes* – Apply from 2019/20 (see **Chapter 18**)

(6) *Further information* – see www.gov.uk/employee-tax-codes.

PAYE and Class 1 NIC – accounting periods

(*SI 2003/2682, regs 69, 70*)

			Payment must clear HMRC's bank account:	
Tax Period	**Tax Month**	**Tax quarter**	**When paid electronically**	**Paid by other means**
6 Apr–5 May	1	–	22 May	19 May
6 May–5 Jun	2	–	22 June	19 June
6 Jun–5 Jul	3	1	22 July	19 July
6 Jul–5 Aug	4	–	22 August	19 August
6 Aug–5 Sep	5	–	22 September	19 September
6 Sept–5 Oct	6	2	22 October	19 October
6 Oct–5 Nov	7	–	22 November	19 November
6 Nov–5 Dec	8	–	22 December	19 December
6 Dec–5 Jan	9	3	22 January	19 January
6 Jan–5 Feb	10	–	22 February	19 February
6 Feb–5 Mar	11	–	22 March	19 March
6 Mar–5 Apr	12	4	22 April	19 April

Notes

(1) *Electronic payment* – HMRC recommend that all employers pay electronically, but employers with 250 or more employees must pay PAYE liabilities electronically.

(2) *Non-banking day* – Where due day falls on a weekend or a bank holiday, the payment must reach HMRC on the previous working day.

(3) *Non-electronic payments* – When paying by post employers must enclose a pre-printed payslip for the correct period. HMRC treat payments as being received on third day after the cheque is received.

(4) *Quarterly payment* – Where the employer has reasonable grounds to believe their 'average monthly amount' will be less than £1,500 he can ask HMRC to for permission to pay quarterly, in which case the payment for all months in the quarter is due after the end of the quarter as shown above. Call the HMRC payment enquiry line: 0300 200 3401 to discuss quarterly or annual payments.

(5) *Further information* – For available payment methods and timings see www.gov.uk/pay-paye-tax.

PAYE PENALTIES

RTI returns from 6 April 2014

(*FA 2009, Sch 55*)

Number of employees in PAYE scheme	Amount of monthly late filing penalty £
1 to 9	100
10 to 49	200
50 to 249	300
250 or more	400

Notes

(1) *Not automatic* – Penalties for late or non-filing of the FPS due within the tax year are only issued to employers after a manual risk assessment by HMRC officers. When the RTI data collection mechanism is sufficiently robust these penalties will be issued automatically (*FA 2009, s 106, Sch 55, paras 6B–6D*).

(2) *One default* – Each PAYE scheme is permitted one default for late filing per tax year when no penalty charged (*FA 2009, Sch 55, para 6C*).

(3) *Grace period* – For periods ending between 6 March 2015 and 5 April 2019 no penalty is applied if the FPS is submitted within three days of the payment date. Employers who persistently file late, but within three days of the payment date may be considered for a penalty.

(4) *New employer* – The first FPS submitted by a new employer within 30 days paying its employees for first time will not attract a penalty.

(5) *Frequency* – Only one penalty is issued per month even if FPS reports are submitted more frequently. Penalties are charged quarterly at the end of: July, October, January and April.

(6) *Tax-geared penalties* – Where FPS is more than three months late, a penalty of 5% of the amount showing on the missing returns applies (*FA 2009, Sch 55 para 6D*).

(7) *Appeals* – Employers can appeal online against the penalty quoting the unique ID shown on the penalty notice, or submit an appeal in writing. The penalty must be paid within 30 days unless an appeal is lodged.

(8) *Specified charge* – An estimated PAYE charge based on the PAYE liability for the previous tax year. It is raised if the employer has not submitted an FPS or EPS for the tax month and the scheme is not registered as annual. The specified charge is payable until it is replaced by EPS or FPS (*SI 2003/2682, reg 75A*).

(9) *Inaccuracies* – The penalty regime for errors or inaccuracies in RTI returns is the same as applies to all other tax returns – see **Chapter 17**: **Structure of penalties** (*FA 2007, s 97, Sch 24, para 1*).

(10) *Further information* – For guidance on RTI penalties see: tinyurl.com/whydrprt.

RTI returns to 5 April 2014

(*FA 2009, s 106, Sch 55*)

RTI report:	2012/13	2013/14
FPS filed in-year	• No late filing penalty. • No inaccuracy penalty	• No late filing penalty. • Inaccuracy penalty may apply.
Final FPS/EPS or EYU for the tax year	• Late filing penalty if final FPS submitted after 19 May 2013. • Inaccuracy penalty may apply.	• Late penalty if final FPS submitted after 19 April 2014. No late filing penalty if EYU submitted by 19 May 2014. • Inaccuracy penalty may apply.
EPS	No penalties but specified charge may apply if no nil EPS submitted	No penalties but specified charge may apply if no nil EPS submitted

Note

(1) *End of year* – Penalty of £100 per 50 employees (or part thereof) for each month (or part-month) that the final FPS or EPS return remains outstanding after 19 April.

Pre-RTI regime

(1) *Late end of year returns* – Penalties for late filing of forms P35 and P14 are (*TMA 1970, s 98A*):

- *Up to 12 months late* – £100 for each 50 employees (or part thereof) for each month the failure continues;

- *Over 12 months late* – penalty up to the amount of PAYE etc due and unpaid at 19 April following year end.

(2) *Inaccurate returns* – Maximum penalty for incorrect PAYE returns is 100% of the difference between the amount payable under the return and the amount payable had the return been correct. For incorrect forms P9D and P11D, the maximum penalty is up to £3,000 per incorrect form (*TMA 1970, ss 98, 98A*).

(3) *Benefits and expenses* – Penalties for late filing of forms P11D and P9D are (*TMA 1970, s 98(1)(b)*):

- Initial penalty of up to £300 per form;
- Continuing penalty of up to £60 for each day on which the penalty continues after imposition of initial penalty.

(4) *Returns of Class 1A NIC* – Penalties for late filing of form P11D(b) are similar to the penalties for the late filing of PAYE returns (*SI 2001/1004, reg 81(2)*).

Late payments of PAYE

(*FA 2009, s 107, Sch 56*)

Default penalties

Number of times payment is late in a tax year	Penalty %
1	No penalty (as long as the payment is less than 6 months late – see below)
2–4	1
5–7	2
8–10	3
11 or more	4

Notes

(1) *Small differences* – From 2014/15 where the difference in PAYE owed (according to HMRC) and the amount paid for the month is £100 or less no penalty will be charged, but interest will still accrue on underpayments.

(2) *Percentage applies to* – From 2014/15: to each late payment due within the tax year, ie each month or quarter, and are charged automatically each quarter. For earlier periods the percentage applies to the total amount which is late in the tax year.

(3) *Further penalties* – In addition to the above, a 5% penalty is imposed:

- Where monthly or quarterly payments remain unpaid after six months; and,
- where payments remain outstanding after 12 months.

Such penalties apply even where only one payment in the tax year is late.

(4) *Small employers* – A small employer who makes quarterly payments can only have a maximum of four failures in a tax year, so the maximum initial default penalty

rate is 1% (CH152550). However, further penalties may still arise for prolonged lateness (see note 3).

(5) *Suspension or reduction* – HMRC may reduce a penalty due to 'special circumstances' at its discretion. Penalties are suspended if the employer has an agreement for deferred payment in place (ie a 'time to pay' arrangement) with HMRC, which is not broken.

(6) *Appeals* – Employers can appeal using HMRC's online PAYE service, or using paper form. Tax agents can submit online appeals for clients. Penalty should be cancelled if there is a 'reasonable excuse' for the failure (*FA 2009, Sch 56, paras 9, 10, 13, 16*).

(7) *Further information* – See: tinyurl.com/PAYEltpd.

Interest on PAYE paid late

(*SI 2003/2682, regs 82, 83*)

(1) *From 2014/15* – Interest is charged on any PAYE payments including specified charges, not paid by the due date within the tax year.

(2) *Years to 2013/14* – Where an employer has not paid HMRC the net tax payable under PAYE within 14 days of the end of the tax year (or 17 days, if the payment is made electronically), the unpaid tax carries interest at the prescribed rate (see **Chapter 17**) from the reckonable date until the date of payment.

(3) *Additional debt* – Interest on late paid PAYE is in addition to and separate from any penalties for late payment of PAYE. Interest is also charged on PAYE penalties which are not paid within 30 days of the penalty notice.

RECOVERY OF TAX DEBTS THROUGH PAYE

(*ITEPA 2003, s 684(2), (3A); SI 2011/1585*)

Debt from:	Maximum recovery in PAYE code
Operation of PAYE	£3,000
Underpaid Class 2 NICs	£3,000
Self-assessment balancing payment	£3,000
Other taxes, overpaid tax credits and penalties where PAYE earnings are:	(see note 4)
less than £30,000	£3,000
£30,000 to £40,000	£5,000
£40,001 to £50,000	£7,000
£50,001 to £60,000	£9,000
£60,001 to £70,000	£11,000
£70,001 to £80,000	£13,000
£80,001 to £90,000	£15,000
Over £90,000	£17,000

Notes

(1) *Amend code* – HMRC may alter an employee's PAYE code, to recover all or part of a relevant debt up to the above limits (*SI 2003/2682, reg 14A(1)*), with effect from 6 April 2012 (*SI 2011/1584, reg 2(2)*).

(2) *Process* – HMRC always write to the taxpayer explaining the intention to code out. The taxpayer has the right to object to coding out, and may arrange to pay the debt by another method.

(3) *Limits* – The total deductions made through the PAYE code cannot exceed 50% of the employee's relevant pay.

(4) *Graduated limits* – Limits above £3,000 apply from 2015/16 (*SI 2014/2483*).

APPRENTICESHIP LEVY

(*FA 2016, Pt 6*)

From	Annual charge on payroll	Annual allowance
6 April 2017	0.5%	£15,000

Notes

(1) *Payable by* – All employers in the UK who have 'pay subject to employers' class 1 NIC'. This includes employers who pay other employment levies such as in the construction, engineering and film industries.

(2) *Pay bill* – This is the total pay of all employees who have earnings liable to NI, including where the NI is due at 0%, such as for apprentices aged under 25. The levy is paid on the entire pay bill, but not on the value of benefits subject to class 1A NIC.

(3) *Allowance* – The levy is only payable to the extent that it is not covered by the annual allowance. Effectively employers with a pay bill of no more than £3 million will not pay the levy. Only one annual allowance can be claimed per group of companies or connected employers, but it can be apportioned amongst the group's PAYE schemes, apportionment being reported on the April EPS and is fixed for the tax year.

(4) *Period of payment* – The levy is payable monthly with PAYE deductions by 22nd of each month, and reported in each month's EPS.

(5) *Apprenticeship funding* – From May 2017 employers in England who pay the apprenticeship levy can access the amount they have paid as levy to fund the cost of training apprentices. Different arrangements apply in Scotland, Northern Ireland and Wales.

(6) *Further information* – See tinyurl.com/jfu78m2.

STUDENT LOANS

(*SI 2009/470, reg 29; SI 2011/784, reg 6*)

Year	Pay deducted	Plan 1 threshold			Plan 2 threshold		
		Annual £	Monthly £	Weekly £	Annual £	Monthly £	Weekly £
2019/20	9%	18,935	1,577.92	364.14	25,725	2,143.75	494.71
2018/19	9%	18,330	1,527.50	352.50	25,000	2,083.33	480.77
2017/18	9%	17,775	1,481.25	341.82	21,000	1,750.00	403.84
2016/17	9%	17,495	1,457.91	336.44	21,000	1,750.00	403.84
2015/16	9%	17,335	1,444.58	333.36	N/A	N/A	N/A
2014/15	9%	16,910	1,409.16	325.19	N/A	N/A	N/A
2013/14	9%	16,365	1,363.75	314.71	N/A	N/A	N/A

Notes

(1) *Payroll deduction* – Employers are responsible for deducting student loan repayments from employees' pay at the percentage shown, and passing the payment to HMRC, who will in turn account for the funds to the Student Loan Company.

(2) *Plan 1* – Where students began their course prior to 1 September 2012 they repay the loan under plan 1, and are due to make loan repayments from gross earnings above this threshold.

(3) *Plan 2* – Students from England & Wales who began their course on or after 1 September 2012 repay student loans under plan 2 from 6 April 2016.

(4) *Post graduate loan (PGL)* – Applies from 6 April 2019 with repayments due at 6% above earnings of £21,000 for 2019/20.

(5) *Reporting* – Student loan deductions must be reported on each FPS, but the loan deductions data will be passed to the Student Loan Company just once after the end of the tax year.

(6) *Further information* – See guidance for employers on the deduction of student loans: www.gov.uk/guidance/special-rules-for-student-loans.

CONSTRUCTION INDUSTRY SCHEME (CIS)

CIS deductions and returns

(*FA 2004, ss 62, 70; SI 2005/2045, regs 4, 7, 8*)

Sub-contractors:	Rate of deduction
Registered to receive payments gross	0%
Registered with HMRC	20%
Not registered with HMRC	30%

Notes

(1) *Returns* – Contractors must file a monthly CIS return online of the deductions taken from payments made to subcontractors, by 19th of the month following the last tax month.

(2) *Payments* – The CIS deductions must reach HMRC by 22nd of the following month if made electronically, or by 19th of that month if paying by post.

(3) *Quarterly payments* – A contractor who believes their 'average monthly amount' will be less than £1,500 can choose to pay tax on a quarterly basis (ie for quarters ending 5 July, 5 October, 5 January and 5 April). The CIS return must be filed monthly.

(4) *'Nil' returns* – Contractors who have not paid any subcontractors in the previous tax month are not required to submit a nil return (*SI 2015/429*).

(5) *Further information* – See: www.gov.uk/what-you-must-do-as-a-cis-contractor.

Late CIS returns

(*FA 2009, s 106, Sch 55, paras 7–13*)

Period	Penalty
Up to 2 months late	£100 automatic
More than 2 months late	£200 automatic
More than 6 months late	Greater of: • 5% of CIS deductions; and • £300
More than 12 months late except where taxpayer withholds information deliberately (see below)	Greater of: • 5% of CIS deductions; and • £300
Information deliberately withheld and more than 12 months late:	
Information withheld but **not** concealed	Greater of: • 70% of CIS tax liability; and • £1,500 (for gross payment contractors)
Information withheld **and** concealed	Greater of: • 100% of CIS tax liability; and • £3,000 (for gross payment contractors)

Notes

(1) *Commencement* – For return periods beginning on or after 6 October 2011 (see Compliance Handbook: CH61120).

(2) *Contractors new to CIS* – For the first CIS return the upper limit for the 'fixed' penalties is £3,000 where the return is less than six months late. This limit does not replace any 'tax geared' penalties, but the £300 minimum that would otherwise be charged, is removed (*FA 2009, Sch 55, para 13*).

Late CIS payments

(*FA 2009, s 107, Sch 56, paras 6–8*)

- *Penalties* – For quantum of penalties for late payment, see **Chapter 17**.
- *Scope* – The taxpayer can incur 'default' penalties for any amount of unpaid CIS deduction at the penalty date, plus two further penalties for CIS deductions which are more than 6 and 12 months late. For HMRC guidance see their Compliance Handbook (CH153000).
- *Appeal or reduction* – Taxpayer can appeal against imposition and/or the amount of the penalty. HMRC may reduce a penalty due to 'special circumstances', which does not include inability to pay. Penalties are suspended if the contractor has a 'time to pay' agreement with HMRC and complies with its terms. The penalty may be removed if there is a 'reasonable excuse' for the failure (*FA 2009, Sch 56, paras 9, 10, 13, 16*).

4

Shares and share options

ADMINISTRATION

Tax-advantaged share schemes

Notes

(1) *Registration* – Employers must register a share scheme with HMRC, whether it is tax advantaged or not, when there is a reportable event for the scheme by 6 July following the end of the tax year in which the scheme commenced.

(2) *Self-certification* – New tax advantaged schemes must be registered and self-certified by 6 July following the end of the tax year in which the scheme is implemented.

(3) *Online filing* – Employers must use the online ERS system to file the annual return for each share scheme by 6 July after the end of the tax year where there is a reportable event in the scheme in that tax year (ERS Bulletin: July 2015).

(4) *Penalties* – An automatic penalty of £100 applies for late submission of an annual share scheme return. Additional penalties of £300 apply on 7 October, and 7 January, following the end of the tax year if the annual return is still not filed by those dates.

(5) *Making good amounts of tax paid* – Where tax is due on the award of shares or options the employee must reimburse the employer any tax and NIC paid by the employer in respect of the shares/options. This must be done by 6 July following the end of the tax year in which that event occurred (*ITEPA 2003, s 222*).

(6) *Further information* – See http://tinyurl.com/emrltdscits.

ENTERPRISE MANAGEMENT INCENTIVES (EMI)

(*ITEPA 2003, Pt 7, Ch 9, Sch 5*)

Action	**Tax & NIC Implications**
Grant of option	No income tax or NICs arise
Exercise of option	No income tax or NIC charges, if exercised within 10 years of grant and no disqualifying events have occurred. Employee must pay at least market value of shares as at the date of grant (*ITEPA 2003, ss 529–530*).

continued

Action	Tax & NIC Implications
Disposal of shares	Gain subject to CGT. Shares disposed of from 6 April 2013 can qualify for entrepreneurs' relief where the option grant date falls at least 1 year before disposal date; the requirement to hold 5% of ordinary share capital is ignored (*FA 2013, Sch 24*).

Notes

(1) *Purpose* – To help small, higher risk companies recruit and retain employees. EMI options must be granted for qualifying purposes (*ITEPA 2003, Sch 5, para 4*).

(2) *Number of employees* – The company must have fewer than 250 'full-time equivalent employees' at the option grant date (sum of all employees of a parent company and qualifying subsidiaries) (*ITEPA 2003, Sch 5, para 12A*).

(3) *Gross assets* – Must not exceed £30 million at the option grant (limit applies to the gross assets of the group as a whole) (*ITEPA 2003, Sch 5, para 12*).

(4) *Maximum company limit* – The total value of shares under EMI options granted by the company must not exceed £3 million (*ITEPA 2003, Sch 5, para 7*).

(5) *Maximum employee entitlement* – An employee may be granted qualifying options over shares with a total value not exceeding £250,000 (*SI 2012/1360*).

(6) *Notice required* – Options granted must be notified to HMRC using the ERS service within 92 days of the option grant (*ITEPA 2003, Sch 5, para 44*). Send reasonable excuse for late notification including unique scheme number, name of the company and scheme name to: shareschemes@hmrc.gsi.gov.uk.

(7) *Annual return* – Employers operating an EMI scheme must submit an annual return using the ERS online service by 6 July in the immediately following tax year (*ITEPA 2003, Sch 5, para 52*).

(8) *Further information* – See HMRC's Employee Tax Advantaged Share Scheme User Manual para ETASSUM50000+.

SHARE INCENTIVE PLAN (SIP)

(*ITEPA 2003, Pt 7, Ch 6, Sch 2; ITTOIA 2005, ss 392–396, 405–408, 770; SI 2001/1004, reg 22(8), Sch 3, Pt 9, para 7*)

Type of share and annual limit per employee	When shares acquired	Shares taken from plan during the first 3 years	Shares taken from plan during years 3 to 5	Shares taken from plan after 5 years
Free shares up to £3,600 and Matching shares (maximum 2:1 to partnership shares)	No income tax or NICs to pay on the value of the shares (*ITEPA 2003, s 490*)	Income tax payable on the market value of the shares when taken out of the plan (*ITEPA 2003, s 505(2)*)	Income tax payable on the lower of the market value of the shares: • when awarded, or • when taken out of plan (*ITEPA 2003, s 505(3)*)	No income tax or NICs to pay

Type of share and annual limit per employee	**When shares acquired**	**Shares taken from plan during the first 3 years**	**Shares taken from plan during years 3 to 5**	**Shares taken from plan after 5 years**
Partnership shares up to £1,800	No income tax or NICs to pay on the money used to buy the shares (*ITEPA 2003, s 492*)	Income tax payable on the market value of the shares when taken out of the plan (*ITEPA 2003, s 506(2)*)	Income tax payable on the lower of: • the pay used to buy the shares, or • the market value of the shares when taken out of the plan (*ITEPA 2003, s 506(3)*)	No income tax or NICs
Dividend shares	No income tax or NICs on dividends used to buy dividend shares (*ITEPA 2003, ss 490(1(b), 493, 496; ITTOIA 2005, s 770(2)*)	Dividends used to buy shares are taxed as a dividend in the year the shares are taken out of the plan (*ITTOIA 2005, ss 394(2), 407(2)*)	No income tax or NICs	No income tax or NICs

Notes

(1) *All employees* – Participation in the SIP cannot be restricted to particular groups or individuals. However, the employer can exclude employees who haven't worked for the company for a minimum period of time, which may be no longer than 18 months (*ITEPA 2003, Sch 2, paras 7, 8, 16*).

(2) *NI exemption* – There is generally no National Insurance liability when an employee acquires shares from a SIP. However, a Class 1 NIC liability (and an income tax charge) may arise if the employee leaves the company, or takes shares out of the plan, within five years of joining it (see National Insurance Manual, NIM06806–06807).

(3) *Further information* – See HMRC's Employee Tax Advantaged Share Scheme User Manual para ETASSUM20000+.

COMPANY SHARE OPTION PLAN (CSOP)

(ITEPA 2003, Pt 7, Ch 8, Sch 4)

Action:	**Tax & NIC Implications**
Grant of option	No income tax or NICs arise, unless option was granted at a discount (*ITEPA 2003, s 526*).
Exercise of option	No income tax or NIC charges if the option is exercised between 3 and 10 years of the date of grant, or under 'good leaver' provisions within 3 years of the grant, (*ITEPA 2003, s 524*).
Disposal of shares	Gains are subject to CGT.

Notes

(1) *Tax advantaged* – The company can only grant share options if the CSOP has been registered and self-certified with HMRC (*ITEPA 2003, Sch 4, Pt 7*).

(2) *Maximum per employee* – Approved options with a market value of no more than £30,000, calculated at the date of grant (*ITEPA 2003, Sch 4, Pt 2).*

(3) *Eligible employees* – The individuals who receive the CSOP options must be either a full-time director or a 'qualifying employee' of the scheme organiser (or constituent company in a group scheme), and must not have a material interest (more than 30% of ordinary share capital) in the company in which the options are granted (*ITEPA 2003, Sch 4, Pt 3*).

(4) *Further information* – See HMRC's Tax Advantaged Share Scheme User Manual para ETASSUM40000+.

SAVE AS YOU EARN (SAYE)

(ITEPA 2003, Pt 7, Ch 7, Sch 3)

Action	**Tax & NIC Implications**
Grant of option	No income tax or NICs arise, unless option was granted at a discount. If options are accidentally granted at a discount to the market value of the shares on the agreed valuation date in excess of the permitted 20%, the option is treated as not having been granted, and will attract no tax advantages.
Exercise of option	No income tax or NIC charges if the option is exercised 3 years or more after the date of grant or if within 3 years of grant, in certain defined circumstances such as injury, disability or redundancy (*ITEPA 2003, s 519*).
Interest and bonuses	No income tax liability arises on interest and any bonus payable under a certified SAYE savings arrangement (*ITTOIA 2005, ss 702–703*). No NIC liability arises when proceeds of savings are used to buy shares.
Disposal of shares	Gains are subject to CGT.

Notes

(1) *Purpose* – SAYE, also known as Sharesave, allows employees to save, by having amounts deducted from their pay after income tax and NIC. This money is used to provide share options to current employees and directors of the scheme organiser or constituent company in a group scheme, to purchase the company's shares in the future, at a price determined at the time of invitation (*ITEPA 2003, Sch 3, Pt 3*).

(2) *Self-certification* – SAYE option schemes must be self-certified by the scheme organiser and registered with HMRC (*ITEPA 2003, Sch 3, Pt 8*).

(3) *Linked savings arrangements* – Individuals may contract to make monthly contributions over a three or five-year period, and may choose to leave the contributions in their accounts for an additional two years (ETASSUM34170–34180).

(4) *Contribution breaks* – Individuals can suspend contributions to the SAYE for up to 12 months without leaving the scheme or their options lapsing (ETASSUM34140).

(5) *Contribution limits* – Maximum contribution permitted is £500 per month. The minimum contribution cannot exceed £10 per month (*ITEPA 2003, Sch 3, Pt 5*).

(6) *Bonus and interest rates* – The bonus rate is set at the time the savings contract is entered into, and is unaffected by any subsequent change to the rate.

(7) *Further information* – See HMRC's Employee Tax Advantaged Share Scheme User Manual para ETASSUM30000+.

EMPLOYEE SHAREHOLDER SHARES

(*ITEPA 2003, ss 226A–226D, 326B; ITTOIA 2005, s 385A; TCGA 1992, ss 236B–236G; CTA 2009, s 1038B*)

Action:	**Tax & NIC implications**
Award of shares before 1 December 2016	Up to £2,000 of shares awarded to each employee are free of income tax and NIC. Employees are deemed to have the value of the shares acquired (*ITEPA 2003, ss 226A–226D*).
Sale of shares back to issuing company	No income tax charge arises where the shares are sold back to the company if the individual is not an employee (or office-holder) of the employer company or of an associated company at the time of disposal (*ITTOIA 2005, s 385A*).
Disposal of shares	Capital gains realised on the disposal of up to £50,000 of shares (valued on acquisition) are exempt from CGT when the employee disposes of them (see notes 7–9) (*TCGA 1992, ss 236B–236G*).

Notes

(1) *Cancelled* – This scheme was effectively cancelled for shares issued from December 2016. If the employee received independent advice on their shareholder agreement prior to 1.30pm on 23 November 2016, the agreement could be signed by 2 December 2016 with the tax reliefs for the shares intact.

(2) *Period of scheme* – The tax and NI exemptions apply to shares awarded to employees who signed an employee shareholder status contract under the *Growth and Infrastructure Act 2013, s 31* on or after 1 September 2013 and before 1 December 2016, or 2 December 2016 as detailed in note 1.

(3) *Taxable* – Income tax and NICs are due on any value of shares awarded that exceeds £2,000.

(4) *Employment rights* – By taking up employee shareholder status, in order to receive the shares, the employee had to opt out of a package of employment rights. The employee was not treated as disposing of an asset by relinquishing the employment rights.

(5) *No connection* – The employee shareholder must not have a 'material interest' in the company (or its parent company) when the shares are issued or allotted, or within one year prior to that date, and must not be connected with an individual with such an interest (*ITEPA 2003, s 226D; TCGA 1992, s 236D*).

(6) *Corporation tax* – The deemed payment of up to £2,000 for the shares for income tax purposes is disregarded for the corporation tax deduction under *CTA 2009, Pt 12,* but where shares worth more than £2,000 are awarded, the excess over £2,000 qualifies for a corporation tax deduction.

(7) *Restricted gains on disposal* – Where the shares were acquired in connection with an employee shareholder agreement entered into on or after 16 March 2016 and before 1 December 2016, the gains made on the disposal of those shares are exempt from CGT up to a maximum of £100,000 for the person making the disposal. This is a lifetime limit.

(8) *Unrestricted gains* – Gains made on disposal of employee shareholder shares acquired from 1 September 2013 and 15 March 2016 do not count towards that £100,000 limit (*FA 2016, s 88*).

(9) *No transfer* – Shares acquired under this scheme enjoy CGT exemption on disposal if and only if they are held by the employee who received them under the shareholder agreement, subject to these limits. Where the shares are transferred to a spouse or civil partner the exemption will not apply on disposal by that spouse/partner.

(10) *Further information* – See http://tinyurl.com/Emshtx.

5

Pensions and investments

PENSION CONTRIBUTIONS

(*FA 2004, Pt 4, Schs 28–36*)

Individual has	Annual maximum relievable contributions
Relevant UK earnings	100% of earnings capped by annual allowance
Little or no UK earnings	£3,600 gross contribution

Notes

(1) *Individual's contributions* – Income tax relief is generally given at the basic rate by the registered pension scheme claiming 25% of the net contribution from HMRC. This also applies to contributions made by individuals who pay no tax, or who are taxed at rates lower than 20%.

(2) *Higher rate relief* – Tax relief is given at the individual's marginal rate of tax (where higher than 20%) by claiming through the tax return or the PAYE code, on relievable contributions are made by the individual within the above annual limits. Additional contributions may be made by the individual, but no further tax relief is available (*FA 2004, s 190*).

(3) *Employer contributions* – The individual's employer may make pension contributions on behalf of the individual up to the limit of the annual allowance (see below). These contributions do not attract income tax relief but in general will be a qualifying deduction for tax purposes for the employer.

(4) *Excluded contributions* – Contributions made after the individual has reached age 75 don't attract income tax relief (*FA 2004, s 188(3)*).

Annual allowances

(*FA 2004, ss 218, 228*)

Tax year:	2019/20 £	2018/19 £	2017/18 £	2016/17 £	2015/16 £	2014/15 £
Annual Allowance	40,000	40,000	40,000	40,000	40,000	40,000
Restricted AA (note 7)	10,000	10,000	10,000	10,000	N/A	N/A
MPAA	4,000	4,000	4,000	10,000	10,000	N/A

Notes

(1) *Annual allowance charge* – This is levied at the individual's marginal income tax rate charged on earned income. Scottish taxpayers pay the charge at their highest Scottish income tax rate. The charge does not apply in the tax year the individual dies, retires due to severe ill-health, or is a deferred member whose benefits cannot increase (*FA 2004, ss 229(3), 230*).

(2) *Scheme to pay* – Where the annual allowance charge exceeds £2,000, the member can ask his pension scheme to pay the liability, with the scheme benefits being actuarially reduced accordingly (*FA 2004, ss 237A, 237B*).

(3) *PIP alignment* – All pension input periods (PIPs) are aligned with the tax year from 2016/17. All earlier PIPs were deemed to end on 8 July 2015 and recommenced on 9 July 2015 to allow for this adjustment (*FA 2004, ss 238ZA, 238ZB*).

(4) *Double allowance* – For 2015/16 only it was possible to enjoy a two annual allowances of £40,000 each; for a PIP ending on 8 July 2015, and for a PIP ending on 5 April 2016. The maximum unused allowance which can be carried forward to 2016/17 is £40,000 (*FA 2004, s 228C*).

(5) *Carry forward* – Unused annual allowance from the three tax years preceding the current tax year may be added to the current year's allowance, using earliest years' allowance first. This does not apply for the MPAA. The taxpayer must have been a member of a registered pension scheme for the years from which the allowance is carried forward (*FA 2004, s 228A*).

(6) *MPAA* – Money purchase annual allowance applies to restrict contributions to the same or other money purchase/defined contribution schemes, where a taxpayer has flexibly accessed their defined contribution scheme or SASS. The MPAA doesn't apply when only the tax-free cash is taken (*FA 2004, 227B*). The MPAA is £20,000 if the flexible access occurred before 9 July 2015 *(FA 2004, s 228C*).

(7) *Restricted allowance* – Where the taxpayer's adjusted net income is more than £150,000, their annual allowance is restricted by £1 for every £2 of income over that threshold. Adjusted net income includes all taxable earnings plus pension contributions made by the taxpayer's employer on their behalf (*F(No 2)A 2015, Sch 4, Pt 4*).

PENSION WITHDRAWALS

Lifetime allowance

(*FA 2004, s 215*)

Tax year	2019/20 £	2018/19 £	2017/18 £	2016/17 £	2015/16 £	2014/15 £
Allowance	1.055m	1.03m	1m	1m	1.25m	1.25m

Notes

(1) *Pension age* – This is the minimum age from which a person can draw their pension. It is normally 55, but members of certain professions and occupations can draw

pension benefits earlier (see protected retirement ages). Pension age is due to be raised in future years.

(2) *Lifetime allowance charge* – This tax charge is calculated as percentage of the excess pension pot above the lifetime allowance, measured at the time benefits are first taken. If the benefits are taken as a pension the charge is 25%: where the benefits are taken as a lump sum the charge is 55%. These rates also apply to Scottish taxpayers.

(3) *Individual protection 2016* – Individuals who expect to have pension savings over £1 million at 5 April 2016 can apply online to protect their lifetime allowance up to £1.25 million, but this needs to happen before pension benefits are taken (*FA 2016, Sch 4*).

(4) *Fixed protection 2016* – Individuals who have not applied for the previous versions of fixed protection can apply to protect their lifetime allowance at £1.25m, where an online election is made from July 2016. To meet the conditions of fixed protection there must be no further contributions into their pension fund from 6 April 2016 onwards (*FA 2016, Sch 4*).

(5) *Further information* – See: HMRC's Pension Tax Manual para PTM094100+.

Tax charges on withdrawals

(*FA 2004, Pt 4, Ch 5*)

Charge	Tax rates
Lifetime allowance charge (*FA 2004, s 215*)	See note 2 under **Lifetime allowance:** 55% on lump sum, 25% on pension
Annual allowance charge (*FA 2004, s 227*)	See note 1 under **Annual allowance:** highest marginal rate
Unauthorised payments charge (*FA 2004, s 208*)	40%
Unauthorised payments surcharge (*FA 2004, s 209*)	15%
Short service refund lump sum charge (*FA 2004, s 205; SI 2010/536*)	20% on first £20,000, 50% on amounts over £20,000. These rates also apply to Scottish taxpayers
Serious ill-health lump sum charge (*FA 2004, s 205A*)	55%
Special lump sum death benefits charge (*FA 2004, s 206*)	55%
Authorised surplus payments charge (*FA 2004, s 207*)	35%
Scheme sanction charge (*FA 2004, s 240*)	5%–40%
De-registration charge (*FA 2004, s 242*)	40%

Notes

(1) *Pension freedoms* – From 6 April 2015 members of defined contribution pension schemes who are aged 55 or over can draw all of their pension savings without restriction, without having to purchase an annuity at that point. However, withdrawals in excess of the 25% tax-free amount are taxed at the individual's marginal tax rate for the year of withdrawal. For 2014/15 the pension access rules were relaxed as described in notes 2 to 4 below (*FA 2014, ss 41–42, Sch 5*).

(2) *Flexible drawdown* – Where the individual has guaranteed pension income of £12,000 (£20,000 before 27 March 2014) all their pension funds can be taken in cash; 25% tax free and the rest is taxed at their marginal income tax rate for earned income.

(3) *Capped drawdown* – Where the individual does not qualify for flexible drawdown, the maximum drawdown cash that can be taken is 150% (120% before 27 March 2014) of the equivalent single life annuity.

(4) *Trivial commutation* – Where an individual over age 60 has total pension rights under all registered pension schemes of less than £30,000 (£18,000 before 27 March 2014) the total can be taken in cash: 25% tax free, the rest taxed at the taxpayer's marginal rate for earned income.

(5) *Small lump sums* – Up to three pension pots with a value of less than £10,000 (£2,000 prior to 27 March 2014) can be taken as a lump sum.

(6) *Tax free pensions advice* – From 6 April 2017 an employer may pay for relevant pensions advice for an employee, former employee, or prospective employee, who is within five years of retirement age. The benefit of receiving this advice is exempt from tax and NIC where the cost doesn't exceed £500 per person per year (*ITEPA 2003, s 308C*). A similar exemption applied from 14 December 2004 for employees only, where the advice cost no more than £150 per person (*SI 2002/205*).

PROTECTED RETIREMENT AGES

(*FA 2004, Sch 36, paras 21, 23; SI 2005/3451, reg 3, Sch 2*)

The following professions and occupations have lower retirement ages than the standard of age 55.

Athletes	**Members of the Reserve Forces**
Badminton players	Motor racing drivers
Boxers	Rugby players
Cricketers	Skiers (downhill)
Cyclists	Snooker or billiards players
Dancers	Speedway riders
Divers (saturation, deep sea and free swimming)	Squash players
Footballers	Table tennis players
Golfers	Tennis players (including real tennis)
Ice hockey players	Trapeze artists
Jockeys – flat and national hunt racing	Wrestlers

Notes

(1) *Normal retirement age* – Retirement benefits can generally only be taken from a registered pension scheme from minimum pension age of 55. Lower pension ages for certain qualifying occupations were generally abolished from 6 April 2006.

(2) *Protected age* – The above occupations and profession have protected pre-existing rights to take benefits under a personal pension scheme or retirement annuity contract before the age of 50. This is the individual's protected pension age (see HMRC's Pensions Tax Manual, PTM062220).

INDIVIDUAL SAVING ACCOUNTS (ISA)

(*ITTOIA 2005, Pt 6, Ch 3; SI 1998/1870, reg 4*)

ISAs	2019/20 £	2018/19 £	2017/18 £	2015/16 & 2016/17 £	1 July 2014– 5 April 2015 £	6 April 2014– 30 June 2014 £
Overall limit	20,000	20,000	20,000	15,240	15,000	11,880
Cash limit	20,000	20,000	20,000	15,240	15,000	5,940
Junior ISA	4,368	4,260	4,128	4,080	4,000	3,840
Lifetime ISA	4,368	4,000	4,000	N/A	N/A	N/A
Help to save	50 per month	N/A	N/A	N/A	N/A	N/A

Notes

(1) *Combination of savings* – From 1 July 2014, investors can invest any combination of cash or shares in an ISA up to the limits shown (*SI 2014/1450*).

(2) *Junior ISA (JISA)* – Available to UK residents who are under 18 and who don't have a Child Trust Fund (CTF) account. The investment limit can be divided between cash and stocks and shares. When the holder reaches age 18, their JISA becomes an adult ISA (*ITTOIA 2005, s 695A*).

(3) *Young people* – Whether or not a person aged 16 to 18 holds a Junior ISA, they may invest in an adult cash ISA up to the cash limit, but not in a stocks and shares ISA.

(4) *Help to buy ISA* – From 1 December 2015 to 30 November 2019 individuals can open a help to buy ISA to save for their first home. The saver may deposit up to £1,000 initially and then up to £200 per month. The Government will contribute a 25% bonus, up to £3,000 per ISA which is paid when the funds are used to buy the home (*Help to Buy ISA factsheet*).

(5) *Lifetime ISA* – From 6 April 2017 UK resident individuals aged between 18 and 40 can open a lifetime ISA. This limit is part of the overall £20,000 for all ISA saving. The Government adds a 25% bonus of up to £1,000 per year. The funds can be withdrawn from age 60 onwards or when the saver is terminally ill. Alternatively, the savings may be used to help purchase the saver's first home worth up to £450,000,

after the account has been open for at least 12 months. The Government bonus is lost if the funds are accessed for other purposes (*Lifetime ISA fact sheet*).

(6) *Inherited ISA allowance* – For deaths on or after 2 December 2014 the surviving spouse/civil partner has an additional ISA allowance for the year of death equivalent to the value of the deceased person's savings at the date of death (*SI 2015/869*).

(7) *Help to save* – From 1 September 2018 individuals receiving tax credits or universal credit can open a help to save account with NS&I. The Government will contribute 50% bonus on the second and fourth anniversaries of opening the account (*SI 2018/87*).

(8) *Further information* – For ISAs see www.gov.uk/individual-savings-accounts. For help-to-buy ISA see http://tinyurl.com/htbisa. For help to save see www.gov.uk/get-help-savings-low-income.

INVESTMENTS FOR CHILDREN BY PARENTS

(*ITTOIA 2005, s 629*)

Assets given by parent to:	Annual income derived	Treated as income of
Their child	Up to £100	Child
Their child	Over £100	Parent
Their child's cash ISA	Up to £100	Child, but tax free
Their child's cash ISA	Over £100	Capital treated as part of parent's ISA limit
Their child's JISA or child trust fund account	Unlimited	Child, but tax free

Notes

(1) *Applies* – Where the child is aged under 18, and is neither married nor in a civil partnership.

(2) *Further information* – ISA guidance notes: http://tinyurl.com/ISAmGn.

ENTERPRISE INVESTMENT SCHEME (EIS)

(*ITA 2007, Pt 5; TCGA 1992, s 150A, Sch 5B*)

Shares issued in:	Maximum investment per tax year £	Rate of income tax relief	Amount permissible to carry back £
2018/19 and 2019/20 (note 1)	2,000,000	30%	All
2012/13 to 2017/18	1,000,000	30%	All
2011/12	500,000	30%	All
2008/09 to 2010/11	500,000	20%	50,000 for 2008/09 See Note 2
2006/07 to 2007/08	400,000	20%	50,000

Notes

(1) *Knowledge intensive* – Any investment over £1 million per tax year must be invested in knowledge intensive companies (*FA 2018, Sch 4*).

(2) *New shareholders only* – For shares issued on or after 18 November 2015, EIS relief can only apply if the shareholder did not previously own any shares in the company other than subscriber shares, or shares issued under the EIS, SEIS or VCT schemes (*ITA 2007, s 164A*).

(3) *Carry-back* – EIS relief is available for the tax year in which the shares are issued, but the investor may carry back some or all of the tax relief to the immediately preceding year, subject to the overriding tax relief limit for that earlier year (*ITA 2007, s 158(4)*).

(4) *Disposal relief* – A gain made on the disposal of EIS shares after holding them for at least three years is exempt from CGT to the extent that full income tax relief was been claimed, and not withdrawn, on the investment (*TCGA 1992, s 150A*).

(5) *Deferral relief* – Where the disposal proceeds from any capital gain are reinvested in a subscription for EIS shares in the four-year period that starts one year before the date of the gain, all or part of the original gain can be deferred. The deferred gain is brought back into charge on the disposal of the EIS shares or on a breach of the investment conditions (*TCGA 1992, Sch 5B*).

(6) *Further information* – See HMRC's Venture Capital Schemes Manual at VCM10000.

SEED ENTERPRISE INVESTMENT SCHEME (SEIS)

(*TCGA1992, ss 150E–150G; ITA 2007, Pt 5A*)

Shares issued in:	Maximum investment £	Rate of income tax relief %	Rate of CGT reinvestment relief %
2013/14 onwards	100,000	50	50
2012/13	100,000	50	100

Notes

(1) *Small companies* – SEIS can be used by companies with gross assets of no more than £200,000, and up to 25 full-time equivalent employees. There is no minimum investment for the investor.

(2) *Scope* – A company can accept up to £150,000 as SEIS investments in any three-year period, but it can go on to raise money under EIS or VCT at a later stage. SEIS cannot be used after permission to use EIS has been granted.

(3) *Income tax relief* – The relief may be claimed in respect of investments in SEIS shares issued on or after 6 April 2012. The relief is given as a reduction in the individual's tax liability for the tax year in which the investment was made.

(4) *Carry back* – A claim can be made to treat the investment as having been made in the immediately preceding tax year (but not before 2012/13). This election is

also effective for CGT reinvestment relief (see HMRC's Venture Capital Manual at VCM45010).

(5) *Reinvestment relief* – This exempts from CGT 100% or 50% of a gain where the disposal proceeds are reinvested in new SEIS shares, within the same tax year in which the disposal occurs (*TCGA 1992, Sch 5BB*). Income tax relief must be given for the SEIS investment and not withdrawn.

(6) *Disposal relief* – A gain on the disposal of SEIS shares after the relevant three-year period is exempt from CGT to the extent that income tax relief has been given, and not withdrawn, for the investment in the shares.

(7) *Further information* – See HMRC's Venture Capital Schemes Manual at VCM30000.

SOCIAL INVESTMENT TAX RELIEF (SITR)

(*ITA 2007, Pt 5B; TCGA 1992, ss 255A–255B, Sch 8B*)

Shares issued in:	Maximum investment per tax year £	Rate of income tax relief	Amount permissible to carry back £
2015/16 to 2018/19	1,000,000	30%	All
2014/15	1,000,000	30%	none

Notes

(1) *Social enterprises* – SITR is a venture capital scheme for investments in social enterprises (eg charities, community interest companies), which have fewer than 500 employees and a maximum of £15 million gross assets.

(2) *Applies to* – Subscriptions for new shares and debt instruments issued by social enterprises on and after 6 April 2014.

(3) *Income tax relief* – Tax relief is given as a tax reduction following a claim, which must be made no later than the fifth anniversary of 31 January following the tax year of investment. The tax relief may be reduced or withdrawn in certain circumstances, broadly on a disposal of the SITR investment or a breach of the investment conditions, within three years.

(4) *Disposal relief* – A gain on the disposal of SITR investment realised at least three years after it was acquired is exempt from CGT to the extent that income tax relief has been given on the investment, and has not been withdrawn.

(5) *Hold-over relief* – Where a gain is reinvested in SITR shares or debt instruments in a four-year period that begins one year before the gain arose, all or part of the original gain can be held-over. That gain is brought back into charge to CGT on the disposal of the SITR investment or a breach of the investment conditions.

(6) *Further information* – Outline guidance is found at: http://tinyurl.com/SIRTapply.

VENTURE CAPITAL TRUSTS (VCT)

(*ITA 2007, Pt 6*)

Shares issued from	**Maximum annual investment £**	**Rate of relief**
6 April 2006	200,000	30%
6 April 2004	200,000	40%
6 April 2000	100,000	20%

Notes

(1) *Income tax relief* – This is given for the tax year in which the shares are issued by the VCT. The relief available is the lower of 30% of the investment value, and the amount which reduces the individual's income tax liability to nil.

(2) *Dividend exemption* – Individual investors are exempt from income tax on dividends in respect of ordinary VCT shares acquired with the above maximum amounts, provided that the shares were acquired for genuine commercial reasons and not for a tax avoidance purpose (*ITTOIA 2005, Pt 6, Ch 5*).

(3) *CGT exemption* – Disposals of VCT shares by individual investors are exempt from CGT (and losses are not allowable) where the shares were acquired within the above permitted maximum amounts, and if certain other conditions are satisfied (*TCGA 1992, ss 151A, 151B*).

(4) *From 6 April 2014* – Tax relief is withdrawn if the VCT shares are disposed of within five years of acquisition and income tax relief is restricted where investments are conditionally linked to a VCT share buy-back or have been made within six months of a disposal of shares in the same VCT (*FA 2014, Sch 10*).

(5) *Further information* – See: HMRC's Venture Capital Schemes Manual at VCM50000.

COMMUNITY INVESTMENT TAX RELIEF (CITR)

(*ITA 2007, Pt 7; CTA 2010, Pt 7*)

Investor:	**Rate of relief of invested amount**	**Given over:**	**Maximum relief:**
Individual	25%	5 years	Unlimited
Company	25%	5 years	€200,000

Notes

(1) *For investments in* – Accredited Community Development Finance Institutions (CDFIs), for a period of at least five years.

(2) *Given as* – Reduction in the investor's tax liability, limited to the amount of tax liability for each year.

(3) *Carry forward* – For investments made from April 2013, the tax relief can be carried forward to the next year or accounting period if it is not fully relieved in the relevant tax year (*ITA 2007, s 335A*; *CTA 2010, s 220A*).

(4) *Claimed for* – Tax year or accounting period in which the investment falls and the four subsequent tax years or accounting periods (*ITA 2007, s 335(3)*; *CTA 2010, s 220(4)*).

(5) *Further information* – See http://tinyurl.com/kxxtpmf.

EMPLOYEE OWNERSHIP TRUST

(*TCGA 1992, ss 236H–236P; ITEPA 2003, Pt 4, Ch 10A; IHTA 1984, ss 13, 28, 75, 86; CTA 2009, s 1292*)

Relief from	**Type of relief**	**Starts from**	**Maximum relief:**
Capital gains tax	No gain, no loss on shares transferred	6 April 2014	unlimited
Inheritance tax	Exempt disposal on transfer to EOT	6 April 2014	unlimited
Income tax	Tax exempt bonuses paid to employees of the company controlled by the EOT	1 October 2014	£3,600 per year per employee
Corporation tax	Deduction given for tax exempt bonuses paid	1 October 2014	£3,600 per year per employee

Notes

(1) *Controlling interest* – The tax reliefs described above apply when shares in a trading company are transferred to an employee-ownership trust (EOT), and within that tax year the EOT has acquired a controlling interest in that company.

(2) *Individuals* – The reliefs are only available for transfers of shares made by individuals, trustees or personal representatives of deceased individuals, not by companies.

(3) *After the disposal* – The transferor must not hold 5% or more of shares in the company, or less than two-fifths of the employees and office holders in the company must hold 5% or more in the company.

(4) *Further information* – HMRC's Capital gains manual CG67800.

6

Business profits

MAKING TAX DIGITAL (MTD)

Timetable

(F(No 2)A 2017, ss 60–62, Sch 14)

Commencing	Businesses which are:	Must report:
VAT periods starting on and after 1 April 2019	VAT registered with VATable turnover of £85,000 or more and are not deferred	Totals as per the 9 boxes on current VAT return
VAT periods starting on and after 1 October 2019	VAT registered and VATable turnover over £85,000 who are deferred (note 2)	Totals as per the 9 boxes on current VAT return
Accounting periods starting no earlier than 6 April 2020	Income taxpayers with turnover over a threshold to be confirmed	Totals per current self-employment section of SA return
Accounting periods starting no earlier than 1 April 2020	Companies	Corporation tax – details to be announced

Notes

(1) *MTD for VAT* – Most VAT registered businesses (see note 5) will be required to enter the MTD regime for VAT periods commencing on and after 1 April 2019 Businesses in deferred categories can't commence filing under MTD for VAT until their first VAT period which begins on or after 1 October 2019 (see note 2).

(2) *Deferred categories* – Businesses who are required to make payments of VAT on account, as they pay VAT of more than £2m per year, plus those in the following categories can't commence VAT filing under MTD until their first VAT period which begins on or after 1 October 2019:

- VAT groups
- VAT divisions
- traders based overseas
- trusts
- unincorporated not-for-profit organisations
- certain public sector bodies and local authorities
- annual account scheme users

(3) *Digital records* – Once within the MTD regime, the business or landlord must keep the accounting or VAT records which are required to make tax or VAT returns, in a digital form. This can be within MTD-functional accounting software or in spreadsheets. Where more than one software package or spreadsheet is used, each package or spreadsheet must be linked digitally so the data is transferred between them without a person retyping it (*SI 2018/261, reg 6*; VAT Notice 700/22, section 7).

(4) *VAT reporting* – The VAT return figures must be submitted to HMRC directly from the MTD-compatible software by way of an API (application programming interface) to HMRC. No further information is required to be, or can be, submitted under MTD at this time.

(5) *Voluntary registered* – Businesses which are VAT registered on a voluntary basis and whose turnover is less than £85,000, can choose to enter the MTD regime and report VAT figures under MTD but they are not required to do so (VAT Notice 700/22, section 2.3).

(6) *Other taxes* – Commencement dates for income tax and corporation tax reporting under MTD have not been announced. The MTD regime won't be extend to other taxes before April 2020, and for corporation tax this may be much later as the public consultation hasn't started yet (Mel Stride written statement HCWS47, 13 July 2017).

(7) *MTD for income tax* – Businesses and landlords will be required to submit summary totals of expenses and receipts on a quarterly basis via MTD-compatible software to HMRC.

(8) *Exemptions* – The conditions for exemption from MTD will vary for each tax. Those already exempt from online filing for VAT will be automatically exempt from MTD for VAT. Other businesses will have to apply to HMRC for an exemption on the grounds of; insolvency, religion, or that it is not reasonably practical to keep digital records by reason of age, disability, remoteness of location, or other reason (VAT Notice 700/22 section 2.2).

(9) *Further information* – See VAT notice 700/22 and Bloomsbury Professional: MTD Tracker, available as part of all Bloomsbury Professional tax packages.

CASH BASIS

Trading business

(*ITTOIA 2005, s 25A, Pt 2, Ch 3A, ss 33A, 51A, 56A, Ch 17A, Pt 3, Ch 3*)

Tax Year	Entry threshold £	Exit threshold £
2019/20	150,000	300,000
2018/19	150,000	300,000
2017/18	150,000	300,000
2016/17	83,000	166,000
2015/16	82,000	164,000
2014/15	81,000	162,000

Notes

(1) *Elect in* – Unincorporated trading businesses can elect to calculate profits/losses for tax purposes on the basis of the cash received and expenses paid out, known as the cash basis. This cash basis replaces the cash basis used by barristers, with some transitional arrangements (*ITTOIA 2005, s 25A*).

(2) *Permitted turnover* – For the first period of using the cash basis turnover must be no more than the entry threshold. Where the business is operated by a universal credit claimant, it can start to use the cash basis up to the exit threshold (*ITTOIA 2005, s 31B*).

(3) *Excluded businesses* – The following businesses cannot use the cash basis (*ITTOIA 2005, s 31C*):

- companies;
- LLPs;
- farmers using the herd basis;
- persons using profit averaging for farmers and artists;
- persons carrying on a mineral extraction trade;
- persons who have claimed business premises renovation allowance or R&D allowance; and
- Lloyd's underwriters.

(4) *Exit* – The business must cease to use the cash basis when its annual turnover exceeds the exit threshold. Alternatively, the business may leave the cash basis when its commercial circumstances change such that the cash basis is no longer appropriate.

(5) *Loan interest* – The deduction for loan interest paid is limited to £500 per year, although a full deduction for hire purchase costs and credit card interest for business purchases is permitted (*ITTOIA 2005, s 57B*).

(6) *Losses* – Trade losses can only be carried forward to the following tax year. No sideways or carry back of loss relief is permitted (*ITA 2007, s 74E*).

(7) *Accounting year* – The business can make up its accounts to any date in the year and use the cash basis.

(8) *Further information* – Outline guidance is found at: www.gov.uk/simpler-income-tax-cash-basis. Technical guidance is provided in HMRC's Business Income Manual at BIM70000.

(9) *Three line accounts* – Where the trader has turnover below the VAT registration threshold he may submit just three totals (turnover, expenses and profit) on the self-employment short SA return (see: tinyurl.com/zvz43uj).

Property businesses

(*ITTOIA 2005, ss 271A–271E, 272ZA, 276A, 307A–307F, 329A, 334A*)

Tax Year	Entry threshold £	Exit threshold £
2019/20	150,000	150,000
2018/19	150,000	150,000
2017/18	150,000	150,000

Notes

(1) *Opt out* – From 6 April 2017 the cash basis for unincorporated property businesses is the default accounting treatment, but the landlord may opt out by making an election on his tax return (*ITTOIA 2005, s 271A(10)*).

(2) *Excluded* – The following are not permitted to use the cash basis for property businesses (*ITTOIA 2005, s 271A(2), (7)*):

- companies;
- LLPs;
- partnerships with one or more partners who are not individuals;
- trustees;
- where the property is jointly owned by spouses or civil partners, and one of those individuals uses the GAAP basis of accounting for their share of the joint property income;
- where the receipts for the year, calculated on the cash basis, exceed £150,000.

(3) *Finance costs* – These costs may be deducted as incurred, subject to a restriction where the capital value of the loans outstanding at the end of the period exceeds the value of the let property when it was first let by the taxpayer plus any improvements made by that landlord since that date (*ITTOIA 2005, ss 307C, 307D*).

(4) *Residential property* – The restriction outlined in note 3 applies before, and in addition to, the restriction on the deduction of finance costs described under Residential Property Lettings below.

FIXED RATE DEDUCTIONS

(*ITTOIA 2005, Ch 5A*)

Optional use – From 6 April 2013 any unincorporated trading business or profession, can use the following fixed rate deductions, also known as simplified expenses, to replace the calculation of actual costs incurred. These rates can be used whether or not the business also opts to use the cash basis (*ITTOIA 2005, s 94B*).

Not companies – Any firm which includes a company as a partner is prohibited from using these fixed rate deductions (*ITTOIA 2005, s 94C*).

Motor expenses

(*ITTOIA 2005, ss 94D–94G*)

Vehicle	Business use	Rate per mile
Car or goods vehicle	First 10,000 miles per year (833 per month)	45p
Car or goods vehicle	In excess of 10,000 miles per year (833 per month)	25p
Motor cycle	All such journeys	24p

Notes

(1) *Other deductions* – These rates do not cover the finance element of a finance lease or hire purchase, which may be claimed in addition to the mileage rate, subject to private use adjustment. In addition, journey-specific costs such as parking, toll and congestion charges may be claimed.

(2) *Excluded vehicles* – Goods vehicles or motorcycles acquired under the cash basis where a full deduction has been made for the cost, and vehicles for which capital allowances have previously been claimed, cannot use these mileage rates (*ITTOIA 2005, s 94E*).

(3) *More than one car* – Where a business uses more than one car, including vehicles used by employees, it must aggregate all business mileage across all the vehicles that qualify for a fixed rate deduction to calculate the overall deduction (*ITTOIA 2005, s 94F*).

(4) *Further information* – See HMRC's Business Income Manual at BIM75005.

Use of home for business purposes

(*ITTOIA 2005, s 94H*)

Home used for working hours per month	Claim per month £
25 to 50 or more	10
51 to 100 or more	18
101 or more	26

Notes

(1) *Which costs* – Businesses that use the home for business purposes can opt to use the above fixed deduction in place of the business proportion of home expenses including; power, telephone, internet or broadband. These rates don't cover council tax (domestic rates in Northern Ireland), insurance and mortgage interest, so a business proportion of those costs can be claimed in addition.

(2) *Separate months* – The fixed rate expense claimed can be different for each month, depending on the use of the property in that month. There is no pro-rata reduction where the home is only used for part of the month.

(3) *Partners* – From 6 April 2016 partners in partnerships can claim the use of home deduction (*FA 2016, s 24*).

(4) *Further information* – See HMRC's Business Income Manual at BIM75010.

Business premises used partly as a home

(*ITTOIA 2005, s 94I*)

Number of relevant occupants	Applicable amount per month £
1	350
2	500
3 or more	650

Notes

(1) *Where it applies* – For business premises, such as a hotel or bed and breakfast, which are used partly for private purposes as a home. The applicable amount is deducted from the actual expenses such that the costs net of private use are deducted in the accounts.

(2) *Relevant occupant* – This is any individual who at any time during the month (or part of the month) occupies the premises as a home, otherwise in the course of the trade. From 6 April 2016 the individual may be a partner in the business (*FA 2016, s 24*).

(3) *Further information* – See Revenue & Customs Brief 14/13, and HMRC's Business Income Manual at BIM75015.

AVERAGING PROFITS FOR FARMERS AND ARTISTS

(*ITTOIA 2005, Pt 2, Ch 16*)

One year's profits are:	Less than 70% of other year	Less than 75% of other year	70% to 75% of other year
	May apply full averaging	Full averaging from 2016/17 onwards	Marginal relief (note 5)

Notes

(1) *Farmers* – Individuals and partnerships (not companies) engaged in farming, market gardening, the intensive rearing in the UK of livestock or fish on a commercial basis for human food production.

(2) *Artists* – Individuals and partnerships (not companies) who personally create literary, dramatic, musical or artistic works or designs.

(3) *Which profits to include* – Profits arising in consecutive tax years. A trading loss is treated as a nil profit for these averaging purposes.

(4) *Averaging period* – From 2016/17 farmers (as defined above) can average their profits and losses over two years (as per earlier years) or over a period of five years (*FA 2016, s 25*).

(5) *Marginal relief* – This form of averaging relief is abolished for 2016/17 onwards. If the profits for one year exceed 70% of the profits for the other, but are less than 75% of those profits, marginal relief is calculated as follows (*ITTOIA 2005, s 223(4)*):

Step 1 – Calculate the adjustment, using the following formula:

$$(D \times 3) - (P \times 0.75)$$

where: D is the difference between the relevant profits for the two years; and

P is the higher relevant profits of the two years

Step 2 – Add the adjustment to the relevant profits of the tax year of which those profits are lower.

Step 3 – Deduct the adjustment from the relevant profits of the tax year of which those profits are higher.

(6) *How to claim* – Claim made in the self-assessment return for the later year, within 12 months of 31 January following the later of the two tax years to be averaged. This time limit may be extended if profits are adjusted for some other reason (*ITTOIA 2005, s 222(6)*; see BIM73155).

(7) *Further information* – See HMRC's Business Income Manual at BIM73000–73190, and HMRC Helpsheets HS224 and HS234.

CAR HIRE COSTS

(*ITTOIA 2005, s 48; CTA 2009, ss 56, 1251(2);* BIM47714 et seq)

(1) *Deduction for lease costs* – For leases commencing on or after 1 April 2018 (for corporation tax) or 6 April 2018 (for income tax), the amount of deduction which would otherwise be allowable is reduced by 15% if the car has CO_2 emissions above 110g/km (130g/km for leases commencing between 1/6 April 2015 and 31 March/5 April 2018).

(2) *No restriction* – The above restriction does not apply to:

- cars first registered before 1 March 2001;
- cars with low CO_2 emissions as defined in *CAA 2001, s 104AA*;
- electrically propelled cars; and
- qualifying hire cars.

RESIDENTIAL PROPERTY LETTINGS

Restriction of finance costs

(*ITTOIA 2005, ss 272A–272B, 274A–274B*)

Tax year	Proportion of finance costs deductible
2017/18	75%
2018/19	50%
2019/20	25%
2020/21 and later	nil

Notes

(1) *Restrictions* – Deductions for finance costs, including interest payments, relating to the letting of residential properties is restricted to the proportions shown above (*ITTOIA 2005, s 272A*).

(2) *Applies to* – Individual landlords, partnerships of individuals and trustees. Corporate landlords are not affected, even where the company carries on a property letting business in partnership with individuals (*ITTOIA 2005, s 272A(5)*).

(3) *Tax credit* – The landlord can claim a tax credit to set against their income tax liability for the year equal to 20% of the lower of:

- finance costs which have been restricted for the tax year;
- profits of the property business for the tax year; or
- total income that exceeds the taxpayer's personal allowances for the tax year (*ITTOIA 2005, s 274AA*).

(4) *Further information* – See tinyurl.com/lndlrds1718tx.

Qualifying periods for FHL

(*ITTOIA 2005, s 325; CTA 2009, s 267*)

Condition:	Applies in accounting period or tax year:
Available for commercial letting	At least 210 days
Actually let commercially	At least 105 days (see Note 2).
Pattern of occupation	No more than 155 days of longer-term occupation.

Notes

(1) *Qualify as FHL* – Furnished accommodation which is let during the tax year (or accounting period, for companies) qualifies as furnished holiday lettings (FHL) for that year or accounting period if all of the conditions set out above are satisfied.

(2) *Longer-term occupation* – A continuous period of more than 31 days during which the accommodation is let to the same person, other than under circumstances that are not normal.

(3) *First or last periods* – When letting starts or finishes count the first or last 12 months as the relevant period (*ITTOIA 2005, s 324; CTA 2009, s 266*).

(4) *Averaging election* – Where several properties are let as FHL the owner can elect for the number of days of actual lettings to be averaged over two or more properties, such that all the properties reach the minimum threshold of 105 days let for the relevant period (see *ITTOIA 2005, s 326; CTA 2009, s 268*).

(5) *'Period of grace' election* – Where a property has qualified as FHL on the actual days let or due to the averaging election in the previous relevant period, the owner can elect to treat the property as continuing to qualify for up to two later years or accounting periods. This applies even though the property does not satisfy the letting condition in those periods. The election must be made in the first tax year or accounting period in which the letting condition is not met (see *ITTOIA 2005, s 326A; CTA 2009, s 268A*).

(6) *Further information* – See HMRC's Property Income Manual at PIM4100, and HMRC's Helpsheet HS253 'Furnished holiday lettings'.

TIME LIMITS FOR CLAIMS AND ELECTIONS

(*TMA 1970, s 43(1)*)

(1) Claims must be made on the tax return or by an amendment to the return. Except where another period is expressly prescribed, a claim for relief in respect of income tax must be within four years after the end of the tax year. For claims relating to companies, see **Chapter 7**.

(2) Specific exceptions in respect of business profits and losses include the following:

Provision	**Time limit**
Averaging of profits of farmers or creative artists (*ITTIOA 2005, ss 222(5), 222A(6)*)	First anniversary of 31 January after the end of the last tax year to which the claim relates
Stock transferred to a connected party on cessation of trade to be valued at higher of cost or sale price (*ITTOIA 2005, s 178(4)*)	First anniversary of 31 January following the tax year of cessation
Herd basis (*ITTOIA 2005, s 124(2); CTA 2009, s 122(2)*)	First anniversary of 31 January following the tax year in which the first relevant period of account ends
Change of accounting date (*ITTOIA 2005, s 217(2)*)	Filing date for the relevant tax return
Post-cessation relief (*ITTOIA 2005, s 257(4); ITA 2007, s 96(4)*)	First anniversary of 31 January following the tax year

continued

Provision	Time limit
Furnished holiday lettings: averaging of letting periods (*ITTOIA 2005, s 326(6)*)	First anniversary of 31 January following the tax year
Furnished holiday lettings: grace period election (*ITTOIA 2005, s 326A(2)*)	First anniversary of 31 January following the tax year
Current and preceding year set-off of trading losses (*ITA 2007, s 64(5)*)	First anniversary of 31 January following the loss-making year
Three year carry back of trading losses in opening years of trade (*ITA 2007, s 72(3)*)	First anniversary of 31 January following the tax year in which the loss is made
Relief for trade etc losses against capital gains of the year in which the loss was made or the previous year (*TCGA 1992, s 261B(8)*)	First anniversary of 31 January following the tax year in which the loss was made

LEASE PREMIUMS

Short leases

(*ITTOIA 2005, s 277; CTA 2009, s 217*)

$$P \times \frac{(50 - \mathrm{Y})}{50}$$

Where:

P is the premium, and

Y is the number of complete periods of 12 months (other than the first) comprised in the effective duration of the lease.

Notes

(1) *What is a short lease* – Broadly a lease with 50 years or less to run.

(2) *Property income* – The amount calculated using the above formula is treated as a property business receipt for the tax year or accounting period in which the lease is granted.

(3) *Capital deduction* – The amount of the premium for the grant of a short lease which is brought into account as a property business receipt is deducted from the consideration taken into account for capital gains purposes, in accordance with *TCGA 1992, Sch 8, paras 5, 7.*

(4) *Which percentage* – The percentages of short lease premium charged as a property business receipt and taken into account for capital gains purposes are summarised in the table below (see PIM1205):

Length of lease in years	Percentage of premium taxable as receipt of property business	Percentage of premium chargeable as a capital gain
More than 50	0	100
50	2	98
49	4	96
48	6	94
47	8	92
46	10	90
45	12	88
44	14	86
43	16	84
42	18	82
41	20	80
40	22	78
39	24	76
38	26	74
37	28	72
36	30	70
35	32	68
34	34	66
33	36	64
32	38	62
31	40	60
30	42	58
29	44	56
28	46	54
27	48	52
26	50	50
25	52	48
24	54	46
23	56	44
22	58	42
21	60	40
20	62	38
19	64	36
18	66	34
17	68	32
16	70	30
15	72	28
14	74	26
13	76	24
12	78	22

continued

Length of lease in years	**Percentage of premium taxable as receipt of property business**	**Percentage of premium chargeable as a capital gain**
11	80	20
10	82	18
9	84	16
8	86	14
7	88	12
6	90	10
5	92	8
4	94	6
3	96	4
2	98	2
1 or less	100	0

Long Leases

- Where the payment relates to a lease of more than 50 years, a premium is treated as being within the lease premium regime if it falls within *ITTOIA 2005 s 303,* or *CTA 2009, s 243.*
- For leases granted on and after 1 April 2013 for companies, and on and after 6 April 2013 for unincorporated businesses, the lease premium relief is limited (*FA 2013, Sch 28*).

Leases which are wasting assets

(*TCGA 1992, Sch 8, para 1*)

A short lease is a wasting asset. The allowable expenditure attributable to a short lease therefore reduces over its term. The rate at which the expenditure is written off is fixed in accordance with the table in *TCGA 1992, Sch 8, para 1* (see **Chapter 8**: **Capital Gains Tax**).

Relief for premiums paid

(*ITTOIA 2005, s 61; CTA 2009, s 63*)

(a) **Tenant occupies the whole of the land**

$$\frac{A}{TRP}$$

Where:

A is the unreduced amount of the taxed receipt; and

TRP is the number of days in the receipt period of the taxed receipt.

(b) Tenant occupies part of the land

$$\frac{F \times A}{TRP}$$

Where:

F is the fraction of the land occupied (calculated on a just and reasonable basis); and

A and TRP have the same meaning as in (a) above.

Notes

(1) *Land used in a trade* – The income element of a short lease premium is allowable as a deduction from the tenant's business profits for income tax or corporation tax purposes. The above formulae are used to calculate the allowable proportion of the 'taxed receipt' (broadly the amount of the lease taxed on the landlord as a rental business receipt) available as a deduction for the tenant. Relief is also available if the land is sub-let.

(2) *Occupation* – The formula in (a) should be used if the tenant occupies the whole of the land for trading purposes. The formula in (b) applies if only part of the land is so used.

7

Taxation of companies

RATES OF CORPORATION TAX

(*CTA 2010, Pt 2, Chs 2, 3, Pt 3*)

	Financial year commencing 1 April				
	2020	**2019**	**2018**	**2017**	**2016**
Main rate	17%	19%	19%	19%	20%
	2015	**2014**	**2013**	**2012**	**2011**
Main rate	20%	21%	23%	24%	26%
Small Profits Rate	–	20%	20%	20%	20%
Small Profits Rate can be claimed by qualifying companies with profits not exceeding	–	£300,000	£300,000	£300,000	£300,000
Marginal Relief Lower Limit	–	£300,000	£300,000	£300,000	£300,000
Marginal Relief Upper Limit	–	£1,500,000	£1,500,000	£1,500,000	£1,500,000
Standard fraction	–	1/400	3/400	2/200	3/200

Notes

(1) *From 1 April 2015* – All profits are charged at a single rate of corporation tax, with an exception for profits made by companies within a ring fence trade (see note 5), (*FA 2014, Sch 1*).

(2) *Prior to 1 April 2015* – The Small Profits Rate applied and the lower and upper limits were reduced proportionately for accounting periods of less than 12 months. The limits are also divided by the number of associated companies carrying on a trade or business for all or part of the accounting period (*CTA 2010, s 25*). The Small Profits Rate did not apply to 'Close Investment Holding Companies' (*CTA 2010, s 18(b)*).

(3) *Patent Box* – For accounting periods beginning on and after 1 April 2013, any company can elect for a reduced rate of corporation tax to be applied to all profits attributable to qualifying intellectual property (see **Patent Box** below).

(4) *Unit trusts and OEICs* – These companies are subject to corporation tax set at the basic income tax rate charged for the tax year beginning on 6 April in that financial

year (*CTA 2010, ss 614, 618*). For financial years 2008 to 2018, the applicable tax rate was 20%.

(5) *Oil and gas* – For companies with ring fence profits from oil-related activities, the Main Rate still applies at 30%, the Small Profits Rate is 19%, and the ring fence fraction is 11/400, all for financial years 2008 to 2018 (*CTA 2010, Pt 8, Ch 3A*). Companies in the oil and gas industries also pay the supplementary charge of corporation tax and petroleum revenue tax (PRT), see HMRC's Oil Taxation Manual.

(6) *Restitution interest* – From 21 October 2015 restitution interest paid to companies when a dispute concerning HMRC's mistake in law is resolved, is taxed at 45% rather than at the normal CT rates. Where HMRC pays restitution interest it withholds tax at 45% from the payment (*F(No 2)A 2015, s 38*).

(7) *Proposal* – The Northern Ireland Assembly is to be given the power to set a special rate of corporation tax (expected to be 12.5%), for companies trading in Northern Ireland. However, the devolution of this power will not commence until the Northern Ireland Executive demonstrates its finances are on a sustainable footing (*Corporation Tax (Northern Ireland) Act 2015*).

Effective marginal rates for small profits

(*CTA 2010, s 19*)

Financial Year (Commencing 1 April)	Marginal Small Profits Rate %
2014	21.25
2013	23.75
2012	25.00
2011	27.50
2010	29.75

Marginal relief

(*CTA 2010, s 19*)

The corporation tax charged on the company's taxable total profits of the accounting period is reduced by an amount equal to:

$$F \times (U - A) \times \frac{N}{A}$$

Where:

F is the standard fraction,

U is the upper limit,

A is the amount of the augmented profits, and

N is the amount of the taxable total profits.

Notes

(1) *The standard fraction* – See table of Rates of Corporation Tax (*CTA 2010, s 19(3)*).

(2) *Augmented Profits* – This is defined as the company's taxable total profits plus any franked investment income received by the company, excluding any franked investment income received by the company from a company which is a 51% subsidiary of the receiving company or a company of which the receiving company is a 51% subsidiary, or from a trading company or relevant holding company that is a quasi-subsidiary of the receiving company.

(3) *Quasi-subsidiary* – This is a company owned by a consortium of which the recipient company is a member, which is not a 75% subsidiary of any company, where no arrangements exist for it to become a 75% subsidiary of any company (*CTA 2010, ss 32, 33*).

RESEARCH AND DEVELOPMENT (R&D)

(*CTA 2009, ss1039–1142; FA 2012, Sch 3*)

Expenditure incurred on and after:	**SME companies**	**Large companies**		
	Enhanced deduction	Enhanced deduction	Vaccines research	RDEC
1 Jan 2018	230%	N/A	N/A	12%
1 April 2017	230%	N/A	N/A	11%
1 April 2016	230%	N/A	140%	11%
1 April 2015	230%	130%	140%	11%
1 April 2014	225%	130%	140%	10%
1 April 2013	225%	130%	140%	10%

Notes

(1) *Company conditions* – To claim R&D tax relief the company must incur qualifying expenditure on qualifying R&D projects which relate to its own trade, or to qualifying R&D projects it works on as a subcontractor for another organisation. The company must also be a going concern as shown in its latest accounts, and from 1 August 2015 it must not be an ineligible company (*CTA 2009, Pt 13*).

(2) *Time limits* – The relief must be claimed in the corporation tax return within two years of the end of the accounting period in which the qualifying R&D expenditure was incurred (*CTA 2009, ss 1044, 1074*).

(3) *Qualifying R&D* – Each R&D project must be carried on in a field of science or technology and be undertaken with an aim of extending knowledge in a field of science or technology, and must fall within the former DTI guidelines (see CIRD 813000).

(4) *Qualifying expenditure* – Restricted to the areas of staffing costs, external workers (conditions apply), software, materials consumed or transformed, utilities (not rent) and payments to clinical volunteers. No minimum spend on qualifying costs is required. From 1 April 2015 materials which are included in a saleable product do not qualify (*CTA 2009, ss 1127–1140*).

(5) *Definition of SME* – For this purpose an SME is a company with fewer than 500 employees and turnover not exceeding €100 million or balance sheet value not exceeding €86 million. SMEs can claim a payable tax credit – see table below (*CTA 2009, ss 1119, 1120*).

(6) *R&D expenditure credit (REDC)* – From 1 April 2016 this is the only means of claiming R&D relief for large companies (*CTA 2009, Pt 3, Ch 6A*).

(7) *Vaccines research* – Abolished from 1 April 2017. It applied to R&D projects connected with research on TB, malaria or AIDS, (see CIRD 75000; *CTA 2009, Pt 13, Ch 7; FA 2016, s 43*).

(8) *Further information* – See: http://tinyurl.com/R-DTXRLF and HMRC's Corporate Intangibles Research and Development Manual at CIRD80000.

Payable tax credit

(*CTA 2009, ss 1054–1060*)

Expenditure incurred in financial year starting 1 April	Percentage of loss given as tax credit
2019	14.50%
2018	14.50%
2017	14.50%
2016	14.50%
2015	14.50%
2014	14.50%
2013	14.50%
2012	11.00%

Notes

(1) *Conditions* – Payable tax credits are only available to SME companies which have not started to trade, or have made a loss after the deduction of R&D enhanced expenditure (*CTA 2009, s 1054*).

(2) *Amount* – The tax credit is given in exchange for the loss, calculated as the percentage of the surrendered loss shown in the table above (*CTA 2009, s 1058*).

(3) *Proposal* – From April 2020 the tax credit paid will be limited to three times the company's total PAYE and NIC contributions for the period (*Budget, 29 October 2018*).

PATENT BOX

(*CTA 2010, Pt 8A*)

Financial Year starting 1 April	Effective patent box rate when companies pay: Main CT rate %	Small profits rate %
2018	10.00	10.00
2017	10.00	10.00
2016	11.00	11.00
2015	12.00	12.00
2014	13.30	12.67
2013	15.20	13.20

Notes

(1) *Election* – Companies may elect for a reduced rate of corporation tax rate for profits attributable to qualifying patents and similar intellectual property (IP). The legislation provides a formula to calculate the deduction (*CTA 2010, s 357A*).

(2) *Time limit* – This election only applies to accounting periods beginning on or after 1 April 2013. It must be made (or revoked) within two years of the end of the accounting period (*CTA 2010, ss 357G, 357GA*).

(3) *Qualifying patents* – The company must own, or exclusively licence, patents issued by the UK Intellectual Property Office, European Patent Office or any of these countries: Austria, Bulgaria, Czech Republic, Denmark, Estonia, Finland, Germany, Hungary, Poland, Portugal, Romania, Slovakia, and Sweden. Plant breeders' rights also qualify (*CTA 2010, s 357BB*).

(4) *Only IP income* – Profits from creating or developing the patented product, or a product containing the patented item, qualify for the relief. Profits from holding patents as investments do not qualify (*CTA 2010, ss 357BC–357BE*).

(5) *Streaming* – Costs and revenues are streamed on a patent-by-patent or product-by-product basis for new entrants from 1 July 2016, and for all eligible companies from 1 July 2021 (*FA 2016, s 64*).

(6) *Cost sharing* – From 1 April 2017 the streaming rules are amended where R&D is undertaken collaboratively by two or more companies under a cost sharing arrangement (*CTA 2010, s 357GC*).

(7) *Further Information* – Outline guidance: tinyurl.com/CTptntbx, for detailed guidance see HMRC's Corporate Intangibles Research & Development Manual (para CIRD200000).

FILM TAX RELIEF

(CTA 2009, Pt 15; SI 2015/1741)

Method of tax relief	From 1 April 2015 (note 2)	To 31 March 2015
Additional deduction		
• Limited budget films:	100% of core expenditure	100% of core expenditure
• Other films:	80% of core expenditure	80% of core expenditure
Payable tax credit		
• Limited budget films:		25% of loss surrendered
• Other films:		20% of loss surrendered
• All films:	25% of loss surrendered, up to 'unused 25% band'; plus 20% of any remaining loss.	

Notes

(1) *Eligible* – Film tax relief (FTR) can by claimed by film production companies in respect of British films intended for commercial release. At least 10% (25% before application of *FA 2014, s 32*) of the core expenditure on the film must be UK expenditure (*CTA 2009, s 1198*).

(2) *Revised rates* – These rates apply to films of which principal photography is not completed before 1 April 2015 (*FA 2015, s 29*).

(3) *Additional deduction* – This is calculated on the basis of UK qualifying core expenditure. Budget films are those with core expenditure up to £20 million (*CTA 2009, ss 1184(2), 1199–1200*).

(4) *Payable tax credits* – If FTR is available, the company may claim a film tax credit for an accounting period in which it has a 'surrenderable loss' (*CTA 2009, ss 1201–1203*).

(5) *Further information* – Outline guidance: tinyurl.com/criTxrlf. Detailed guidance in HMRC's Film Production Company Manual.

CREATIVE INDUSTRIES TAX RELIEFS

(CTA 2009, Pts 15A, 15B)

Method of tax relief	Relief rate
Additional deduction	100% of qualifying core expenditure (see Note 2)
Payable tax credit	25% of loss surrendered

Notes

(1) *Available to* – Companies in the creative sectors including; TV and video game production, theatre productions, orchestras and museums. All cultural reliefs follow the structure of film tax relief, and some require a 'British' cultural test to be passed to qualify (*SI 2015/86*).

(2) *Qualifying core expenditure* – For most of the creative sector reliefs at least 25% of the core expenditure must be on goods or services used or provided from within the EEA countries, but see note (3). The additional deductions, and the payable tax credit, are calculated on the basis of UK core expenditure, up to a maximum of 80% of the total qualifying expenditure by the eligible company (*CTA 2009, ss 1216CG, 1217CG*).

(3) *High-end TV* – From 1 April 2013, relief for production of TV programmes of 30 minutes or more intended for broadcast to the general public, which may be: drama, documentary and animation, but not: advertising, current affairs, entertainment shows, competitions, live performances or training programmes. From 1 April 2015 at least 10% of the core expenditure must be in the UK (*CTA 2009, Pt 15A, Ch 3*).

(4) *Video games development* – From 1 April 2014, relief for the production of video games intended for supply to the general public which are not produced for advertising, promotional or gambling purposes (*CTA 2009, Pt 15B*).

(5) *Theatre productions* – From 1 September 2014, relief for costs of dramatic or ballet productions performed live to the general public, but not for productions including wild animals, or which are made to promote goods or services. The tax credit available is 25% for touring productions and at 20% for other productions (*CTA 2009, Pt 15C*).

(6) *Children's TV* – From 1 April 2015, relief for producing programmes intended for children aged under 15 (*CTA 2009, Pt 15A*).

(7) *Orchestral concerts* – From 1 April 2016, relief for the cost of live orchestral concerts performed before a paying audience. There must be at least 12 musicians and most of the instruments must not be electronically or directly amplified (*CTA 2009, Pt 15D*).

(8) *Museums and galleries* – From 1 April 2017, relief for the costs of new exhibitions including those which are toured. Maximum amount which can be paid to the company per exhibition is £100,000 for a touring exhibition, or £80,000 for a non-touring exhibition (*CTA 2009, Pt 15E*).

(9) *Further information* – Outline guidance at: tinyurl.com/criTxrlf. Detailed guidance in following HMRC manuals: Museums and Galleries Exhibition Tax Relief Manual, Orchestra Tax Relief, Television Production Company Manual, Theatre Tax Relief Manual, Video Games Development Company Manual.

DISINCORPORATION RELIEF

(FA 2013, ss 58–61)

Applies to	**Period/value**
Transfers of a business as a going concern made in:	1 April 2013 to 31 March 2018.
Qualifying assets:	Goodwill and interests in land, worth up to £100,000

Notes

(1) *Applies to* – Transfers of a business as a going concern from a company to some or all of its shareholders made before 31 March 2018. The recipients of the qualifying assets must be individuals who are not trading together as an LLP (*FA 2013, s 59*).

(2) *Election* – A claim for disincorporation relief must be made jointly in writing by the company and the shareholders who receive the assets and the company (*FA 2013, s 60)*.

(3) *Effect* – No corporation tax applies on the transfer of the specified assets, and the recipients inherit the base costs of those assets (*TCGA 1992, ss 162B–162C)*. However, the shareholders are taxed on the distribution of those assets.

(4) *Further information* – Outline guidance: tinyurl.com/ctdiscorlf. Detailed guidance in HMRC's Capital Gains Manual at para CG65800–CG65850.

LOANS TO PARTICIPATORS

(*CTA 2010, Pt 10, Ch 3*)

Loan advanced:	**Before 6 April 2016**	**From 6 April 2016**
Rate of charge	25% of loan value	32.5% of loan value

Notes

(1) *When the charge applies* – If a close company makes a loan or advances money to any of the following who are participators or associates of a participator in the company:

- an individual (or company acting in a representative capacity for the individual);
- a trustee in a settlement where trustees or actual or potential beneficiaries are participators;
- a member of a LLP or other partnership (*CTA 2010, s 455*).

(2) *Charge treated as* – Corporation tax chargeable for the accounting period in which the loan or advance is made. It is not payable in respect of the portion of loan repaid, released or written off before the CT becomes payable. Can choose which outstanding loan a repayment is set against.

(3) *When charge is repaid* – Where the loan or advance is subsequently repaid, released or written off, the tax charge can be reclaimed (*CTA 2010, s 458*).

(4) *Replacing the loan* – From 20 March 2013 additional conditions must be met for a repayment of a loan to be counted as a repayment for the purposes of *CTA 2010, s 455* see notes (5) to (8) below.

(5) *30-day rule* – Where a loan of £5,000 or more is repaid to the company, but within 30 days amounts totalling £5,000 or more are borrowed by the same borrower or one of his associates, the first loan is treated as not having been repaid and is treated as continuing for the purposes of calculating the corporation tax charge (*CTA 2010, s 464C(1)*).

(6) *Arrangements in place* – Where the loan is £15,000 or more, the 30-day rule is ignored if, at the time of the repayment of the first loan arrangements are in place for it to be replaced by the company with an amount of at least £5,000. If the later loan is made, it is treated as a continuation of the first loan (*CTA 2010, s 464C(3)*).

(7) *Taxed income* – Where the repayments made in (5) or (6) above give rise to an income tax charge on the participator or associate who took out the loan (eg the repayment was made as a declared dividend or bonus), that repayment is not caught by the rules in *CTA 2010, s 464C* (*CTA 2010, s 464C(5)*).

(8) *Conferring a benefit* – A charge at the rate in the table above applies to the value of the benefit is due when arrangements which confer a benefit on a participator (eg by transferring value from the company to the participator in an indirect fashion) such that is it not caught by *CTA 2010, s 455*. The charge can be reclaimed if the benefit is returned to the company (*CTA 2010, ss 464A, 464B*).

(9) *Benefit in kind* – See **Chapter 2** for the benefit in kind tax charge that arises on the individual who receives an employment related loan.

(10) *Further information* – See HMRC Corporation Tax Manual para CTM61500+.

COMPANY TAX RETURNS AND PAYMENTS

Filing dates

(*FA 1998, Sch 18, para 14*)

The filing date for a company tax return is the later of the following periods:

(a) 12 months from the end of the return period;

(b) If the company's relevant period of account is less than 18 months; 12 months from the end of that period;

(c) If the company's relevant period of account is longer than 18 months; 30 months from the beginning of that period; or

(d) three months from the date of a notice by HMRC to deliver the return.

Notes

(1) *Relevant period of account* – In relation to a return for an accounting period this is defined as the period of account of the company in which the last day of that accounting period falls.

(2) *Online filing* – Corporation tax returns (with a very few exceptions) must be filed online using iXBRL. This requires the majority of the figures in the company accounts and tax return to be 'tagged'. For further information see: http://tinyurl.com/l9v375a.

Due dates for CT payments

(TMA 1970, ss 59D, 59E, 59G, 59H; SI 1998/3175; ITA 2007, Pt 15, Ch 15; CTA 2010, s 455(3); SI 2017/1072)

Liability	Due Date
Mainstream corporation tax	9 months and 1 day following the end of the accounting period
Mainstream corporation tax payable by large companies (notes 1& 2)	1st – 6 months and 13 days from the start of the accounting period (or date of final instalment, if earlier); 2nd – 3 months after 1st instalment; 3rd – 3 months after 2nd instalment; 4th – 3 months and 14 days from the end of the accounting period.
Mainstream corporation tax payable by very large companies (note 4)	1st – 2 months and 13 days from the start of the accounting period (or date of final instalment, if earlier); 2nd – 3 months after 1st instalment; 3rd – 3 months after 2nd instalment; 4th – 3 months after 3rd instalment.
Income tax on interest, annual payments etc.	14 days after end of return period see note 3
Charge on loans to participators in close companies (*CTA 2010, s 455*)	9 months and 1 day after the end of the accounting period in which the loan or advance was made.

Notes

(1) *Instalment payments* – Large companies are liable to pay corporation tax in quarterly instalments: see note 2. From 1 April 2015 a 'large' company is one with annual taxable profits exceeding £1.5 million, divided by 1 plus the number of related 51% group companies. For earlier periods the number of associated companies were counted.

(2) *Not large* – A company is not large if its profits are £10,000 or less (reduced proportionately for periods shorter than 12 months), or if its profits for the accounting period are up to £10 million and it was not a large company in the 12 months preceding that accounting period (*TMA 1970, s 59E; SI 1998/3175*).

(3) *Amount due* – The CT due for each instalment is calculated using the following formula (*SI 1998/3175, regs 5–8*):

$$3 \times \frac{CTI}{n}$$

where:

CTI = the amount of the company's total liability for that accounting period; and

n = the number of whole months in the accounting period, plus the 'appropriate decimal' (ie broadly the proportion of a whole 30-day month, rounded to 2 decimal places).

(4) *Very large companies* – For accounting periods starting on and after 1 April 2019, where the annual profits are over £20 million for the company or group, instalments of CT will be payable at advanced intervals as shown in table above (*SI 2017/1072*).

(5) *Taxes withheld* – Tax deducted from interest, annual payments and royalties paid overseas must be reported on a form CT61 for the quarterly periods ending on 31 March, 30 June, 30 September and 31 December and at the end of an accounting period. For further information see HMRC's Corporation Tax manual at CTM35000.

(6) *Section 455 charge* – This tax is not payable in respect of any loan or advance repaid before the date on which the tax under *CTA 2010, s 455* would otherwise become due. See **Loans to Participators** above.

TIME LIMITS FOR CLAIMS AND ELECTIONS

A claim or election for corporation tax purposes must generally be made in writing within four years of the end of the accounting period to which it relates, ie in the absence of any provisions to the contrary (*FA 1998, Sch 18, para 55*, see also *SI 2009/403*). Other common time limits are given below.

Provision	**Time limit**
Appropriation of asset to trading stock: election to adjust trading profit by the amount of the gain or loss on the deemed disposal at market value (*TCGA 1992, s 161(3)*).	2 years from the end of the accounting period in which the asset is appropriated as trading stock.
Reallocation of chargeable gain or an allowable loss within a group (*TCGA 1992, s 171A(5)*).	2 years from the end of the transferring company's accounting period in which the gain or loss accrues.
Stock transferred to a connected person on the cessation of trade to be valued at higher of cost or selling price (*CTA 2009, s 167(4)*).	2 years from the end of the accounting period of cessation. Election must be made jointly by both parties.
Relief for trading losses against total profits of the same, or an earlier, accounting period (*CTA 2010, s 37(7)*).	2 years from the end of the loss making accounting period.
Terminal loss relief on the cessation of trade (*CTA 2010, s 39*).	2 years from the end of the loss making accounting period.
Group relief (*FA 1998, Sch 18, para 74*).	Group relief claims must be made or withdrawn by the later of the following: (1) 12 months from the filing date for the claimant company's tax return for the accounting period of the claim; (2) 30 days after the completion of an enquiry into that return;

Provision	Time limit
	(3) 30 days after the issue of a notice of amendment by HMRC following the completion of an enquiry; or (4) 30 days after the determination of any appeal against an HMRC amendment (in (3) above).
Capital allowances (*FA 1988, Sch 18, para 82*).	As for group relief (see above).
Surrender of company tax refund within group (*CTA 2010, s 963(3)*).	Before the refund is made to the surrendering company.
Intangible fixed assets: election to write down cost for tax purposes at a fixed rate (*CTA 2009, s 730*).	2 years from the end of the accounting period in which the company creates or acquires the asset.
Set-off of loss on disposal of shares in unquoted trading company against income of investment company (*CTA 2010, s 70(4)*).	2 years from the end of the accounting period in which the loss was incurred.
Company distributions – election that distribution should not be treated as exempt (*CTA 2009, s 931R*).	2 years from the end of the accounting period in which the distribution is received.
Relief for a non-trading deficit on loan relationships (including any non-trading exchange losses) (*CTA 2009, ss 458(2), 460(1)*).	• Claim to carry forward the deficit to later accounting periods – 2 years from the end of the accounting period following the deficit period. • Claim to set off deficit against profits of the deficit period or earlier periods – 2 years from end of period in which deficit arises.

Notes

(1) *Extended time limits* – In some cases, HMRC may allow a longer claim period at its discretion.

(2) *Group relief* – The above references to an enquiry do not include a restricted enquiry into an amendment of a return (ie where the restriction arises because the time limit for enquiring into that return has expired), where the amendment consists of a group relief claim or the withdrawal of such a claim (*FA 1998, Sch 18, para 74(4)*).

INDEXATION ALLOWANCE

(TCGA 1992, Ch IV)

Retail Prices Index (RPI)

	Jan	Feb	Mar	Apr	May	Jun	Jul	Aug	Sep	Oct	Nov	Dec
1982			79.44	81.04	81.62	81.85	81.88	81.90	81.85	82.26	82.66	82.51
1983	82.61	82.97	83.12	84.28	84.64	84.84	85.30	85.68	86.06	86.36	86.67	86.89
1984	86.84	87.20	87.48	88.64	88.97	89.20	89.10	89.94	90.11	90.67	90.95	90.87
1985	91.20	91.94	92.80	94.78	95.21	95.41	95.23	95.49	95.44	95.59	95.92	96.05
1986	96.25	96.60	96.73	97.67	97.85	97.79	97.52	97.82	98.30	98.45	99.29	99.62
1987	100.0	100.4	100.6	101.8	101.9	101.9	101.8	102.1	102.4	102.9	103.4	103.3
1988	103.3	103.7	104.1	105.8	106.2	106.6	106.7	107.9	108.4	109.5	110.0	110.3
1989	111.0	111.8	112.3	114.3	115.0	115.4	115.5	115.8	116.6	117.5	118.5	118.8
1990	119.5	120.2	121.4	125.1	126.2	126.7	126.8	128.1	129.3	130.3	130.0	129.9
1991	130.2	130.9	131.4	133.1	133.5	134.1	133.8	134.1	134.6	135.1	135.6	135.7
1992	135.6	136.3	136.7	138.8	139.3	139.3	138.8	138.9	139.4	139.9	139.7	139.2
1993	137.9	138.8	139.3	140.6	141.1	141.0	140.7	141.3	141.9	141.8	141.6	141.9
1994	141.3	142.1	142.5	144.2	144.7	144.7	144.0	144.7	145.0	145.2	145.3	146.0
1995	146.0	146.9	147.5	149.0	149.6	149.8	149.1	149.9	150.6	149.8	149.8	150.7
1996	150.2	150.9	151.5	152.6	152.9	153.0	152.4	153.1	153.8	153.8	153.9	154.4
1997	154.4	155.0	155.4	156.3	156.9	157.5	157.5	158.5	159.3	159.5	159.6	160.0
1998	159.5	160.3	160.8	162.6	163.5	163.4	163.0	163.7	164.4	164.5	164.4	164.4
1999	163.4	163.7	164.1	165.2	165.6	165.6	165.1	165.5	166.2	166.5	166.7	167.3
2000	166.6	167.5	168.4	170.1	170.7	171.1	170.5	170.5	171.7	171.6	172.1	172.2
2001	171.1	172.0	172.2	173.1	174.2	174.4	173.3	174.0	174.6	174.3	173.6	173.4
2002	173.3	173.8	174.5	175.7	176.2	176.2	175.9	176.4	177.6	177.9	178.2	178.5
2003	178.4	179.3	179.9	181.2	181.5	181.3	181.3	181.6	182.5	182.6	182.7	183.5
2004	183.1	183.8	184.6	185.7	186.5	186.8	186.8	187.4	188.1	188.6	189.0	189.9
2005	188.9	189.6	190.5	191.6	192.0	192.2	192.2	192.6	193.1	193.3	193.6	194.1
2006	193.4	194.2	195.0	196.5	197.7	198.5	198.5	199.2	200.1	200.4	201.1	202.7
2007	201.6	203.1	204.4	205.4	206.2	207.3	206.1	207.3	208.0	208.9	209.7	210.9
2008	209.8	211.4	212.1	214.0	215.1	216.8	216.5	217.2	218.4	217.7	216.0	212.9
2009	210.1	211.4	211.3	211.5	212.8	213.4	213.4	214.4	215.3	216.0	216.6	218.0
2010	217.9	219.2	220.7	222.8	223.6	224.1	223.6	224.5	225.3	225.8	226.8	228.4
2011	229.0	231.3	232.5	234.4	235.2	235.2	234.7	236.1	237.9	238.0	238.5	239.4
2012	238.0	239.9	240.8	242.5	241.8	242.8	242.1	243.0	244.2	245.6	245.6	246.8
2013	245.8	247.6	248.7	249.5	250.0	249.7	249.7	251.0	251.9	251.9	252.1	253.4
2014	252.6	254.2	254.8	255.7	255.9	256.3	256.0	257.0	257.6	257.7	257.1	257.5
2015	255.4	256.7	257.1	258.0	258.5	258.9	258.6	259.8	259.6	259.5	259.8	260.6
2016	258.8	260.0	261.1	261.4	262.1	263.1	263.4	264.4	264.9	264.8	265.5	267.1
2017	265.5	268.4	269.3	270.6	271.7	272.3	272.9	274.7	275.1	275.3	275.8	278.1

Acknowledgement: Office for National Statistics website: www.ons.gov.uk

Indexation formula

The formula for calculating indexation factors is as follows (*TCGA 1992, s 54(1)*):

$$\frac{(RD - RI)}{RI}$$

Where:

RD is the RPI for the month of disposal; and

RI is the RPI for March 1982 (or the month in which the expenditure was incurred, if later).

The resulting figure is applied to each item of qualifying expenditure in the computation, by multiplying the expenditure by the relevant indexation factor as calculated.

Notes

(1) *Which periods* – For disposals made in periods from 31 March 1982 to 31 December 2017. The allowance adjusts the base value of the asset for the effects of inflation as measured by the RPI.

(2) *Who can use it* – Only companies within the charge to corporation tax (*TCGA 1992, s 52A*). It can reduce an unindexed gain to nil, but it cannot be applied to create or increase a loss (*TCGA 1992, s 53(1)*).

(3) *Publication* – Tables showing the indexed rise in respect of disposals taking place in particular months can be found here: http://tinyurl.com/odelvrk.

Capital Gains Tax

RATES AND ANNUAL EXEMPTIONS

(TCGA 1992, ss 3, 4, Sch 1)

Tax Year	Annual exempt amount		Tax rate paid by		
	Individuals, PRs and trusts for disabled	General trusts	Individuals within:		Trustees and PRs
			Basic rate band	Higher tax bands	
	£	£	%	%	%
2019/20 (note 1)	12,000	6,000	10	20	20
2018/19 (note 1)	11,700	5,850	10	20	20
2017/18 (note 1)	11,300	5,650	10	20	20
2016/17 (note 1)	11,100	5,550	10	20	20
2015/16	11,100	5,550	18	28	28
2014/15	11,000	5,500	18	28	28
2013/14	10,900	5,450	18	28	28

Notes

(1) *Upper rates* – From 6 April 2016 taxable gains made on the disposal of residential property and carried interest gains are taxed at 18% (within the taxpayer's basic rate income tax band) or 28% where the gain is made by trustees or lies within the higher or additional rate income tax bands (*TCGA 1992, ss 4(2A), 4BB*).

(2) *Scottish taxpayers* – From 6 April 2016 these taxpayers are treated as if they are **not** Scottish taxpayers, so they use the tax bands which apply in the rest of the UK, for the purposes of calculating the applicable rates of CGT (*TCGA 1992, s 4(10)*).

(3) *Personal representatives* – The annual exemption is available to personal representatives in the tax year of death and the following two years (*TCGA 1992, s 3(7)*).

(4) *Trustees* – The annual exemption for trustees is divided by the number of qualifying settlements created by one settlor, subject to a lower limit of 10% of the annual exemption for individuals for that tax year (*TCGA 1992, Sch 1, para 2*).

(5) *Remittance basis users* – An individual who claims to use the remittance basis for a tax year is not entitled to the annual exempt amount for that year (*ITA 2007, s 809G*).

However the annual exempt amount remains available where the remittance basis applies without a claim – eg where the individual's unremitted foreign income and gains are less than £2,000 for the year (*ITA 2007, s 809D*).

(6) *Entrepreneurs' relief* – From 23 June 2010 a 10% rate of CGT applies in respect of gains brought within a claim for entrepreneurs' relief (*TCGA 1992, s 169N(3);* see **Entrepreneurs' relief**).

(7) *Investors' relief* – From 6 April 2019 a 10% rate of CGT applies in respect of gains qualifying for investors' relief (*TCGA 1992, s 169VC(2)*; see **Investors' relief**).

CHATTEL EXEMPTION

(*TCGA 1992, s 262*)

	Exemption (max sale proceeds)	**Marginal relief (max chargeable gain)**
From 1989/90 onwards	£6,000	5/3 of the excess over £6,000

ENTREPRENEURS' RELIEF

(*TCGA 1992 ss 169H–169S*)

Date of disposal	**Lifetime limit**	**Calculation of relief**
From 6 April 2011	£10 million	10% of net gains
23 June 2010–5 April 2011	£5 million	10% of net gains

Conditions

(1) *Qualifying disposals* – Disposals made by an individual or by certain trustees qualify if the disposal consists of:

- all or part of a trade carried on alone or in partnership (see note 7);
- assets used by a partnership or company which are disposed of in association with a disposal of an interest in the partnership or company (see note 8);
- assets of such a trade following cessation; or
- shares or securities in the individual's 'personal company'(see note 2), where the company is a trading company (or the holding company of a trading group) and the individual is an officer or employee of the company (or of a trading group member) (*TCGA 1992, ss 169H, 169I*); and
- the relevant conditions are met throughout a period of at least 24 months (12 months for disposals before 6 April 2019) ending with the date of disposal or cessation of trade (*TCGA 1992, s 169I*).

(2) *Personal company* – The taxpayer must hold at least 5% of the ordinary share capital and control at least 5% of the voting rights of the company. For disposals made on and after 29 October 2018 the taxpayer must also hold a right to at least 5% of the distributable profits available to the equity holders, and have a right to at least

5% of the assets available for distribution to equity holders on the winding up of the company (*F(No 3)B 2017–19, cl 38, Sch 15*).

(3) *Diluted shares rights* – Where the company raises more equity capital by issuing new shares on or after 6 April 2019, which results in the rights of an existing shareholder being reduced below the 5% thresholds set out in note 2, that shareholder can elect to claim entrepreneurs' relief on the accrued gain to that date (*TCGA 1992, ss 169SB–169SH*).

(4) *Trust assets* – Trust assets used for business purposes can be eligible for relief if a qualifying beneficiary of the trust has an interest in possession in the whole or a relevant part of the settled property, and all the above conditions for the relief are satisfied by the beneficiary (*TCGA 1992, s 169J*).

(5) *Transitional rules* – These may allow relief to be claimed where a gain made before 6 April 2008 has been deferred using QCBs, EIS or VCT and becomes chargeable on or after that date (*FA 2008, Sch 3, paras 7, 8*).

(6) *EMI shares* – Gains made on shares from 6 April 2013 which were acquired through exercising EMI options on or after 6 April 2012 can qualify for entrepreneurs' relief, even if the taxpayer holds less than 5% of the ordinary share capital and voting rights of the company.

(7) *Goodwill* – The relief is restricted for gains arising on the transfer of goodwill to a close company on or after 3 December 2014 (*TCGA 1992, s 169LA*).

(8) *Deferred gains* – Gains that have been deferred under EIS or SITR can qualify for entrepreneurs' relief when the deferred gain falls back into charge on or after 3 December 2014 (*TCGA 1992, Pt 5, Ch 4*).

(9) *Associated disposals* – From 18 March 2015 for a gain to qualify for ER as an associated disposal, it must be connected with a disposal of at least 5% of the ordinary share capital of the individual's personal company or at least a 5% interest in the partnership assets of the partnership of which he is a member. This rule is relaxed for a retiring partner and an additional condition is added for assets acquired on and after 13 June 2016 (*TCGA 1992, s 169K*).

(10) *Further information* – Chapter 12 of *Capital Gains Tax 2018/19* (Bloomsbury Professional).

INVESTORS' RELIEF

(*TCGA 1992, ss 169VA–169VR, Sch 7ZB*)

Date of disposal	Lifetime limit	Calculation of relief
From 6 April 2019	£10 million	10% of net gains

Conditions

(1) *Qualifying shares* – Only gains made on the disposal of qualifying shares are eligible for this relief. The shares must be:

- subscribed for on or after 17 March 2016 by the taxpayer who is disposing of them;

- issued by an unquoted trading company or unquoted holding company of a trading group;
- held by the investor for a continuous period of at least three years to date of disposal, which cannot be before 6 April 2019.

(2) *Connection to company* – The investor can become an employee of the company six months or more after acquiring the shares, but he must not be offered that employment as a condition of subscribing for the shares. Alternatively, the investor may become an unpaid director of the company (*TCGA 1992, s 169VB*).

(3) *Receipt of value* – The relief cannot apply where the investor has received value from the company at any time in the period starting one year before the issue of the shares to three years after the share issue (*TCGA 1992, Sch 7ZB*).

(4) *Further information* – Chapter 17 of *Capital Gains Tax 2018/19* (Bloomsbury Professional).

ROLLOVER RELIEF FOR BUSINESS ASSETS

(*TCGA 1992, Pt 5, Ch 1*)

Qualifying assets (*TCGA 1992, s 155*):

Class of asset	Description
1A	Land and buildings occupied (and used) only for the purposes of a trade
1B	Fixed plant or machinery (not forming part of a building)
2	Ships, aircraft and hovercraft
3	Satellites, space stations and spacecraft (including launch vehicles)
4	Goodwill
5	Milk & potato quotas (both abolished)
6	Ewe and suckler cow premium quotas
7	Fish quotas
7A	Payment entitlements under Single Payment for farmers
7B	Payment entitlement under Basic Payment Scheme for farmers (note 2)
8A	Lloyd's underwriters' syndicate capacity
8B	Lloyd's members' agent pooling arrangements

Notes

(1) *Corporate claims* – For the purposes of corporation tax, assets in categories 4 to 7A listed above, if owned by a company at any time on or after 1 April 2002, would fall within the intangible assets regime and are therefore excluded from business asset rollover relief (see *TCGA 1992, s 156ZB*).

(2) *Farmers' subsidies* – From 20 December 2013 the disposal of entitlements to the Basic Payment Scheme under EU regulation 1307/2013 qualifies for rollover relief (*FA 2014, s 61*).

(3) *Companies and intangibles* – From 19 March 2014, companies are specifically prohibited from claiming rollover relief where the proceeds on disposal of a tangible asset are reinvested in an intangible fixed asset (*CTA 2009, s 870A*).

MAIN RESIDENCE RELIEF

(*TCGA 1992, ss 222–226B*)

Deemed occupation due to:	Maximum period permitted:
Delay in taking up occupation	1 year under ESC D49
Job-related accommodation	No limit (*TCGA 1992, s 222(8)*)
Working outside the UK	No limit (*TCGA 1992, s 223(3)(b)*)
Absence for any reason	3 years, if occupied property before and after, and if no other qualifying residence in that period (*TCGA 1992, s 223(3)(a)*)
Final period of ownership (note 10)	18 months for disposals on or after 6 April 2014, or 36 months where owner or spouse is disabled or has moved to residential care home, and for earlier disposals (*TCGA 1992, s 225E*).

Notes

(1) *The relief* – Also known as principal private residence relief (PPR). Relief from CGT is given on the disposal of (or of an interest in) a dwelling which has been the individual's only or main residence, and on land enjoyed with that residence as its garden or grounds up to half a hectare, or more if the additional land is required for the reasonable enjoyment of the property.

(2) *Period of occupation* – The relief is time apportioned for periods of occupation, and for certain periods of deemed occupation. Relief for the final period of ownership is given, if the property was at some time the individual's only or main residence (*TCGA 1992, s 223(1)*).

(3) *Election* – Where an individual has two or more properties which he uses as a home, the owner may elect within two years of the second or subsequent property becoming their home, which property is to be treated as the main residence (*TCGA 1992 s 222(5)*). Where the property is located in a country in which the owner is not resident for tax purposes, the property may only be subject to that election if the owner spends at least 90 midnights in the property in the tax year (*TCGA 1992, s 222A*).

(4) *Married couples and civil partners* – Such couples may have only one main residence at any time between them which qualifies for the relief (*TCGA 1992, s 222(6)*).

(5) *Lettings relief* – If the main residence has been wholly or partly let as residential accommodation at any time in the period of ownership, lettings relief can provide an exemption for gains limited to the lower of:

- the gain attributable to the let period;
- £40,000 per owner; and
- the gain exempt as main residence relief.

(6) *Non-residents* – From 6 April 2015 owners who are not resident for tax purposes in the UK are subject to non-resident CGT (NRCGT) on gains on the disposal of UK residential property. Individual non-resident owners can claim main residence relief, but only if they are present in the property for at least 90 midnights during the tax year (*FA 2015, Sch 7*).

(7) *ATED-related* – Where a UK residential property disposed of before 6 April 2019 was subject to the Annual Tax on Enveloped Dwellings (ATED) (see **Chapter 13**), the part of the gain that accrues after 5 April 2013 is subject to an ATED-related CGT charge at 28%.

(8) *Rate of CGT* – Any gain on a residential property interest which is not covered by a relief above, and is not subject to ATED-related CGT, is charged to CGT at 28%, (18% within basic rate band) for disposals made on and after 6 April 2016.

(9) *Further information* – Chapter 11 of *Capital Gains Tax 2018/19* (Bloomsbury Professional).

(10) *Proposals* – For disposals on and after 6 April 2020, lettings relief (note 5) will be restricted to periods during which the home-owner is in joint occupancy with the tenant and relief for the final period will be cut to nine months (*Budget, 29 October 2018*).

ASSETS OF NEGLIGIBLE VALUE

(*TCGA 1992, s 24(2)*)

Claim by	Time limit	Claim to be made
Individuals and trustees	2 years from end of tax year in which asset value became negligible or was noticed to be so.	In tax return or by later amendment
Companies	2 years from end of accounting period in which asset value became negligible or was noticed to be so.	In tax return or by later amendment

Notes

(1) *Conditions* – The asset must have **become** of negligible value during the period of ownership, and it must still be of negligible value and be owned by the taxpayer at the date of claim.

(2) *Effect* – The claimant is treated as having sold and immediately reacquired the asset at the time of the claim or (subject to certain conditions) at any earlier time specified in the claim, for consideration equal to the value specified in the claim.

(3) *Form CG34* – This form may be used to establish whether the asset has a negligible value, which can then be used in a later claim on the tax return. See **Chapter 17: HMRC clearances** for the procedure to use form CG34.

(4) *Negligible value list* – HMRC publishes a list of shares or securities formerly quoted on the London Stock Exchange, which have been officially declared of negligible value for the purposes of a claim under *TCGA 1992, s 24(2)* by HMRC Shares and Assets Valuation (SAV), see: http://tinyurl.com/NegValshs.

(5) *Further information* – See HMRC Help Sheet HS286, HMRC's Capital Gains Manual at CG13128, and Share Valuation Manual at SVM107150.

CULTURAL GIFT SCHEME

Gifts of pre-eminent objects

(*FA 2012, s 49, Sch 14*)

	Taxes to be reduced	Tax credit as percentage of the gift
Individuals	Income tax and/or CGT	30%
Companies	Corporation tax	20%

Notes

(1) *Applies from* – Tax years or accounting periods starting on or after 1 April 2012 (*SI 2013/587*).

(2) *Relief given* – A reduction in specified taxes is available where the donor makes a 'qualifying gift' of 'pre-eminent property' to be held for the benefit of the public or the nation. The gift offer must be registered and accepted under the Cultural Gifts Scheme.

(3) *Individuals* – An individual (not trustee or PR) can allocate the tax reduction to the tax year in which the offer is registered and/or any of the following four tax years. Unless otherwise instructed, the tax reduction is first applied against income tax liabilities, then against CGT liabilities.

(4) *Companies* – The tax reduction is treated as arising when the company's corporation tax liability for the period in which the gift is made becomes due, or the registration date of the gift, if later.

(5) *Capital gains* – A gain on the gift of an object under the scheme is exempt from CGT or corporation tax (*TCGA 1992, s 258(1A)*).

(6) *Inheritance tax* – Gifts of property under the scheme are exempt from inheritance tax under *IHTA 1984, s 25(3)*.

(7) *Further information* – Administered by the Department for Culture Media and Sport and the Arts Council, see: http://tinyurl.com/Cltgiftschm.

Charities and CASCs

(*TCGA 1992, ss 256, 257*)

(1) Gains accruing to charities which are both applicable and applied for charitable purposes are generally exempt for CGT purposes.

(2) Relief from CGT generally applies to gifts to charities and certain other bodies. The relief was extended from 6 April 2002 to asset disposals to Community Amateur Sports Clubs (CASCs).

LEASES WHICH ARE WASTING ASSETS

(TCGA 1992, Sch 8, para 1)

Depreciation table

Years	%	Monthly increment (note 2)
50 or more	100	–
49	99.657	0.029
48	99.289	0.031
47	98.902	0.032
46	98.490	0.034
45	98.059	0.036
44	97.595	0.039
43	97.107	0.041
42	96.593	0.043
41	96.041	0.046
40	95.457	0.049
39	94.842	0.051
38	94.189	0.054
37	93.497	0.058
36	92.761	0.061
35	91.981	0.065
34	91.156	0.069
33	90.280	0.073
32	89.354	0.077
31	88.371	0.082
30	87.330	0.087
29	86.226	0.092
28	85.053	0.098
27	83.816	0.103
26	82.496	0.110
25	81.100	0.116

Years	%	Monthly increment (note 2)
24	79.622	0.123
23	78.055	0.131
22	76.399	0.138
21	74.635	0.147
20	72.770	0.155
19	70.791	0.165
18	68.697	0.175
17	66.470	0.186
16	64.116	0.196
15	61.617	0.208
14	58.971	0.221
13	56.167	0.234
12	53.191	0.248
11	50.038	0.263
10	46.695	0.279
9	43.154	0.295
8	39.399	0.313
7	35.414	0.332
6	31.195	0.352
5	26.722	0.373
4	21.983	0.395
3	16.959	0.419
2	11.629	0.444
1	5.983	0.470
0	0	0.499

Notes

(1) *Formula* – Fraction of expenditure disallowed:

$$\frac{A-B}{A}$$

Where:

A is the percentage for duration of lease at acquisition or expenditure; and

B is the percentage for the duration of the lease at disposal.

(2) *Fraction of years* – Add one-twelfth of the difference between the percentage for the whole year and the next higher percentage for each additional month. For a period of less than one month, odd days under 14 are not counted; 14 or more odd days are rounded up and treated as a month.

Short lease premiums

(*ITTOIA 2005, s 277*)

See **Chapter 6: Lease premiums** as to the calculation of the proportion of any premium received in respect of a lease of less than 50 years which is partly chargeable to capital gains tax, and that part which is chargeable to income tax as property business profits.

EXEMPT GILT-EDGED SECURITIES

(*TCGA 1992, ss 16(2), 115, Sch 9*)

Gains on the following securities are not chargeable gains and any losses are not allowable losses.

2.50%	Annuities 1905 or after redeemed 5 July 2015
2.75%	Annuities 1905 or after redeemed 5 July 2015
2.50%	Consolidated Stock 1923 or after redeemed 5 July 2015
3.50%	War Loan 1952 or after redeemed 9 March 2015
4.00%	Consolidated Loan 1957 or after redeemed 1 Feb 2015
3.50%	Conversion Loan 1961 or after redeemed 1 April 2015
3.00%	Treasury Stock 1966 or after Redeemed 8 May 2015
2.50%	Treasury Stock 1975 or after Redeemed 6 July 2015
4.25%	Treasury Gilt 2011
9.00%	Conversion Loan 2011
9.00%	Conversion Loan 2011 'A'
9.00%	Conversion Loan 2011 'B'
9.00%	Conversion Loan 2011 'C'
9.00%	Conversion Loan 2011 'D'
3.25%	Treasury Gilt 2011
5.50%	Treasury Stock 2008–2012
9.00%	Treasury Stock 2012

9.00%	Treasury Stock 2012 'A'
5.00%	Treasury Stock 2012
5.25%	Treasury Gilt 2012
2.50%	Index-Linked Treasury Stock 2013
8.00%	Treasury Stock 2013
4.50%	Treasury Gilt 2013
2.25%	Treasury Gilt 2014
5.00%	Treasury Stock 2014
7.75%	Treasury Loan 2012–2015
2.75%	Treasury Gilt 2015
4.75%	Treasury Stock 2015
8.00%	Treasury Stock 2015
8.00%	Treasury Stock 2015 'A'
2.50%	Treasury Stock 1986–2016
2.50%	Index-Linked Treasury Stock 2016
2.50%	Index-Linked Treasury Stock 2016 'A'
4.00%	Treasury Gilt 2016
2.00%	Treasury Gilt 2016
12.00%	Exchequer Stock 2013–2017
1.0%	Treasury Gilt 2017
1.25%	Index-Linked Treasury Gilt 2017
1.75%	Treasury Gilt 2017
8.75%	Treasury Stock 2017
8.75%	Treasury Stock 2017 'A'
1.25%	Treasury Gilt 2018
5.00%	Treasury Gilt 2018
0.125%	Index-linked Treasury Gilt 2019
1.75%	Treasury Gilt 2019
3.75%	Treasury Gilt 2019
4.50%	Treasury Gilt 2019
2.50%	Index-linked Treasury Stock 2020
2.00%	Treasury Gilt 2020
4.75%	Treasury Stock 2020
3.75%	Treasury Gilt 2020
8.00%	Treasury Stock 2021
3.75%	Treasury Gilt 2021
1.5%	Treasury Gilt 2021
1.75%	Treasury Gilt 2022
1.875%	Index-Linked Treasury Gilt 2022
4.00%	Treasury Gilt 2022
0.50%	Treasury Gilt 2022

continued

2.25%	Treasury Gilt 2023
0.125%	Index-linked Treasury Gilt 2024
2.50%	Index-linked Treasury Stock 2024
2.75%	Treasury Gilt 2024
5.00%	Treasury Stock 2025
2.00%	Treasury Gilt 2025
0.125%	Index-Linked Treasury Gilt 2026
1.5%	Treasury Gilt 2026
1.25%	Index-Linked Treasury Gilt 2027
4.25%	Treasury Gilt 2027
6.00%	Treasury Stock 2028
0.125%	Index-linked Treasury Gilt 2029
4.125%	Index-Linked Treasury Stock 2030
4.75%	Treasury Gilt 2030
1.25%	Index-linked Treasury Gilt 2032
4.25%	Treasury Stock 2032
0.75%	Index-linked Treasury Gilt
4.50%	Treasury Gilt 2034
2.00%	Index-Linked Treasury Stock 2035
4.25%	Treasury Stock 2036
0.125%	Index-Linked Treasury Stock 2036
1.125%	Index-Linked Treasury Gilt 2037
1.75%	Treasury Gilt 2037
4.75%	Treasury Stock 2038
4.25%	Treasury Gilt 2039
0.625%	Index-linked Treasury Gilt 2040
4.25%	Treasury Gilt 2040
0.625%	Index-linked Treasury Gilt 2042
4.50%	Treasury Stock 2042
0.125%	Index-linked Treasury Gilt 2044
3.25%	Treasury Gilt 2044
3.5%	Treasury Gilt 2045
4.25%	Treasury Gilt 2046
0.125%	Index-Linked Treasury Gilt 2046
0.75%	Index-Linked Treasury Gilt 2047
1.50%	Treasury Gilt 2047
4.25%	Treasury Gilt 2049
0.50%	Index-linked Treasury Gilt 2050
0.25%	Index-linked Treasury Gilt 2052
3.75%	Treasury Gilt 2052
1.25%	Indexed-linked Treasury Gilt 2055

4.25%	Treasury Gilt 2055
0.125%	Index-linked Treasury Gilt 2058
4.00%	Treasury Gilt 2060
0.375%	Index-linked Treasury Gilt 2062
0.125%	Index-Linked Treasury Stock 2065
2.50%	Treasury Gilt 2065
0.125%	Index-linked Treasury Gilt 2068
3.5%	Treasury Gilt 2068

IDENTIFICATION OF SECURITIES

(*TCGA 1992, ss 104–109*)

Disposals by individuals and trustees

Disposals on or after 6 April 2008 are to be identified with acquisitions in the following order:

(1) Same day acquisitions (*TCGA 1992, s 105(1)(b)*) (subject to an election under *s 105A* (see below));

(2) Acquisitions within the following 30 days on the basis of earlier acquisitions in that period, rather than later ones (a FIFO basis) (*TCGA 1992, s 106A(5)*); and

(3) Securities within the expanded *TCGA 1994, s 104* holding, which specifically does not include acquisitions under (1) and (2) above, on the basis of later acquisitions before earlier ones (a LIFO basis) (*TCGA 1992, s 106A*).

Where the number of securities which comprise the disposal exceed those identified under the above rules, that excess is identified with subsequent acquisitions beyond the 30-day period referred to above, taking the earliest one first.

Disposals by companies

Order of identification:

(1) Any acquisition on the same day (*TCGA 1992, s 105(1)(b)*);

(2) Acquisitions within the previous 10 days (*TCGA 1992, s 107(3)*) (on a 'first in, first out' (FIFO) basis);

(3) Acquisitions since 1 April 1982 ('the *s 104* holding', previously termed 'the new holding') (*TCGA 1992, s 107(7), (8)*);

(4) Acquisitions in the period 6 April 1965 to 31 March 1982 ('the 1982 holding') (*TCGA 1992, s 107(7), (9)*), and

(5) Those held on 6 April 1965, in respect of which no election has been made to include them in the pre-1982 pool; these will be identified on a last-in, first-out (LIFO) basis (*TCGA 1992, s 107(7), (9)*).

For disposals before 5 December 2005, where a company or group of companies held at least 2% of the shares or securities of that class, acquisitions and disposals within one month (for most quoted shares or securities) or six months (for other disposals) could be matched.

TIME LIMITS FOR ELECTIONS AND CLAIMS

The general time limit for claims and elections is four years from the end of the tax year or accounting period (*TMA 1970, s 43(1)*). HMRC may allow an extension of the normal time limit for certain elections and claims.

Provision	**Time limit**	**References**
Asset of negligible value	2 years from end of tax year (or accounting period, if a company) in which deemed disposal/reacquisition takes place	*TCGA 1992, s 24(2)*
Re-basing of all assets to 31 March 1982 values	For companies only: 2 years from end of accounting period of disposal	*TCGA 1992, s 35(6)*
50% relief if deferred charge on gains before 31 March 1982 (pre 06/04/08 disposals)	2 years from end of accounting period of disposal (if a company)	*TCGA 1992, s 36, Sch 4 para 9(1)*
Variation of a will so not to constitute a disposal for CGT purposes	Within 2 years of death; instrument of variation must contain a statement relying on *TCGA 1992, s 62(6)* (see *TCGA 1992, s 62(7)*)	*TCGA 1992, s 62(6)*
Employee share schemes – identifying disposals with acquisitions on "same day" transactions	Within 12 months from 31 January next following the tax year of the first disposal	*TCGA 1992, s 105B(2)*
Earn-out right to be treated as a security	Within 12 months from 31 January next following the tax year in which the right is conferred (or 2 years from end of accounting period, if a company)	*TCGA 1992, s 138A(5)*
Replacement of business assets (roll-over relief)	4 years from the end of the tax year (or accounting period) Note: Replacement asset to be purchased between 12 months before and 3 years after disposal of old asset (see *TCGA 1992, s 152(3)*)	*TCGA 1992, s 152(1)*
Asset appropriated to trading stock: trading profits to be adjusted by gain or loss on the deemed disposal at market value	Within 12 months from 31 January next following the year of assessment in which ends the period of account in which the asset is appropriated to trading stock (or 2 years from the end of the accounting period in which the asset is appropriated to trading stock, if a company)	*TCGA 1992, s 161(3A)*

Provision	Time limit	References
Disapplication of incorporation relief under *TCGA 1992, s 162*	2 years from 31 January following the end of the year of assessment in which the business is transferred If all the new assets have been disposed of by the end of the year of assessment following the one in which the business transfer took place, the time limit is 12 months from 31 January next following the tax year of the business transfer	*TCGA 1992, s 162A(3), (4)*
Hold-over of relief for gifts of business assets	4 years from the end of the tax year	*TCGA 1992, s 165(1)*
Entrepreneurs' relief	Within 12 months from 31 January following the tax year in which the qualifying business disposal is made	*TCGA 1992, s 169M(3)*
Deemed disposal/ reacquisition on expiry of mineral lease	4 years from the relevant date	*TCGA 1992, s 203(2)*
Main residence notification	2 years from date the second or subsequent property is used as a residence. Non-resident taxpayers give notice in the NRCGT return submitted within 30 days of disposal of the property	*TCGA 1992, ss 222(5), 222A(6)*
Small part disposals of land: consideration to be deducted from allowable expenditure on a subsequent disposal	Within 12 months from 31 January next following the tax year of disposal (or 2 years from end of accounting period of disposal, if a company)	*TCGA 1992, s 242(2A)*
Irrecoverable loan to a trader	4 years from the end of the tax year (or accounting period)	*TCGA 1992, s 253(3)*
Hold-over relief for gifts on which IHT is immediately chargeable etc	4 years from the end of the tax year.	*TCGA 1992, s 260(1)*
Trading losses relieved against gains	12 months from 31 January next following the tax year in which loss arose	*TCGA 1992, s 261B(8)*
Post-cessation expenses relieved against gains	12 months from 31 January next following the tax year in which expenses paid	*TCGA 1992, s 261D(6)*
Delayed remittances of foreign gains	4 years from the end of the tax year (or accounting period)	*TCGA 1992, s 279(5)*
Loss on disposal of right to deferred unascertainable consideration to be treated as accruing in an earlier year	Within 12 months from 31 January next following the year of the loss	*TCGA 1992, s 279D(8)*

9

Inheritance tax, gifts and deceased estates

IHT THRESHOLDS

(IHTA 1984, s 7, Sch 1)

Period	Nil rate band	Residential nil rate band
	£	£
2020/21	325,000	175,000
2019/20	325,000	150,000
2018/19	325,000	125,000
2017/18	325,000	100,000
2009/10 to 2016/17	325,000	N/A
2008/09	312,000	
2007/08	300,000	
2006/07	285,000	
2005/06	275,000	
2004/05	263,000	
2003/04	255,000	
2002/03	250,000	
2001/02	242,000	
2000/01	234,000	
1999/2000	231,000	
1989/99	223,000	
1997/98	215,000	
1996/97	200,000	
1995/96	154,000	
10 March 1992 to 5 April 1995	150,000	
6 April 1991 to 9 March 1992	140,000	
1990/91	128,000	
1989/90	118,000	
15 March 1988 to 5 April 1989	110,000	
17 March 1987 to 14 March 1988	90,000	
18 March 1986 to 16 March 1987	71,000	

Notes

(1) *Scope* – The above thresholds apply to cumulative lifetime transfers and transfers on death or within seven years before death.

(2) *Nil rate band (NRB)* – Covers value of the estate and gifts made within seven years of death, IHT is paid on any excess value subject to RNRB and other reliefs (*FA 2010, s 8*). Unused proportion of NRB may be inherited from deceased spouse or civil partner. The NRB has been frozen for all tax years 2015/16 to 2020/21 (*FA 2014, Sch 25, para 2* and *F(No 2)A 2015, s 10*).

(3) *Residential nil rate band (RNRB)* – Where individual dies on or after 6 April 2017, and their estate is above the NRB, the RNRB may also be deducted if all the conditions apply.

(4) *Conditions for RNRB* – The whole or a part share in the value of deceased's home is passed to a direct descendent on death. The maximum value of RNRB is the lower of: value of the home passed on, and the amount in the table above. RNRB is tapered away at £1 for every £2 by which the value of the total estate exceeds £2 million (*IHTA 1984, ss 8D–8M*).

(5) *Liabilities* – For deaths occurring on or after 17 July 2013, a debt owed by the deceased may be deducted from the value of the estate only if it is actually discharged out of the estate on or after the death, unless certain conditions are satisfied (*IHTA 1984, s 175A*).

(6) *Grossing up* – Applies at the rates of: 1/4 for net lifetime transfers and 2/3 for net transfers on death (not bearing own tax). Where the will specifies tax-free legacies and the estate residue passes to persons who are not eligible to receive the gift exempt of IHT, there is no requirement to gross-up to tax-free legacies.

Capital transfer tax (IHT thresholds) – 13 March 1975 to 17 March 1986

From	To	Limit
6 April 1985	17 March 1986	£67,000
13 March 1984	5 April 1985	£64,000
15 March 1983	12 March 1984	£60,000
9 March 1982	14 March 1983	£55,000
26 March 1980	8 March 1982	£50,000
27 October 1977	25 March 1980	£25,000
13 March 1975	26 October 1977	£15,000

Estate duty (IHT thresholds) – 16 August 1914 to 12 March 1975

England, Wales and Scotland

From	To	Limit
22 March1972	12 March 1975	£15,000
31 March1971	21 March 1972	£12,500
16 April1969	30 March 1971	£10,000
4 April 1963	15 April 1969	£5,000
9 April 1962	3 April 1963	£4,000
30 July 1954	8 April 1962	£3,000
10 April 1946	29 July 1954	£2,000
16 August 1914	9 April 1946	£100

Northern Ireland

From	To	Limit
22 March1972	12 March 1975	£15,000
5 May1971	21 March 1972	£12,500
4 June1969	4 May 1971	£10,000
22 May1963	3 June 1969	£5,000
4 July1962	21 May 1963	£4,000
1 November 1954	3 July 1962	£3,000
29 August1946	31 October 1954	£2,000
16 August 1914	28 August 1946	£100

RATES OF IHT

(*IHTA 1984, Sch 1A*)

Period in which transfer occurs:	Life-time transfers	On death	Reduced rate on death
2012/13 to 2019/20	20%	40%	36%
18 March 1986 to 5 April 2012	20%	40%	N/A

Notes

(1) *Reduced rate* – Available where at least 10% of the base-line net value of the estate is left to charities or CASCs on death (*IHTA 1984, Sch 1A, para 1*).

(2) *Variations* – Where an Instrument of Variation is executed, leaving or increasing a legacy to charity, the variation will only be treated as being made by the deceased where it is shown that the charity has been notified of the variation (*IHTA 1984, s 142(3A)*).

(3) *Further information* – For outline guidance on the reduced rate see: tinyurl.com/36rate. For detailed guidance, see HMRC's Inheritance Tax Manual at para IHTM45000+.

GIFT EXEMPTIONS

Annual and small gifts

(*IHTA 1984, ss 19, 20*)

Period	Annual exemption £	Small Gift exemption (to the same person) £
From 6 April 1981	3,000	250
6 April 1980 to 5 April 1981	2,000	250
6 April 1976 to 5 April 1980	2,000	100

Notes

(1) *Carry forward* – To the extent that the annual exemption is unused for a particular tax year, it can be carried forward to the next tax year but not beyond.

(2) *Priority* – The current year exemption must be used in priority over any brought forward exemption (*IHTA 1984, s 19(2)*).

In consideration of marriage or civil partnership

(*IHTA 1984, s 22*)

Donor	Limit
Parent of party to the marriage/civil partnership	£5,000
Remoter ancestor than parent of party to the marriage/civil partnership	£2,500
Party to the marriage/civil partnership	£2,500
Any other person	£1,000

Notes

(1) *Before marriage* – The gift must be made on or before the date of the marriage, and it is not IHT free if the marriage does not take place.

(2) *Excess gifts* – If the value of the gift is greater than the amount of the available exemption, it is an exempt transfer up to the amount of the available exemption, and the excess is chargeable.

Non-UK domiciled spouse or civil partner

(*IHTA 1984, s 18*)

Transfers	Limit
From 6 April 2013 (Note 1)	£325,000
9 March 1982–5 April 2013	£55,000

Notes

(1) *Nil rate band alignment* – With effect for gifts made on and after 6 April 2013, the IHT-exempt amount that a UK-domiciled individual can transfer to their non-UK domiciled spouse or civil partner is increased to the prevailing nil rate band limit (*IHTA 1984, s 18(2)*)

(2) *Election* – Individuals who are domiciled outside the UK and who have a UK-domiciled spouse or civil partner can elect to be treated as domiciled in the UK for IHT purposes. This election can be made at any time after marriage or civil partnership and within two years of the death where that occurs on or after 6 April 2013. The election can be back-dated up to seven years to the later of the date of the marriage or 6 April 2013 (*IHTA 1984, ss 267ZA–267ZB*).

AGRICULTURAL AND BUSINESS PROPERTY RELIEF

(IHTA 1984, Pt V, Chs 1, 2)

Agricultural property (APR)	
Nature of property	**Relief %**
Vacant possession or right to obtain it within 12 months	100
Tenanted land with vacant possession value (note 4)	100
Agricultural land let on or after 1 September 1995	100
Any other circumstances	50

Business Property (BPR)	
Nature of property	**Relief %**
Business or interest in a business	100
Quoted company: controlling shareholding	50
Unquoted company: any shareholding	100
Settled property used in life tenant's business: transferred with the business on death	100
Settled property used in life tenant's business	50
Land, buildings, machinery or plant used by a company controlled by transferor or by transferor's partnership	50

Notes

(1) *Applies from* – The rates of relief in the tables above apply to disposals made on and after 6 April 1996.

(2) *Location of land* – Agricultural property located in an EEA State, Channel Islands or Isle of Man, at the time of the chargeable event is eligible for relief (*IHTA 1984, s 115(5)*).

(3) *Grazing land* – If land is let to graze animals or take grass from land for a season, and vacant possession reverts to the landowner within a year, any agricultural property relief due will be at the 100% rate (IHTM24142).

(4) *Old tenancies* – Land let on a tenancy commencing before 10 March 1981 may qualify for relief at 100% in certain circumstances, ie broadly if the transferor owned the land before 10 March 1981, the land would have qualified for relief (under *FA 1975, Sch 8*) had it been transferred before that date, and the transferor did not have vacant possession (or entitlement to it) from then until the date of death/transfer (*IHTA 1984, s 116(2), (3)*).

(5) *Liabilities* – Where a debt is incurred or refinanced on or after 6 April 2013 to acquire an asset on which relief is due under APR, BPR or woodlands relief, the debt must be first deducted from the value of that asset before application of APR/BPR with any excess debt is deducted from the value of the total estate (*IHTA 1984, s 162B*).

QUICK SUCCESSION RELIEF

(*IHTA 1984, s 141*)

Years between transfers		Percentage
More than	**Not more than**	**(applied to formula – see below) %**
0	1	100
1	2	80
2	3	60
3	4	40
4	5	20

Formula:

$$\text{Percentage} \times \text{Tax charge on earlier transfer} \times \frac{\text{Increase in value of transferee's estate}}{\text{Value of earlier chargeable transfer}}$$

TAPER RELIEF

(*IHTA 1984, s 7(4)*)

Period between gift and death	**% of full charge at death rates**
3 years or less	100
Over 3 years but not more than 4 years	80
Over 4 years but not more than 5 years	60
Over 5 years but not more than 6 years	40
Over 6 years but not more than 7 years	20

Notes

(1) *Lifetime gifts* – The relief provides for a reduced tax charge on gifts made within seven years before death. The amount of relief depends on the length of time the deceased survived following the transfer. The tax otherwise due at the death rates is reduced by applying the percentages in the preceding table.

(2) *Not applicable* – If IHT on a chargeable lifetime transfer is recalculated on death with taper relief and produces a lower IHT figure than originally calculated at lifetime rates, the original figure stands (*IHTA 1984, s 7(5)*).

PRE-OWNED ASSETS

(*FA 2004, s 84, Sch 15*)

Asset type	**Chargeable amount calculated as:**
Land	R × DV/V less actual rent paid under a legal obligation
Chattels	N × DV/ V less amounts paid for use of chattel under a legal obligation
Intangible property in settlor-interested settlements	N – T

Where: R is the rental value of the relevant land for the taxable period;

DV is the value at the valuation date of the interest in the relevant land or chattel that was disposed of by the chargeable person or, where the disposal was a non-exempt sale, the appropriate proportion of that value; and

V is the value of the relevant land or chattel at the valuation date.

N is the notional interest for the taxable period, at the official rate of interest at the start of the period, on the value of the property or chattel at the valuation date.

T is the amount of income tax or capital gains tax payable by the chargeable person in the taxable period by virtue of gains from contracts of life assurance, income from settlements where the settlor retains an interest, transfer of assets abroad, the charge on settlors with an interest in settlements and the attribution of gains to settlors with an interest in non-resident or dual resident settlements for capital gains tax purposes.

Notes

(1) *The charge* – An income tax charge arises where a UK resident individual continues to benefit from property in the categories above, which was previously owned by them.

(2) *Exemption* – No tax is payable if the chargeable amount does not exceed £5,000. If the chargeable benefits exceed £5,000, the tax is due on the full amount.

(3) *Further Information* – HMRC's Inheritance Tax Manual at IHTM44000+.

DELIVERY OF IHT ACCOUNTS

Due dates

(IHTA 1984, s 216)

Type of transfer	Due Date
Chargeable lifetime transfer	Later of: – 12 months after end of month in which transfer occurred – 3 months after person became liable
Transfers on death	Later of: – 12 months after end of month in which death occurred – 3 months after personal representatives first act in that capacity
Potentially exempt transfers which have become chargeable	12 months after end of month in which the transferor died
Gifts subject to reservation included in donor's estate at death	12 months after end of month in which death occurred
National heritage property or woodlands (on disposal)	6 months after end of month in which chargeable event occurred
Relevant property trust IHT charges	6 months after end of month in which chargeable event occurred

Excepted transfers

From 6 April 2007

(*SI 2008/605, reg 4*)

For chargeable transfers from 6 April 2007, no account is necessary where:

- the transfer is in cash or quoted shares or securities and the value of the transfer and other chargeable transfers made in the preceding seven years does not exceed the IHT threshold; or
- the value of the transfer (ignoring business and agricultural property relief) and other chargeable transfers made in the preceding seven years does not exceed 80% of the IHT threshold, and the value of the transfer does not exceed the net amount of the threshold available to the transferor at the time of the transfer.

Similar rules apply in determining whether the termination of an interest in possession in settled property is excepted from the requirement to deliver an account (*SI 2008/605, reg 5*).

Excepted estates

(*SI 2004/2543; SI 2006/2141; SI 2011/214*)

Deaths from	Before	Excepted estate limit	Assets held outside UK – limit	Total value of settled property	Specified transfers – limit	Specified exempt transfers – limit
6 April 2009	5 April 2021	325,000	100,000	150,000	150,000	1,000,000
6 April 2008	5 April 2009	312,000	100,000	150,000	150,000	1,000,000
6 April 2007	5 April 2008	300,000	100,000	150,000	150,000	1,000,000

Notes

(1) *General* – The regulations provide for three categories of excepted estate:

(a) The 'low value' estate;

(b) The 'exempt estate'; and

(c) The 'foreign domiciliaries' estate.

(2) *Transferable nil rate band* – For deaths on and after 6 April 2010, the low value and exempt estate categories are expanded to twice the nil rate band. This only applies if a claim is made for 100% of the nil rate band to be transferred from an earlier deceased spouse or civil partner, subject to other conditions being satisfied. The excepted estate return form IHT205, or C5 in Scotland, must be used (*SI 2011/214*).

(3) *Alternatively secured pension funds* – For deaths occurring from 6 April 2011 the conditions relating to the alternatively secured pension fund do not have effect (*SI 2004/2543, reg 4(10)*).

(4) *Further information* – See Chapter 6 of *Inheritance Tax 2018/19* (Bloomsbury Professional) and HMRC's IHT Manual at IHTM06011+.

Excepted settlements

(*IHTA 1984, ss 216, 256; SI 2008/606*)

No account is necessary of settled property in which no qualifying interest in possession subsists for chargeable events from 6 April 2007, broadly where:

Either:

- Cash has always been the only property comprised in the settlement;
- The settlor has added no further property to the settlement;
- The trustees have been UK resident since the settlement commenced;
- The gross value of settled property has not exceeded £1,000 since the settlement commenced; and
- There are no related settlements.

or

- The settlor was UK domiciled when the settlement was made, and remained so until the chargeable event, or until death (whichever is earlier);
- The trustees have been UK resident since the settlement commenced; and
- There are no related settlements; and *either*
- For ten-year anniversary IHT charge purposes, the value of the notional aggregate chargeable transfer (in *IHTA 1984, s 66(3)*) does not exceed 80% of the nil rate band; *or*
- On a chargeable event before the settlement's first ten-year anniversary, the value of the notional aggregate chargeable transfer (in *IHTA 1984, s 68(4)*) does not exceed 80% of the nil rate band; *or*
- On a chargeable event between ten-year anniversaries, the value of the notional aggregate chargeable transfer (in *IHTA 1984, s 66(3)*, taking account of *s 69*) does not exceed 80% of the nil rate band; *or*
- Where an IHT charge arises in respect of an 'age 18 to 25' trust (under *IHTA 1984, s 71E*), the value of the notional aggregate chargeable transfer (as adjusted in accordance with *IHTA 1984, s 71F(8)*) does not exceed 80% of the nil rate band.

Note

Further guidance – See HMRC's Inheritance Tax Manual at IHTM06120+.

Personal representatives' allowable expenses

(SP 2/04)

Gross value of estate	Allowable expenditure for deaths after 5 April 2004
Not exceeding £50,000	1.8% of the probate value of assets sold by the personal representatives.
Over £50,000 but not exceeding £90,000	£900, divided among all assets of the estate in proportion to their probate values and allowed in those proportions on assets sold by the personal representatives.
Over £90,000 but not exceeding £400,000	1% of the probate value of assets sold.
Over £400,000 but not exceeding £500,000	£4,000, divided among all assets of the estate in proportion to their probate values and allowed in those proportions on assets sold by the personal representatives.
Over £500,000 but not exceeding £1,000,000	0.8% of the probate value of assets sold.
Over £1,000,000 but not exceeding £5,000,000	£8,000, divided among all assets of the estate in proportion to their probate values and allowed in those proportions on assets sold by the personal representatives.
Over £5,000,000	0.16% of the probate value of the assets sold, subject to a maximum of £10,000.

DUE DATES FOR PAYMENT OF IHT

(*IHTA 1984, s 226*)

Transfer	Due Date
Chargeable transfers other than death made between:	
6 April and 30 September	30 April in following year
1 October and 5 April	6 months after end of month in which transfer was made
Chargeable transfers which have conditional exemptions for heritage Charge to tax on disposals of trees or underwood	6 months after end of month in which chargeable event occurred
Transfers on death	Earlier of : – 6 months after end of month in which death occurs; or – delivery of account by personal representatives
Chargeable transfers and potentially exempt transfers within 7 years of death	6 months after end of month in which death occurs

Notes

(1) *Relevant property trusts* – For relevant property trust IHT charges arising on or after 6 April 2014, the IHT must generally be paid within six months after the end of the month in which the chargeable event occurs (*IHTA 1984, s 223(3C)*).

(2) *Penalties and interest* – For details of the penalties for late payment and interest that may be charged see **Chapter 17**.

DISTRIBUTION OF INTESTATE ESTATES

England and Wales

(*Administration of Estates Act 1925, s 46; Inheritance and Trustees' Powers Act 2014*)

See **Chapter 18** for Scottish estates

Distributions on and after 1 October 2014

Spouse or civil partner and issue survive	
Spouse or civil partner receives	*Issue receives*
• All personal chattels; • £250,000 absolutely (or the entire interest where this is less); and • One-half of residue (if any) in trust for the survivor absolutely.	• One half of residue (if any) on statutory trusts.

Spouse or civil partner survives without issue
Spouse or civil partner receives:
Residue in trust for the survivor absolutely.

Notes

(1) *No Will* – The distribution of a deceased individual's estate, and the IHT liability in respect of the estate, can be affected if the individual died without having made a valid will.

(2) *Location* – The above tables only apply to deaths occurring in England, Wales and Northern Ireland. For deaths in Scotland see **Chapter 18**.

(3) *From 1 Oct 2014* – The fixed sum of £250,000 is determined by *AEA 1925, Sch 1A*, and is subject to possible future amendment by statutory instrument.

(4) *Civil partners* – The surviving civil partner effectively acquires the same rights as a surviving spouse in cases of intestacy.

(5) *Survivorship* – The above provisions in favour of the deceased's spouse or civil partner are subject to a 28-day survival period (*AEA 1925, s 46(2A)*).

(6) *No spouse or civil partner survives* – The estate is held in the following order in such cases, with no class beneficiaries participating unless all those in a prior class have predeceased. Statutory trusts may apply except under (b), (e) and (h):

(a) Issue of deceased.

(b) Parent(s).

(c) Brothers and sisters (or issue).

(d) Half-brothers and half-sisters (or issue).

(e) Grandparent(s).

(f) Uncles and aunts (or issue).

(g) Half-brothers and half-sisters of deceased's parents (or issue).

(h) The Crown, the Duchy of Lancaster or the Duke of Cornwall.

(8) *Further information* – See HMRC's Inheritance Tax manual at IHTM12101.

Capital Allowances

PLANT AND MACHINERY

(*CAA 2001, Pt 2*)

Annual investment allowance (AIA)

(*CAA 2001, s 51A*)

Expenditure incurred in period:	**AIA cap** **£**
From 1 January 2019 to 31 December 2020	1,000,000
From 1 January 2016 to 31 December 2018	200,000
April 2014 to 31 Dec 2015	500,000
1 Jan 2013 to March/April 2014	250,000
April 2012 to 31 Dec 2012	25,000
April 2010 to April 2012	100,000

Notes

(1) *Temporary increase* – The AIA cap is temporarily increased to £1m for 2019 and 2020 (*F(No 3)B 2017–2019, cl 31*).

(2) *Non-qualifying* – The AIA cannot be claimed by a trust or by a partnership where one or more members is a company, and there are restrictions to the amount of the AIA claimable by groups of companies and related companies (*CAA 2001, ss 38A, 51B –51N*).

(3) *Exclusions* – The AIA cannot be claimed in respect of; the purchase of cars, for the final period of the trade, or where tax avoidance is the motive (*CAA 2001, s 38B*).

(4) *Changes* – The changes at 31 December/1 January apply for both corporation tax and income tax. The changes in March/ April were effective from 1 April for corporation tax and from 6 April for income tax. There are transitional rules for periods that straddle the dates of change (see notes (6) & (7)).

(5) *Chargeable periods* – The AIA is given for a chargeable period. As a general rule, the annual cap is proportionately increased or decreased for chargeable periods longer or shorter than 12 months.

(6) *Periods straddling 1 January 2019* – The AIA cap is found by splitting the chargeable period at the dates of changes in the maximum AIA cap.

For example, a business with a chargeable period that began on 1 March 2019 would calculate its AIA cap for that period in two parts:

(a) three months to 31 March 2019 = 3/12 × £1,000,000; and

(b) nine months to 31 December 2018 = 9/12 × £200,000;

However, the calculation of AIA cap is subject to additional transitional rules about the maximum allowance for expenditure actually incurred, which can restrict the available AIA for particular periods.

(7) *Periods straddling 1 January 2016* – The AIA cap is the sum of the maximum cap as if the chargeable period was split at 31 December 2015 and the resulting periods were treated as separate chargeable periods:

(a) the period from the first day of the chargeable period and ending with 31 December 2015;

(b) the period beginning 1 January 2016 and ending with the last day of the chargeable period.

However, for expenditure incurred in that part of the chargeable period falling after 31 December 2015, the maximum AIA cap is the amount calculated in accordance with transitional rules (*FA 2014, Sch 2*).

(8) *Further information* – See: http://tinyurl.com/CAAIAgd.

Writing down allowances (WDAs)

(*CAA 2001, s 56*)

	Main rate %	Special rate %
From April 2019	18	6
From April 2012 to April 2019	18	8
April 2008 to April 2012	20	10

Notes

(1) *Changes* – The changes in WDA rates apply from 1 April for corporation tax and from 6 April for income tax (*FA 2011, s 10*).

(2) *Straddling periods* – For chargeable periods which straddle the above relevant dates, the rate of WDA is a hybrid of the rates before and after the changes.

(3) *Further information* – Brief guidance is found here: http://tinyurl.com/CAwdwgd. For technical guidance see HMRC Capital Allowances manual at CA23200.

First year allowances (FYAs)

(*CAA 2001, s 52*)

FYAs at a rate of 100% are available for the following types of expenditure incurred by businesses of any size, subject to general exclusions listed below (see **First year allowances: general exclusions**).

Expenditure on	Section in *CAA 2001*
Energy-saving plant or machinery (note 1)	*s 45A*
Cars with low CO_2 emissions	*s 45D*
Goods vehicles with zero emissions (note 3)	*s 45DA*
Plant or machinery for gas refuelling stations (note 4)	*s 45E*
Plant or machinery for electric vehicle charging points (note 5)	*s 45EA*
Plant or machinery for use by a company wholly in a ring fence trade	*s 45F*
Environmentally beneficial plant or machinery (note 1)	*s 45H*
Certain new investment by companies in new plant or machinery in designated assisted areas in Enterprise Zones (see **Enterprise Zones**)	*s 45K*

Notes

(1) *ECA* – Enhanced capital allowances are only available for items included on the Energy Technology List (http://tinyurl.com/ECAengtech) or the Water Technology List. The ECA will be abolished from 1 April 2020 for companies and 6 April 2020 for unincorporated businesses (*Budget, 29 October 2018*).

(2) *Energy tariffs* – From April 2012 plant or machinery that generates electricity or heat (or produces biogas or biofuels) and which attracts tariff payments under the Feed-in Tariff (FiT) or Renewable Heat Incentive (RHI) schemes do not qualify for ECA (*CAA 2001, s 45AA*).

(3) *Zero-emission goods vehicles* – The vehicle must be new and unused (not second hand), and must be acquired in the period from 1 or 6 April 2010 to 31 March 2021 or 5 April 2021 (*CAA 2001, s 45DA*). Firms in financial difficult or in certain industrial sectors can't claim allowances for zero emissions vehicles (*CAA 2001, s 45DB*).

(4) *Gas refuelling equipment* – FYAs for plant and machinery used in gas, biogas and hydrogen refuelling stations apply for acquisitions to 31 March 2021 (*CAA 2001, s 45E*).

(5) *Electric charging points* – FYAs for plant and machinery used in electric vehicle charging points apply for expenditure from 23 November 2016 to 31 March 2023 (corporation tax), or 5 April 2023 (income tax) (*CAA 2001, s 45EA*).

First year allowances: general exclusions

(*CAA 2001, s 46(2)*)

No first year allowances are available for the following types of expenditure:

- incurred in the chargeable period in which the qualifying activity is permanently discontinued;

- cars (other than those with low CO_2 emissions);
- certain ships (within *CAA 2001, s 94* but see *FA 2013, s 70*);
- certain railway assets (exclusion removed by *FA 2013, s 70*);
- expenditure that would be long-life asset expenditure but for transitional provisions (in *CAA 2001, Sch 3, para 20*);
- expenditure on the provision of plant or machinery for leasing (whether in the course of a trade or otherwise) (subject to exceptions in *CAA 2001, s 46(5)*);
- certain anti-avoidance cases where the obtaining of a FYA is linked to a change in the nature or conduct of a trade;
- plant and machinery that was initially acquired for purposes other than those of the qualifying activity;
- plant or machinery that was provided for long funding leasing but later starts to be used for other purposes; and
- plant and machinery that was acquired by way of gift.

CARS

(*CAA 2001, ss 45D, 52, Pt 2, Ch 10A*)

CO_2 emissions in g/km				**Rate of capital allowance**
2009/10 to 2012/13	**2013/14 to 2014/15**	**2015/16 to 2017/18**	**2018/19 to 2020/21**	
Up to 110	Up to 95	Up to 75	Up to 50	FYA at 100% (note 1)
111 to 160	96 to 130	76 to 130	51 to 110	Main rate pool
Over 160	Over 130	Over 130	Over 110	Special rate pool

Notes

(1) 100% FYA – The car must be new and unused (not second hand) (*CAA 2001, s 45D*).

(2) *Cars with private use* – The main or special rates apply as above (depending on CO2 emissions) but the car is retained in a single asset pool (see HMRC's Capital Allowances Manual at CA23535). Allowances are restricted for private use.

(3) *Leased cars* – See **Chapter 6: Business Profits**.

(4) *Capital allowances rates* – For WDA rates in respect of the main rate pool and special rate pool, see **Writing down allowances** (WDAs) above.

BUILDINGS AND FIXTURES

Structures and Buildings (SBA)

(*F(No 3)B 2017–2019, cl 29*)

Costs included:	Rate of allowance
Construction or conversion Improvement, renovation or repair Demolition Preparing the land New and unused building acquired from developer or builder.	Flat rate 2% of qualifying expenditure.

Notes

(1) *Covers* – Expenditure incurred on or after 29 October 2018 in the categories lists above, where the resulting building starts to be used for a qualifying purpose within seven years of construction.

(2) *Excluded costs* – Acquiring the land, associated SDLT (or similar taxes), professional fees and any planning permission costs are not covered.

(3) *Excluded buildings* – Any building used as a dwelling house, or ancillary to a dwelling, or any building used for holiday or overnight accommodation of a prescribed kind. Where a building is partially used for a qualifying purpose an apportionment of costs may be allowed.

(4) *How relief is given* – The cost of each building must be calculated separately and spread over 50 years, with flat 2% of the total cost claimed as an allowance in year full year. When a building is sold the 2% flat rate allowance can be claimed by the new owner for each year the building is used for a qualifying purpose. There will be no balancing allowances or balancing charges for the former owner.

(5) *Further information* – The definitions required for the SBA will be provided for in regulations which are the subject of consultation (*HMRC Technical Note, 29 October 2018*).

Integral Features

(*CAA 2001, ss 33A, 33B, 104A(1), 104D*)

Included:	Excluded:
Electrical and lighting systems. Cold water systems. Space or water heating systems, powered systems of ventilation, air cooling or air purification, and any floor or ceiling comprised in such systems. Lifts, escalators and moving walkways. External solar shading.	Assets used to insulate or enclose the interior of a building, or to provide an interior wall, floor or ceiling intended to remain permanently in place.

Notes

(1) *Special rate pool* – Expenditure on integral features is included in the special rate pool, but can qualify for the AIA.

(2) *Repairs* – The cost of repairs are treated as replacements of the integral feature if the expenditure exceeds 50% of the item's replacement cost in a 12 month period (*CAA 2001, s 33B*).

(3) *Solar panels* – Expenditure on solar panels incurred on or after 1 April 2012 (corporation tax) or 6 April 2012 (income tax) must be included in the special rate pool whether integral or not (*CAA 2001, s 45AA*).

Fixtures

(*CAA 2001, Pt 2, Ch 14*)

The availability of capital allowances to a purchaser of fixtures on or after 1 April 2012 (for corporation tax) or 6 April 2012 (for income tax) is conditional on either:

(a) the seller and purchaser using one of two pre-existing procedures (a joint election under *CAA 2001, ss 198–199* or determination by the First-tier Tribunal) to fix the value of the fixtures transferred within two years of the transfer, or

(b) the past owner providing a written statement of the amount of the disposal value of fixtures which he had some time earlier been required to bring into account.

From April 2016 it is necessary to show that the business expenditure on qualifying fixtures had been pooled before a subsequent transfer on to another person (*CAA 2001, s 187A*).

SHORT-LIFE ASSETS

Expenditure incurred	Period of short life
From April 2011	8 years
Before April 2011	4 years

Notes

(1) *Why* – Where an asset is expected to have a short useful life the business can elect for the asset to be allocated to a single asset pool, so its value is not pooled with other assets. This ensures the full value of the asset is relieved for tax purposes over its useful life (*CAA 2001, s 83*).

(2) *Excluded assets* – Cars, ships, leased assets, and assets restricted to the special rate pool are all excluded from being treated as short life assets, (*CAA 2001, s 84*).

OTHER ALLOWANCES

(*CAA 2001, ss 298–306, Pts 3A, 4A, 5–10*)

Allowances	Date of expenditure	Initial allowance	Writing down allowance
Business premises renovation	From 11 April 2007 to 31 March 2017 or 5 April 2017	100%	25% (Notes 1, 2)
Dredging	From 1 April 1986	–	4% (Note 1)
Enterprise zones	Expenditure on industrial or commercial buildings if: (a) incurred within 10 years of site being included within the enterprise zone; or (b) contracted within that 10-year period and incurred within 20 years after site being included in the zone.	100%	25% (Notes 1, 3)
Know-how	From 1 April 1986	–	25% (Note 5)
Mineral extraction: acquisition of mineral asset	From 1 April 1986	–	10%
Mineral extraction: other expenditure	From 1 April 1986	–	25%
Patents	From 1 April 1986	–	25% (Note 5)
Research and development	From 5 November 1962	100%	

Notes

(1) *WDAs on straight line* – These WDAs are given on a 'straight line' basis rather than a 'reducing balance' basis.

(2) *Business Property Renovation Allowance (BPRA)* – From April 2014 the categories of expenditure that may qualify for BPRA are strictly defined (*CAA 2001, Pt 3A*).

(3) *Enterprise Zones* – Allowances for industrial and commercial buildings in 'old' ten-year enterprise zones were abolished with effect from 1 April 2011 (corporation tax) and 6 April 2011 (income tax) (*FA 2008, s 84*).

See **Enterprise Zones** as to 100% enhanced capital allowances in relation to designated assisted areas within enterprise zones.

(4) *Patents and know-how* – Replaced for most corporation tax purposes by the intangible assets regime with effect from 1 April 2002, but the allowances still apply for income tax.

TIME LIMITS FOR ELECTIONS AND CLAIMS

(*FA 1998, Sch 18, Part IX; CAA 2001, ss 3, 85(2), 198, 201, 260(6), 266, 569–570*)

Claim	Time Limit
Capital allowances: general (*CAA 2001, s 3; FA 1998, Sch 18, Part IX*)	Later of: • 12 months after the filing date for the return in respect of the tax year or accounting period to which the claim relates; • 30 days after a closure notice issued on completion of an enquiry; • 30 days after notice of amendment to a return issued following completion of an enquiry; or • 30 days after the determination of any appeal against an HMRC amendment.
'Short life' asset election (income tax) (*CAA 2001, s 85(2)*)	12 months from 31 January next following the tax year in which the relevant chargeable period ends (ie generally the chargeable period in which the qualifying expenditure was incurred)
'Short life' asset election (corporation tax) (*CAA 2001, s 85(2)*)	2 years from the end of the relevant chargeable period (ie generally the chargeable period in which the qualifying expenditure was incurred)
Purchase of interest in land that includes a fixture – election to fix apportionment of disposal proceeds (*CAA 2001, ss 198, 201*)	2 years from the date of purchase
Lease of interest in land that includes a fixture – election to fix apportionment of disposal proceeds (*CAA 2001, ss 199, 201*)	2 years from the date the lease is granted
Set-off of capital allowances on special leasing (corporation tax) (*CAA 2001, s 260(6)*)	2 years from end of accounting period
Business successions – transfers between connected parties of plant and machinery at tax written down value (*CAA 2001, s 266*)	2 years from the date on which the succession took place
Connected parties and controlled sales treated as being at market value: election for sale to be treated as being for an alternative amount (*CAA 2001, s 570(5)*)	2 years from the date of sale

Notes

(1) *Claims in return* – Capital allowances must generally be claimed in the tax return or as an amendment to the return (*CAA 2001, s 3(2)*).

(2) *Exceptions* – The following capital allowance claims may be made outside the tax return (*CAA 2001, s 3(4), (5)*):

- Special leasing plant and machinery allowances; and
- Patent allowances on non-trading expenditure (in income tax cases).

ENTERPRISE ZONES

(*CA 2001, ss 45K–45N, SI 2018/485*)

EZ location	EZ name	FYAs*
Anglesey (Wales)	Anglesey	N
Basingstoke & Deane, East Hampshire & Runnymede	Enterprise M3	Y
Birmingham (England)	Birmingham Curzon street	N
Black Country (England)	Black Country	Y
Buckinghamshire (England)	Aylesbury Vale	N
Cambridge (England)	Alconbury Enterprise Campus	N
Cambridge (England)	Cambridge Compass	N
Cardiff (Wales)	Central Cardiff	N
Cardiff (Wales)	Cardiff Airport and St. Athan	N
Cheshire & Warrington	Cheshire Science Corridor	Y
Cumbria	Carlisle Kingmoor Park	Y
Cornwall & Isles of Scilly (England)	Aerohub	Y
Derby & Nottingham	Nottingham and Derby	Y
Deeside (Wales)	Deeside	Y
Dorset	Dorset Green	N
Dundee (Scotland)	Dundee Claverhouse (Dundee City)	Y
Dundee (Scotland)	Dundee Port (Dundee City)	Y
Ebbw Vale (Wales)	Ebbw Vale	Y
Harlow (England)	Harlow	N
Haven Waterway (Wales)	Haven Waterway	Y
Hereford (England)	Hereford	N
Hertfordshire	Enviro-tech	N
Humber (England)	Humber	Y
Irvine (Scotland)	Irvine (N. Ayrshire)	Y
Kent (England)	Discovery Park	N
Samlesbury & Warton (England)	Lancashire	N
Lancashire	Blackpool Airport	Y
Leeds (England)	Leeds City region	Y
Leeds region	M62 Corridor	N
Leicester (England)	MIRA Technology Park	N

EZ location	EZ name	FYAs*
Liverpool (England)	Sci-Tech Daresbury	N
Liverpool (England)	Mersey Waters	N
London (England)	Royal Docks	N
Luton	Luton Airport	Y
Manchester (England)	Greater Manchester Life Science	N
Nigg (Scotland)	Nigg (Highland)	Y
Norfolk and Suffolk (England)	Great Yarmouth and Lowestoft	N
Northampton (England)	Northampton Waterside	N
Northern Ireland	Coleraine	Y
North East (England)	North East	Y
North West (England)	Hillhouse International	Y
Nottingham (England)	Nottingham	Y
Oxfordshire (England)	Science Vale UK	N
Oxfordshire	Didcot Growth Accelerator	N
Port Talbot (Wales)	Port Talbot	Y
Sheffield (England)	Sheffield City Region	Y
Snowdonia (Wales)	Snowdonia	N
South West England	Heart of South west	N
Stoke and Staffordshire	Ceramic Valley	Y
Gosport, Hampshire (England)	Solent	N
Tees Valley (England)	Tees Valley	Y
West of England	Bristol Temple Quarter & Bath & Somer valley	N
Yorkshire	York Central	N

*The FYAs may be restricted to designated areas within the Enterprise Zones.

Notes

(1) *Available to* – 100% FYAs are available to companies (not unincorporated businesses) for the cost of new and unused plant or machinery used primarily in designated assisted areas within Enterprise Zones. The expenditure must be incurred for the purposes of a qualifying activity, and must be new investment rather than replacement assets and not exceed £125 million for the investment project.

(2) *Limited period* – The expenditure must be incurred in an eight-year period starting from the date the area is designated as an assisted area, as defined by the *Assisted Areas Orders 2014* and *2016, SI 2014/1508* and *SI 2016/751* (*CAA 2001, s 45K*). The relief is only available up to 31 March 2020.

(3) *Exclusions* – Expenditure does not qualify for 100% FYAs if it is made by a firm in difficulty or in certain industrial sectors, incurred on means of transport or subject to grant finance (*CAA 2001, s 45M*).

(5) *Further information*:

- maps of English enterprise zones offering 100% FYA: http://tinyurl.com/EngEZFYA
- Wales: http://tinyurl.com/WalesEZ
- Scotland: http://tinyurl.com/ScotEZ
- Northern Ireland: http://tinyurl.com/NIrEZ

11

Stamp Taxes

STAMP DUTY LAND TAX (SDLT)

Residential property

(*FA 2003, s 55; SDLTA 2015*)

Property value	Main rates %	Higher rates %
Up to £125,000	0	3
£125,001–£250,000	2	5
£250,001–£925,000	5	8
£925,001–£1,500,000	10	13
Over £1,500,000	12	15

Notes

(1) *Calculation of duty* – SDLT is calculated as a percentage of the chargeable consideration (normally the purchase price) which lies in the appropriate band. Eg a single purchase for over £1.5m will have portions of the consideration taxed at each of the five rates of SDLT (*FA 2003, s 55(1B)*).

(2) *Main rates* – These apply from 4 December 2014. Where contracts were agreed before 3 December 2014 but completion hadn't taken place, purchasers can choose whether to use the old slab system (see below) or the progressive system and rates for paying SDLT on the purchase (*SDLTA 2015, s 2*).

(3) *Higher rates* – These rates include the 3% supplement for second home, which applies to purchases completed on and after 1 April 2016, where the conditions in note 4 apply. Where the contracts were agreed for the purchase before 26 November 2015 and completed on or after 1 April 2016, the higher rates don't apply as long as the contract was not altered or assigned, see: http://tinyurl.com/asdlt3-rt (*FA 2003, Sch 4ZA*).

(4) *Additional home* – Where the purchaser owns an interest in two or more homes after the transaction, and the property is not a replacement for their main home, the 3% supplement applies. A purchase by a company of a residential freehold for £40,000 or more, or leasehold with more than 21 years to run, is always subject to the higher rates. Separate rules apply to trustee purchasers. The period in which a reclaim of overpaid SDLT on a home can be made, was extended where the previous home was sold on after 29 October 2018, to within 12 months of the sale of that previous main

residence, or within 12 months of the filing date of the return relating to the new residence, whichever is later (*Budget, 29 October 2018*).

(5) *First-time buyers* – From 22 November 2017, where all the purchasers have never owned an interest in a residential property, SDLT on the first £300,000 is charged at 0%, if the purchase price does not exceed £500,000. This relief is extended to buyers of shared ownership properties and back dated to 22 November 2017, (*Budget, 29 October 2018, FA 2018, s 41*).

(6) *Mixed property* – Where the transaction consists of a mixture of residential and non-residential property the whole consideration is taxed as non-residential, see rates below.

(7) *Multiple dwellings* – Relief can be claimed for transactions which include the acquisition of interests in more than one dwelling. The rate of SDLT is determined by reference to the consideration divided by the number of dwellings, but subject to a minimum rate of 1%. Also a purchase in a single transaction of six or more dwellings is regarded as non-residential (*FA 2015, s 69; FA 2003, s 58D, Sch 6B*).

(8) *Penal high rate* – SDLT is due at 15% on the entire consideration where a residential property is purchased by a non-natural person (corporate, mixed partnership or collective investment structure) for over £500,000, unless one of the exemptions in *FA 2003, Sch 4A* applies (*FA 2014, s 111*). No equivalent penal rate for LBTT or LTT.

(9) *Scotland* – From 1 April 2015 Land and Buildings Transaction Tax (LBTT) applies for sales and leases of properties located in Scotland, see **Chapter 18**.

(10) *Wales* – From 1 April 2018 Land Transaction Tax (LTT) applies for sales and leases of property located in Wales, see **Chapter 18**.

Non-residential or mixed property

(*FA 2003, s 55, Sch 5*)

Property value	Rates from 17 March 2016 %
Up to £150,000	0
£150,001–£250,000	2
Over £250,000	5

Notes

(1) *Calculation of duty* – SDLT is calculated as a percentage of the amount of relevant consideration which lies in the appropriate band. Eg, a single purchase for over £250,000 will have portions of the consideration taxed at each of the three rates of SDLT (*FA 2003, s 55(1B)*).

(2) *VAT inclusive* – Where VAT is due on disposal, SDLT is charged on the VAT inclusive price, as VAT is part of consideration (*VATA 1994, s 19*).

(3) *Charities* – Exemption from SDLT applies to purchases by charities and where the property is intended to be held for charitable purposes (*FA 2003, Sch 8*).

(4) *Penalties and interest* – See **Chapter 17**.

Slab system

(*FA 2003, s 55; FA 2010, s 7*)

Residential property **22 March 2012 to 3 December 2014**	**Non-residential or mixed property** **8 September 2008 to 16 March 2016**	**Rate %**
Up to £125,000	Up to £150,000	0
£125,001–£250,000	£150,001–£250,000	1
£250,001–£500,000	£250,001–£500,000	3
£500,001–£1,000,000 (note 3)	£500,001 and over	4
£1,000,001–£2,000,000 (note 3)	n/a	5
£2,000,001 and over (note 3)	n/a	7

Notes

(1) *Calculation of duty* – SDLT was calculated as a single percentage of the entire amount of chargeable consideration for the land or property according to the highest rate applicable to the transaction (*FA 2003, s 55(1)*).

(2) *VAT inclusive* – Where VAT is due on disposal SDLT is charged on the VAT inclusive price as VAT is part of consideration (*VATA 1994, s 19*).

(3) Penal high rate – Non-natural persons are required to pay SDLT at 15% for purchases of residential properties worth over £2m (from 21 March 2012), and over £500,000 (from 20 March 2014), if one of the exemptions in *FA 2003, Sch 4A* is not met (*FA 2014, s 111*).

(4) *Avoidance schemes* – SDLT avoidance schemes that rely on the sub-sales rules are subject to anti-avoidance measures from 21 March 2012, which specify that the grant or assignment of an option cannot be a 'transfer of rights' (*FA 2012, s 212*; *FA 2013, s 194*).

Lease rentals

(*FA 2003, s 56, Sch 5*)

Effective Date	**Residential property** **NPV of rents**	**Non-residential or mixed property** **NPV of rents**	**Rate %**
From 17 March 2016	Up to £125,000	Up to £150,000	0
	over £125,000	£150,001 to £5 million	1
	N/A	Over £5 million	2
From 1 January 2010	Up to £125,000	Up to £150,000	0
	over £125,000	over £150,000	1

Notes

(1) *Calculation* – Where the chargeable consideration includes rent, SDLT is payable on the lease premium and on the 'net present value' (NPV) of the rent payable. SDLT calculators are available on gov.uk to work out the tax due for both leasehold and freehold transactions: http://tinyurl.com/SDLTCLT.

(2) *Annual rent* – Where the annual rent for the lease of non-residential property amounts to £1,000 or more, the 0% SDLT band is unavailable in respect of any lease premium (*FA 2003, Sch 5, para 9A*).

STAMP DUTY

(*FA 1986, s 67; FA 1999, s 112, Schs 13, 15*)

Transfers	Rate
Shares valued at no more than £1,000	Nil
Stocks or shares for more than £1,000	1%
Depository receipts	1.5%
Bearer instruments	1.5%

Notes

(1) *Rounding* – Stamp duty is rounded up to the nearest multiple of £5 (*FA 1999, s 112(1)(b)*).

(2) *Fixed duty* – This applies at the rate of £5 for certain instruments effecting land transactions (*FA 2008, Sch 32, para 22*).

(3) *Growth markets* – Stamp duty and SDRT does not apply to transfers of securities in recognised growth markets such as AIM and the ISDX with effect from 28 April 2014 (*FA 2014, Sch 24*).

(4) *Exemptions* – Exempt instruments for transfer of shares valued at no more than £1,000 and which are properly certified, do not need to be presented to HMRC stamping or adjudication.

(5) *Penalties and interest* – See **Chapter 17**.

(6) *Further information* – See *Stamp Taxes 2018/19* (Bloomsbury Professional).

STAMP DUTY RESERVE TAX (SDRT)

(*FA 1986, Pt IV; FA 1999, Sch 19, Pt II*)

Charge	Rate
Standard rate (*FA 1986, s 87*)	0.5%
Higher rate (*FA 1986, ss 93, 96*)	1.5%

Notes

(1) *Scope* – SDRT operates alongside the stamp duty charge on transfers of securities which are operated without a paper contract.

(2) *Standard rate* – Applies to transactions in securities (*FA 1986, s 87*).

(3) *Higher rate* – Applies to the transfer of securities into depository receipt schemes and clearance services (*FA 1986, ss 93, 96*).

(4) *Rounding* – The above charges are rounded up to the nearest penny (*FA 1986, s 99(13)*).

(5) *Unit trusts and OEICs* – Surrenders by investors of units or shares in unit trusts and open-ended investment companies are exempt from SDRT from 30 March 2014 (*FA 1999, Sch 19, Pt 2*). However, from that date the principal SDRT charge applies to non-pro rata in specie distributions (*FA 2014, s 114*).

12

VAT

REGISTRATION AND DEREGISTRATION LIMITS

UK taxable supplies

(*VATA 1994, Sch 1 paras 1, 4*; VAT Notices 700/1 and 700/11)

Effective date	Registration turnover: £	Registration exception: turnover not exceeding £	Deregistration turnover £
1 April 2017 to 31 March 2022	85,000	83,000	83,000
1 April 2016	83,000	81,000	81,000
1 April 2015	82,000	80,000	80,000
1 April 2014	81,000	79,000	79,000
1 April 2013	79,000	77,000	77,000
1 April 2012	77,000	75,000	75,000

Notes

(1) *Freezing of thresholds* – The VAT registration and deregistration thresholds will be frozen until 31 March 2022 (*Budget, 29 October 2018*).

(2) *'Turnover'* – Includes all taxable and zero-rated sales. It doesn't inlcude supplies that are exempt, non-business or outside the scope, capital assets (excluding any supplies of land on which the option to tax has been exercised) or taxable supplies which would not be taxable supplies apart from *VATA 1994, s 7(4)* (ie in connection with 'distance selling'). Any supplies or acquisitions to which *VATA 1994, s 18B(4)* (last acquisition or supply of goods before removal from fiscal warehousing) applies, and supplies treated as made by him under *s 18C(3)* (self-supply of services on removal of goods from warehousing), are also disregarded (*VATA 1994, Sch 1, para 1(7)–(9)*).

(3) *Compulsory registration* – A trader becomes liable to be registered if the registration threshold has been exceeded in the last 12 months to date or is expected to be exceeded in the next 30-days, subject to the exception, see note 5 (*VATA 1994, Sch 1, para 1*).

(4) *Going concern* – If all or part of a business is transferred as a going concern to a person who isn't VAT registered at the time of transfer, the transferee becomes liable to be registered if: the one-year or 30-day limits above are exceeded, subject to the exception (note 5) (*VATA 1994, Sch 1, para 2*).

(5) *Exception* – A person does not become liable to be registered under the mandatory (note 3) or the going concern (note 4) rules using the one-year turnover test, if HMRC are satisfied that the value of his taxable supplies in the one-year period beginning when he would otherwise become liable to be registered doesn't exceed the exception threshold (*VATA 1994, Sch 1, para 3*).

(6) *Non-UK established businesses* – From 1 December 2012, businesses without a UK establishment who make any UK taxable supplies must register for UK VAT, regardless of the value of taxable supplies they make in the UK (*VATA 1994, Sch 1A*).

(7) *Deregistration* – The turnover threshold applies to the value of taxable supplies in the next 12 months.

(8) *Voluntary deregistration* – A business can ask HMRC to cancel its VAT registration if its annual VAT taxable turnover falls, or is expected to fall in the next 12 months, below the deregistration threshold. Registration can't be cancelled if the reduction in turnover is due to the intention of the business to stop or suspend trading for 30 days or more in the next 12 months (VAT Notice 700/11, para 2.2).

(9) *Compulsory deregistration* – A business which is registered due to making taxable supplies in the UK must cancel the registration in certain circumstances, eg ceasing to make taxable supplies, or if the business intended to make taxable supplies but no longer intends doing so (VAT Notice 700/11, para 2.1).

(10) *Making Tax Digital* – VAT-registered businesses, who also have annual VATable turnover of £85,000 or more, must submit VAT returns using MTD-compliant software for VAT periods beginning on and after 1 April 2019, for deferred categories of buisnesses: VAT periods beginning on and after 1 October 2019 (see **Chapter 6**).

RATES AND FRACTIONS

(*VATA 1994, s 2(1)*)

Effective date	Standard rate %	VAT fraction
4 January 2011	20.0	1/6
1 January 2010	17.5	7/47
1 December 2008	15.0	3/23
1 April 1991	17.5	7/47

Notes

(1) *Reduced rate* – Set at 5% for certain supplies made, and acquisitions taking place, after 31 October 2001 (*VATA 1994, s 29A, Sch 7A*), see page 132. VAT fraction = 1/21.

(2) *VAT Fraction* – The VAT fraction is used to calculate the VAT element of VAT-inclusive goods and services at the appropriate rate.

(3) *Penalties and interest* – See **Chapter 17**.

ZERO-RATED SUPPLIES

(*VATA 1994, Sch 8*)

Group Number	Subject matter
1	Food (note 1)
2	Sewerage services and water
3	Books, etc (note 2)
4	Talking books for the blind and handicapped and wireless sets for the blind
5	Construction of buildings, etc
6	Protected buildings
7	International services
8	Transport (note 3)
9	Caravans and houseboats (note 4)
10	Gold
11	Bank notes
12	Drugs, medicines, aids for the handicapped, etc
13	Imports, exports etc
15	Charities etc
16	Clothing and footwear for children and babies
18	Goods supplied to European Research Infrastructure Consortium

Notes

(1) *Hot food and sports drinks* – From 1 October 2012, standard rate VAT is imposed, where it didn't already apply, to hot food and sports drinks. However, pre-baked hot products which are allowed to cool naturally are zero rated (see VAT Notices 701/14 and 709/1).

(2) *Books, etc* – From 19 July 2011, zero-rating is withdrawn from printed matter where the printed matter is ancillary to a differently rated service, and where, if the service and printed matter had been supplied by a single company, the two supplies would have been treated as a single standard-rated, reduced-rated or exempt supply (*FA 2011, s 74*).

(3) *'Qualifying aircraft'* – From 1 January 2011, zero-rating applies to supplies of aircraft used by an airline operating for reward chiefly on international routes (*VATA 1994, Sch 8, Group 8, Note A1(b)*).

(4) *Caravans* – From 6 April 2013, the rate of VAT applied to supplies of holiday caravans depends on the size of the caravan (over/under 7 metres) and whether it complies with standard BS 3632 (see VAT Notice 701/20).

REDUCED RATE SUPPLIES

(*VATA 1994, Sch 7A*)

Group Number	Subject matter
1	Supplies of domestic fuel or power
2	Installation of energy-saving materials (note 2)
3	Grant-funded installation of heating equipment or security goods or connection of gas supply.
4	Women's sanitary products (note 4)
5	Children's car seats (note 3)
6	Residential conversions
7	Residential renovations and alterations
8	Contraceptive products (from 1 July 2006: *SI 2006/1472*)
9	Welfare advice or information (from 1 July 2006: *SI 2006/1472*)
10	Installation of mobility aids for the elderly (from 1 July 2007: *SI 2007/1601*)
11	Smoking cessation products (from 1 July 2008: *SI 2008/1410*)
12	Caravans (from 6 April 2013)
13	Cable-suspended passenger transport systems (from 1 April 2013)

Notes

(1) *Effective from* – Reduced VAT rate (5%) applies with effect for certain supplies made, and acquisitions taking place, after 31 October 2001 (*VATA 1994, s 29A*).

(2) *Installation of energy-saving materials* – From 1 August 2013, buildings solely used for a relevant charitable purpose are removed from the scope of the reduced rate of VAT for the installation of energy-saving materials (*VATA 1994, Sch 7A, Pt 2, group 2*, see VAT Notice 708/6).

(3) *Children's car seats* – Extended to related base units from 1 July 2009 (*SI 2009/1359*).

(4) *Women's sanitary products* – From a date to be confirmed these products will be classifed as zero rate, but until then the products carry VAT at 5% (*FA 2016, s 126*).

EXEMPT SUPPLIES

(*VATA 1994, Sch 9*)

Group Number	Subject matter
1	Land (note 5)
2	Insurance
3	Postal services (note 1)
4	Betting, gaming and lotteries
5	Finance
6	Education

continued

Group Number	Subject matter
7	Health and welfare
8	Burial and cremation
9	Subscriptions to trade unions, professional and other public interest bodies
10	Sport, sports competitions and physical education
11	Works of art etc
12	Fund-raising events by charities and other qualifying bodies
13	Cultural services etc (from 1 June 1996: *SI 1996/1256*)
14	Supplies of goods where input tax cannot be recovered (from 1 March 2000: *SI 1999/2833*)
15	Investment gold (from 1 January 2000: *SI 1999/3116*)
16	Supplies of services by groups involving cost sharing

Notes

(1) *Postal services* – From 31 January 2011 postal services are supplies of public postal services and incidental goods made by a universal service provider (ie the Royal Mail) (*F(No 3)A 2010, s 22*).

(2) *Cost sharing* – Exempts from VAT the supply of services by a group which consists of persons engaged in exempt or non-taxable activities so long as the services are supplied to group members at cost and for the purposes of those activities. The exemption aims to reduce a barrier that might otherwise prevent businesses and organisations that have exempt and/or non-business activities for VAT purposes from joining with others to share costs.

(3) *Supplies by public bodies* – Government departments, local authorities and analogous institutions are not generally subject to VAT when making supplies of goods or services (*VATA 1994, s 41A*).

(4) *Small packages* – Small non-commercial consignments can be sent into the UK from outside the EU, without VAT applied if the value of the goods does not exceed £34 (*SI 2015/2015*).

(5) *Land* – There are many exceptions to this exemption, so VAT on the supply of land or buildings can apply at any rate of VAT (see VAT notice 742). For example the hire of hairdressers' chairs is standard rated, as are self-storage facilities (see VAT information sheet 10/13).

SUPPLIES BETWEEN EU MEMBER STATES

Supplies into the UK (distance selling)

(*VATA 1994, Sch 2;* VAT Notice 700/1, section 5, Notice 700/11, section 3)

Effective date	Registration threshold for goods £
1 January 1993	70,000

Notes

(1) *Goods only* – A taxable person in another EU state which supplies and delivers goods to non-VAT registered customers in the UK broadly becomes liable to register in the UK if in a calender year the value of its relevant supplies exceeds the above limit.

(2) *Excise goods* – Special rules apply to the sale of excise goods (eg alcohol and tobacco) sold in the UK (see VAT Notice 700/1, section 6.6).

(3) *Cancel registration* – If the business was registered because it exceeded the distance sales threshold, it may apply to cancel its registration when:

(a) the value of its distance sales in the year ending 31 December did not exceed the threshold; and

(b) the value of its distance sales in the year following, beginning 1 January, will not exceed the threshold.

(4) *Compulsory deregistration* – The registration must be cancelled if either the business ceases to make distance sales, or if the business intended to make distance sales but no longer intends to do so and is not eligible or liable for registration as a result of any taxable supplies, acquisitions or relevant supplies (VAT Notice 700/11, para 3.1).

(5) *Voluntary deregistration* – If the business was registered because the UK was the place of supply for its distance sales, and had made supplies, the business remains registered in the UK for at least two calendar years from the date of first supply following registration. However, if the business opted but did not start to make supplies, the business may apply for cancellation of registration (VAT Notice 700/11, para 3.2).

Services supplied to other EU states

Effective date	Registration threshold for digital services £
1 January 2019	8,818

(1) *Digital services* – From 1 January 2015 traders who sell electronic services, broadcasting or telecoms, to non-businesses in other EU countries (B2C sales) must charge VAT at the rate applicable for the service in the country where the customer belongs (see **EU VAT Rates** below). The UK trader must either register for VAT in the country where the customer belongs or use the VAT mini one stop shop (VAT MOSS) to comply with the EU VAT regulations and pay the VAT due.

(2) *Threshold* – From 1 Janaury 2019 businesses which supply digitial services as defined in note (1), of less than £8,818 to customers in EU member states in a calendar year, and supplied digital services of less than £8,818 in the previous year, do not have to regiser for VAT MOSS (*SI 2018/1194*).

(3) *VAT MOSS registration* – The trader must be registered for VAT in the UK in order to register to use VAT MOSS. However, where the business turnover is under the UK VAT registration threshold the trader can register for VAT and VAT MOSS in one go and is NOT required to charge VAT to its UK customers until its UK turnover reaches the VAT registration threshold.

(4) *VAT MOSS returns* – VAT MOSS returns must be submitted online by 20th of the month following the end of the calender quarter, so by 20 April, 20 July, 20 October and 20 January. The VAT due must also be paid by the same date by electronic means, but not by direct debit.

(5) *Further information* – See **Place of Supply of Services** below and HMRC guidance at: tinyurl.com/VTMSS.

Acquisitions from EU member states

(*VATA 1994, Sch 3*; VAT Notice 700/1, Section 6; Notice 700/11, section 4.2)

Effective date	Registration threshold £
1 April 2017	85,000
1 April 2016	83,000
1 April 2015	82,000
1 April 2014	81,000
1 April 2013	79,000
1 April 2012	77,000

Notes

(1) *Threshold* – The registration threshold for relevant acquisitions from other EU Member States will remain at £85,000 until 31 March 2022 (*Budget, 29 October 2018*).

(2) *No intended supply* – Where an unregistered business or organisation, which does not make or intend to make any taxable supplies in the UK, buys goods from a VAT registered supplier in another EU state to bring to the UK, these are known as relevant acquisitions. This would typically apply to a business making exempt supplies only or using the goods to make non-business supplies only.

(3) *Annual measure* – The business must register for VAT where the value of relevant acquisitions exceeds the registration limit in the calendar year to 31 December, or if there are reasonable grounds for believing that the value of relevant acquisitions will exceed the registration limit in the next 30 days.

(4) *Cancel registration* – If the business may apply to cancel its registration where:

(a) the value of its relevant acquisitions in the year ending 31 December did not exceed the threshold; and

(b) the value of its relevant acquisitions in the year following, beginning 1 January, will not exceed the threshold.

(5) *Compulsory deregistration* – The registration must be cancelled if the business ceases to make relevant acquisitions, or if the business intended to make relevant acquisitions but no longer intends doing so and is not eligible or liable for registration as a result of any taxable supplies, distance sales or relevant supplies (VAT Notice 700/11, para 4.1).

(6) *Voluntary deregistration* – Where value of relevant acquisitions in the year ending 31 December did not exceed the threshold, and the value of relevant acquisitions in the following year will not exceed the threshold. However, a business which voluntarily registered for relevant acquisitions will remain registered in the UK for at least two calendar years unless entitlement to be registered has ceased (VAT Notice 700/11, para 4.2).

ANNUAL ACCOUNTING SCHEME

(*VAT Regulations 1995, SI 1995/2518, regs 49–55*; VAT Notice 732)

Effective date	**Joining threshold £**	**Leaving threshold £**
1 April 2006	1,350,000	1,600,000

Notes

(1) *Joining threshold* – A business can use this scheme if its estimated taxable supplies for the coming year are not expected to exceed the joining threshold, subject to certain other criteria (see *SI 1995/2518, reg 52*; VAT Notice 732, paras 2.1 and 2.6).

(2) *Leaving threshold* – A business must leave the scheme if at the end of the current accounting year (or transitional accounting period) the value of taxable supplies in that year (or period) exceeds the leaving threshold (*SI 1995/2518, reg 53*).

(3) *MTD regime* – A business which uses the annual accounting scheme can not join the MTD regime until the first VAT period that begins on or after 1 Ocotber 2019 (see **Chapter 6**).

CASH ACCOUNTING SCHEME

(*SI 1995/2518, regs 56–65*; VAT Notice 731)

Effective date	**Joining threshold £**	**Leaving threshold £**
1 April 2007	1,350,000	1,600,000

Notes

(1) *Joining threshold* – A business can use the scheme if estimated taxable supplies in the next year is not expected to exceed the joining threshold, and subject to certain other criteria (see *SI 1995/2518, reg 58*; VAT Notice 731, para 2.1).

(2) *Leaving threshold* – A business must leave the scheme if the value of taxable supplies for a 12-month period (ending at the end of a tax period) has exceeded the leaving threshold (*SI 1995/2518, reg 60*; VAT Notice 731, para 6.2).

(3) *'One-off' sales increases* – A business may remain on cash accounting where it exceeds the leaving threshold because of a one-off increase in sales resulting from a genuine commercial activity, provided there are reasonable grounds for believing that the value of its taxable supplies in the next 12 months will be below the joining threshold (see VAT Notice 731, para 2.6).

FLAT-RATE SCHEME FOR SMALL BUSINESSES

(*SI 1995/2518, regs 55A–55V*; VAT Notice 733)

Category of business	**From 1 April 2017** %	**From 4 January 2011** %
Limited cost trader (note 6)	16.5	N/A
Accountancy or book-keeping	14.5	14.5
Advertising	11.0	11.0
Agricultural services	11.0	11.0
Any other activity not listed elsewhere	12.0	12.0
Architect, civil and structural engineer or surveyor	14.5	14.5
Boarding or care of animals	12.0	12.0
Business services that are not listed elsewhere	12.0	12.0
Catering services including restaurants and takeaways	12.5	12.5
Computer and IT consultancy or data processing	14.5	14.5
Computer repair services	10.5	10.5
Dealing in waste or scrap	10.5	10.5
Entertainment or journalism	12.5	12.5
Estate agency or property management services	12.0	12.0
Farming or agriculture that is not listed elsewhere	6.5	6.5
Film, radio, television or video production	13.0	13.0
Financial services	13.5	13.5
Forestry or fishing	10.5	10.5
General building or construction services*	9.5	9.5
Hairdressing or other beauty treatment services	13.0	13.0
Hiring or renting goods	9.5	9.5
Hotel or accommodation	10.5	10.5
Investigation or security	12.0	12.0
Labour-only building or construction services (note 4)	14.5	14.5
Laundry or dry-cleaning services	12.0	12.0
Lawyer or legal services	14.5	14.5
Library, archive, museum or other cultural activity	9.5	9.5
Management consultancy	14.0	14.0

Category of business	From 1 April 2017 %	From 4 January 2011 %
Manufacturing fabricated metal products	10.5	10.5
Manufacturing food	9.0	9.0
Manufacturing that is not listed elsewhere	9.5	9.5
Manufacturing yarn, textiles or clothing	9.0	9.0
Membership organisation	8.0	8.0
Mining or quarrying	10.0	10.0
Packaging	9.0	9.0
Photography	11.0	11.0
Post offices	5.0	5.0
Printing	8.5	8.5
Publishing	11.0	11.0
Pubs	6.5	6.5
Real estate activity not listed elsewhere	14.0	14.0
Repairing personal or household goods	10.0	10.0
Repairing vehicles	8.5	8.5
Retailing food, confectionery, tobacco, newspapers or children's clothing	4.0	4.0
Retailing pharmaceuticals, medical goods, cosmetics or toiletries	8.0	8.0
Retailing that is not listed elsewhere	7.5	7.5
Retailing vehicles or fuel	6.5	6.5
Secretarial services	13.0	13.0
Social work	11.0	11.0
Sport or recreation	8.5	8.5
Transport or storage, including couriers, freight, removals and taxis	10.0	10.0
Travel agency	10.5	10.5
Veterinary medicine	11.0	11.0
Wholesaling agricultural products	8.0	8.0
Wholesaling food	7.5	7.5
Wholesaling that is not listed elsewhere	8.5	8.5

Notes

(1) *Eligibility* – The flat-rate scheme is open to businesses who expect their taxable supplies (excluding exempt and outside the scope supplies) in the next year to be no more than £150,000 **excluding VAT** (VAT Notice 733, para 3.1). Admission to the scheme is also subject to certain other criteria (see *SI 1995/2518, reg 55L*; VAT Notice 733, para 3.6).

(2) *Withdrawal* – The business must leave the scheme when its annual flat rate turnover (excluding sales of capital assets but including all exempt and outside the scope

income) exceeds £230,000 **including VAT**. The business must also leave the scheme if its total turnover in the next 30 days alone can reasonably be expected to exceed £230,000 including VAT. A business may leave the scheme voluntarily on giving notice and when it becomes ineligible for other reasons. For the effective date of leaving the scheme see VAT Notice 733 para 12.2 (*SI 1995/2518, reg 55M*).

(3) *Discount* – A business is entitled to a 1% discount on the normal flat rate percentage until the day before its first anniversary of becoming VAT registered. This also applies to limited cost traders see note (6) (*SI 1995/2518, reg 55JB*; VAT Notice 733, para 4.7).

(4) *Labour only* – This means building or construction services where the value of materials supplied is less than 10% of relevant turnover from such services; any other building or construction services are "general building or construction services".

(5) *Which category* – The business should use normal English to describe its activities and pick the category which is the best fit for the majority of its activities. See HMRC flat rate scheme manual paras FRS7200 and FRS7300.

(6) *Limited cost trader* – From 1 April 2017 where the business has not acquired relevant goods in the VAT period equal to at least 2% of its gross sales, and at least £1,000 per year, it must use 16.5% as its flat rate percentage for that period. 'Relevant goods' excludes:

- goods not used entirely for business purposes;
- capital items of any value;
- motor fuel and parts, unless the business is in the transport sector and owns of leases a vehicle;
- food and drink for consumption by the business owner or staff;
- goods for resale, leasing, letting or hiring out if the main business activity doesn't ordinarily consist of selling, leasing, letting or hiring out such goods;
- goods intended for re-sell or hire out, unless selling or hiring is the main business activity; and
- goods for disposal as promotional items, gifts or donations.

(*SI 1995/2518, reg 55A(4)*; VAT Notice 733, para 4.4–4.6).

PARTIAL EXEMPTION *DE MINIMIS* LIMITS

(*SI 1995/2518, regs 105A–107*; VAT Notice 706)

Exempt input tax not exceeding:
• £625 per month on average; and
• 50% of total input tax for the period concerned

Notes

(1) *De-minimis threshold* – Businesses which have both taxable and exempt income can recover all their exempt input tax, provided that amount is below the *de minimis* limits in the table above. The input tax claimed in each tax period is provisional until any under or over recovery of input tax is accounted for in an annual adjustment.

(2) *Simplified tests* – If the business passes either the original test in table above or one of the optional tests in notes (3) to (5) below, it may treat itself as *de minimis* and provisionally recover input tax relating to exempt supplies, but it must still check its over/ under recovery of input tax on an annual basis and make any annual adjustment as necessary (see *SI 1995/2518, reg 107*; VAT Information Sheet 04/10).

(3) *Test 1* – Total input tax incurred is no more than £625 per month on average and the value of exempt supplies is no more than 50% of the value of all supplies.

(4) *Test 2* – Total input tax incurred, less input tax directly attributable to taxable supplies, is no more than £625 per month on average and the value of exempt supplies is no more than 50% of the value of all supplies.

(5) *Prior year test* – The business may treat itself as *de minimis* throughout a tax year if it was *de minimis* in the previous tax year.

CAPITAL GOODS SCHEME (CGS)

(*SI 1995/2518, Part XV*; VAT Notice 706/2)

Asset	**No of intervals in adjustment period**
Single items of computer equipment costing £50,000 or more excluding VAT	5
Ships boats and aircraft costing £50,000 or more excluding VAT	5
An interest in land, buildings or civil engineering works costing £250,000 or more excluding VAT	10

Notes

(1) *Applies to* – Input tax recovered by partially exempt traders and businesses that have business/non-business use on property, computers, aircraft, ships and boats.

(2) *Land and buildings* – This includes the purchase or construction of a building, as well as alterations, constructions of extensions or annexes, refurbishments and civil engineering works (*SI 1995/2518, reg 113*). Prior to 1 January 2011, building alterations and constructions of extensions or annexes were only included where additional floor space of 10% or more was created by the works.

(3) *Adjustments* – Input tax is initially recovered under the normal partial exemption rules. Section 7 of VAT Notice 706/2 explains how to make subsequent adjustments under the scheme.

VAT INVOICES

(*SI 1995/2518, reg 14*)

In the UK a VAT invoice must show the following:

- A sequential number based on one or more series which uniquely identifies the document.
- The time of the supply.

- The date of the issue of the document.
- The name, address and registration number of the supplier.
- The name and address of the person to whom the goods or services are supplied.
- A description sufficient to identify the goods or services supplied.
- For each description, the quantity of the goods or the extent of the services, and the rate of VAT and the amount payable, excluding VAT, expressed in any currency.
- The gross total amount payable, excluding VAT, expressed in any currency.
- The rate of any cash discount offered.
- The total amount of VAT chargeable, expressed in sterling.
- The unit price.
- Where the VAT invoice includes zero-rated or exempt goods or services, the total of those values separately showing clearly that there is no VAT payable on them.
- Where a margin scheme is applied under *VATA 1994, s 50A* (see Note 3) or *53* (certain supplies made by a tour operator), a relevant reference or any indication that a margin scheme has been applied.
- Where a VAT invoice relates in whole or part to a supply where the reverse charge rules apply, an indication that the customer is liable to pay the tax.
- Where issued by the customer under a self-billing agreement it must say 'Self Billing' on the face of the invoice.

Notes

(1) *Retailers' invoices* – A retailer who makes a sale of goods or services for £250 or less (including VAT) can issue a simplified invoice (where the customer asks for a VAT invoice), if the supply is other than to a person in another member state. The VAT invoice need only contain the following particulars (*SI 1995/2518, reg 16*):

- The name, address and registration number of the retailer;
- The time of the supply;
- A description sufficient to identify the goods or services supplied;
- The total amount payable including VAT; and
- For each rate of VAT chargeable, the gross amount payable including VAT, and the VAT rate applicable.

(2) *Overseas customers* – Where a VAT invoice is provided for a person in another EU member state (see EU VAT rates below), separate requirements apply, unless HMRC allow otherwise (*SI 1995/2518, reg 14(2)*).

(3) *Margin schemes – VATA 1994, s 50A* applies to supplies of works of art, antiques or collectors' items, motor vehicles, second-hand goods, and any supply of goods through a person who acts as an agent, but in his own name, in relation to the supply. An invoice in relation to such supplies must include a relevant reference. Similar provisions apply to certain supplies made by tour operators (*VATA 1994, s 53*).

(4) *Relevant reference* – Examples of relevant references or indications that a margin scheme has been applied are if the invoice includes: 'This invoice is for a second-hand margin scheme supply' or 'This is a tour operators' margin scheme supply' (*SI 1995/2518, reg 14(8)*).

(5) *Electronic invoices* – Invoices sent electronically must include the same information as paper invoices. When an invoice is attached as a document to an email, HMRC recommend using PDF or XML format for the invoice.

(6) *Further information* – HMRC guidance: tinyurl.com/vrkvin.

PRIVATE FUEL SCALE CHARGES

(*VATA 1994, ss 56(7), 57*)

Shown here on a VAT-inclusive basis.

Fuel scale charge from 1 May 2018 to 30 April 2019

Description of vehicle: vehicle's CO_2 emissions figure (but see Note 2 below)	12-month period £	3-month period £	1-month period £
120 or less	562	140	46
125	842	210	70
130	900	224	74
135	954	238	79
140	1,013	252	84
145	1,067	266	88
150	1,125	280	93
155	1,179	295	98
160	1,238	309	102
165	1,292	323	107
170	1,350	336	111
175	1,404	351	116
180	1,463	365	121
185	1,517	379	125
190	1,575	393	130
195	1,630	407	135
200	1,688	421	140
205	1,742	436	145
210	1,801	449	149
215	1,855	463	154
220	1,913	477	159
225 or more	1,967	491	163

Fuel scale charge from 1 May 2017 to 30 April 2018

Description of vehicle: vehicle's CO_2 emissions figure (but see Note 2 below)	12-month period £	3-month period £	1-month period £
120 or less	563	140	46
125	842	211	70
130	901	224	74
135	955	238	79
140	1,013	252	84
145	1,068	267	88
150	1,126	281	93
155	1,180	295	98
160	1,239	309	102
165	1,293	323	107
170	1,351	337	111
175	1,405	351	116
180	1,464	365	121
185	1,518	379	125
190	1,577	393	131
195	1,631	408	136
200	1,689	422	140
205	1,743	436	145
210	1,802	449	149
215	1,856	463	154
220	1,914	478	159
225 or more	1,969	492	163

Fuel scale charge from 1 May 2016 to 30 April 2017

Description of vehicle: vehicle's CO_2 emissions figure (but see Note 2 below)	12-month period £	3-month period £	1-month period £
120 or less	497	116	38
125	699	175	58
130	747	186	61
135	792	197	65
140	841	209	69
145	886	221	73
150	934	233	77
155	979	245	81
160	1,028	256	85

Description of vehicle: vehicle's CO_2 emissions figure (but see Note 2 below)	12-month period £	3-month period £	1-month period £
165	1,073	268	89
170	1,121	279	92
175	1,166	291	96
180	1,214	303	101
185	1,259	314	104
190	1,308	326	108
195	1,353	338	112
200	1,401	350	116
205	1,446	362	120
210	1,495	373	123
215	1,540	384	128
220	1,588	396	132
225 or more	1,633	408	135

Fuel scale charge from 1 May 2015 to 30 April 2016

Description of vehicle: vehicle's CO_2 emissions figure (but see Note 2 below)	12-month period £	3-month period £	1-month period £
120 or less	536	133	44
125	802	200	66
130	857	213	70
135	909	227	75
140	965	240	80
145	1,016	254	84
150	1,072	267	88
155	1,123	281	93
160	1,179	294	97
165	1,231	308	102
170	1,286	320	106
175	1,338	334	111
180	1,393	347	115
185	1,445	361	119
190	1,501	374	124
195	1,552	388	129
200	1,608	401	133
205	1,660	415	138

continued

Description of vehicle: vehicle's CO_2 emissions figure (but see Note 2 below)	12-month period £	3-month period £	1-month period £
210	1,715	428	142
215	1,767	441	146
220	1,822	455	151
225 or more	1,874	468	155

Fuel scale charge from 1 May 2014 to 30 April 2015

Shown here on a VAT-inclusive basis.

Description of vehicle: vehicle's CO_2 emissions figure (but see Note 2 below)	12-month period £	3-month period £	1-month period £
120 or less	627	156	52
125	939	234	78
130	1,004	251	83
135	1,064	266	88
140	1,129	282	94
145	1,190	297	99
150	1,225	313	104
155	1,315	328	109
160	1,381	345	115
165	1,441	360	120
170	1,506	376	125
175	1,567	391	130
180	1,632	408	136
185	1,692	423	141
190	1,757	439	146
195	1,818	454	151
200	1,883	470	156
205	1,943	485	161
210	2,008	502	167
215	2,069	517	172
220	2,134	533	177
225 or more	2,194	548	182

Notes

(1) *How to use the tables* – If a business pays for any fuel used for private motoring by its owners, directors or employees, it has to pay VAT on the VAT-inclusive fuel scale charge listed above at the rate applicable at the time the charge is due. To calculate standard rate VAT from the VAT inclusive amount, multiply the VAT inclusive scale charge by the appropriate VAT fraction.

(2) *Not for car benefits* – The tables above are not the same as those used to calculate car benefit charge for income tax purposes. See **Chapter 2: Expenses and Benefits** for the latest advisory fuel rates for use by company car drivers. A business can reclaim the VAT element on the amount attributable to fuel of mileage allowances paid to employees or subcontractors.

(3) *Rounding down* – Where the CO_2 emissions figure of a vehicle is not a multiple of five, the figure is rounded down to the next multiple of five to determine the level of the charge. For a bi-fuel vehicle which has two CO_2 emissions figures, the lower of the two figures should be used. For cars which are too old to have a CO_2 emissions figure, HMRC have prescribed a level of emissions by reference to the vehicle's engine capacity (VAT Notice 700/64, para 9.3).

(4) *Further information* – For information on fuel scale charges and motor expenses see VAT Notice 700/64 and tinyurl.com/VTFLSCS.

EU VAT RATES FOR CROSS-BORDER SALES

(*SI 1995/2518, reg 2*)

EU country	Country code	Standard rates & for electronic services %	Other reduced rates %	B2C invoice required?
Austria	AT	20	10 & 13 & 0	No
Belgium	BE	21	6 & 12 & 0	No
Bulgaria	BG	20	9 & 0	No R
Croatia	HR	25	5 &13 & 0	Yes Alt
Cyprus	CY	19	5 & 9 & 0	Yes
Czech Republic	CZ	21	15 &10 & 0	No
Denmark	DK	25	0	No
Estonia	EE	20	9 & 0	No
Finland	FI	24	10 & 14 & 0	No
France	FR	20 & 5.5	10 & 2.1 & 0	No Alt
Germany	DE	19	7 & 0	No
Greece	EL	24	6 &13 & 0	No Alt
Hungary	HU	27	18 & 5 & 0	No R
Ireland	IE	23	4.8 & 9 & 13.5 & 0	No
Italy	IT	22 & 4	10 & 5 & 0	No
Latvia	LV	21	12 & 5 & 0	No R
Lithuania	LT	21	5 & 9 & 0	No
Luxembourg	LU	17	8 & 14 & 3 & 0	No
Malta	MT	18	5 & 7 & 0	No
Netherlands	NL	21	6 & 0	No
Poland	PL	23	5 & 8 & 0	No R

continued

EU country	Country code	Standard rates & for electronic services %	Other reduced rates %	B2C invoice required?
Portugal	PT	23	13 & 6 & 0	No
Romania	RO	19	0 & 5 & 9	No Alt
Slovak Republic	SK	20	10 & 0	No
Slovenia	SI	22	9.5 & 0	Yes
Spain	ES	21	10 & 4 & 0	Yes
Sweden	SE	25	6 &12 & 0	No
United Kingdom	GB	20	5 & 0	No

Notes

(1) *Rates* – Electronic services, broadcasting and telecommunications services are generally subject to VAT at the standard rate, but when another rate also applies it is detailed in the notes below. VAT rates change frequently, check the pull-down menu on VATMOSS return page.

(2) *Cyprus* – Those areas under the control of the Government of the Republic of Cyprus and including the UK Sovereign Base Areas of Akrotiri and Dhekelia.

(3) *Italy* – Excludes: Livigno, Campione d'Italia, the Italian waters of Lake Lugano, San Marino, and the Vatican City.

(4) *France* – Includes Monaco but excludes overseas departments: Guadeloupe, Martinique, Reunion, St. Pierre and Miquelon, and French Guiana. Excludes Andorra. Reduced rates apply digital newspapers: 2.1%.

(5) *Germany* – Excludes Büsingen and the Isle of Heligoland.

(6) *Not in EU* – The following are not part of the EU VAT area:

- The Åland Islands
- Liechtenstein
- Mount Athos (Agion Poros).

(7) *Portugal* – Includes the Azores and Madeira.

(8) *Spain* – Includes the Balearic Islands but excludes Ceuta, Melilla and the Canary Islands. Excludes Gibraltar and Andorra which are not part of the EU.

(9) *United Kingdom* – The UK and the Isle of Man are part of the EU VAT area, but sales to the UK and/or the Isle of Man should not be included on the EC Sales List (ESL). The Channel Islands are not part of the EU.

(10) *Further information* – For the VAT number formats for each EU country and links to foreign language enquiry letters see: tinyurl.com/VATNFMT and VAT Notice 725. For rates applicable to digital services: tinyurl.com/EUVTrtsdig.

(11) *Invoices* – 'R' means must be supplied on request, 'Alt' means alternatives to a VAT invoice may be accepted.

PLACE OF SUPPLY – SERVICES

(*VATA 1994, s 7A, Sch 4A*)

Customers within the EU

From 1 January 2010, the general rule for the place of supply of services where the customer is within the EU is:

- *For business to business (B2B) supplies* – where the customer belongs (EC Sales List needs to be completed).
- *For business to customer (B2C) supplies* – where the supplier belongs, except for digital services – see last line of exceptions table below.

Customers outside the EU

Where the customer belongs outside the EU the place of supply is where the customer belongs for both B2B and B2C services.

Exceptions

Exceptions to the above general rules are as follows:

	Place of supply of services	
Category of service:	**B2B supplies**	**B2C supplies**
Relating to land and property	Where the land is situated	Where the land is situated
Physical performances eg: artistic, cultural, educational, training, sporting, entertainment, exhibitions, conferences, meetings; and any ancillary services.	Subject to the general rule for B2B services – where the customer belongs	Where the event actually takes place
Admission to cultural, artistic, sporting, scientific, educational, entertainment, fairs and exhibitions; and any ancillary services relating to admission to such events	Where event takes place	Where the event takes place
Work on, or valuation of moveable goods and ancillary transport services	Subject to the general rule for B2B services – where the customer belongs	Where the services are physically performed
Restaurant and catering	Where the services are physically carried out	Where the services are physically carried out
Passenger transport	Where it takes place, (Note 3)	Where it takes place, (see Note 3)

continued

	Place of supply of services	
Category of service:	**B2B supplies**	**B2C supplies**
Freight transport	Subject to the general rule for B2B services – where the customer belongs	
B2C international freight transport (between the EC and non-EC countries, or wholly outside the EC)		Where the transport takes place
B2C intra-EC freight transport		The Member State in which the transportation begins
Short-term hire of means of transport (see Note 4)	Where the means of transport is put at the disposal of the hiree	Where the means of transport is put at the disposal of the hiree
Long-term hire of means of transport	Subject to the general rule for B2B services – where the customer belongs	Where the recipient/ customer belongs, unless the hire is long-term hire of a pleasure boat where it will be the place where the pleasure boat is put at the disposal of the customer
Supplies of telecommunications, broadcasting and e-services (digital services)	Taxed where the supplier belongs.	Where the consumer is located (see note 5).

Notes

(1) *Place of supply: 'Use and enjoyment'* – There are additional rules for the letting on hire of goods, electronically supplied services, telecommunications services and radio and television broadcasting services in either of the following situations:

- the place of supply would be the UK (because the supplier or customer belongs in the UK) but the services are effectively used and enjoyed outside the EC, or
- the place of supply would be outside the EC (because the supplier or customer belongs outside the EC) but the services are effectively used and enjoyed in the UK.

In these circumstances, the place of supply is where their effective use and enjoyment takes place. Where this is the UK, the services are subject to UK VAT.

(2) *Use and enjoyment: Accounting procedures* – The accounting procedures taking account of the use and enjoyment provisions are:

If your B2B supply is:	You are:
to a customer belonging in the UK	not required to account for UK VAT to the extent that the customer uses and enjoys the services outside the EC
to a customer belonging outside the EC	required to account for UK VAT to the extent that the customer uses and enjoys the services in the UK
to a customer belonging outside the EC and the customer uses and enjoys the services in another Member State	not required to account for UK VAT as those services are supplied in that Member State but you may be required to register and account for VAT in that Member State

(3) *Passenger transport* – To the extent that the transport takes place outside the UK, it is outside the scope of UK VAT. However, if a journey involves travel through another Member State, the supply of passenger transport will be made in that Member State to the extent that the transport takes place there. In effect VAT is due in each member state the transport passes through in proportion to the total length of the journey.

(4) '*Short-term hire*' – Means for a continuous period not exceeding 90 days if the means of transport is a vessel and not exceeding 30 days for any other means of transport.

(5) *Digital Services* – Traders who sell B2C digital services in other EU countries can use VAT MOSS to make a single return of the VAT due in all other EU countries on those B2C sales of digital services, see **Services supplied to other EU states** above.

INTRASTAT REPORTING

(*Council Regulation (EC) No 638/2004*)

Effective date	Arrivals £	Dispatches £	Delivery terms £
1 Jan 2015	1,500,000	250,000	24,000,000
1 Jan 2014	1,200,000	250,000	24,000,000
1 Jan 2010	600,000	250,000	16,000,000
1 Jan 2009	270,000	270,000	16,000,000
1 Jan 2008	260,000	260,000	14,500,000

Notes

(1) *Reporting* – VAT registered businesses are required to submit an Intrastat declaration or Supplementary Sales Declaration (SSD) each month if their purchases from other EU Member States exceed the thresholds above. The SSD must be submitted online by 21st day following the month to which it relates.

(2) *Further information* – For detailed guidance see: www.uktradeinfo.com and HMRC Notice 60.

EC SALES LIST (ESL)

(SI 1995/2518, Part IV)

Effective date	Goods to other EU countries £	Services £
1 January 2014	35,000	No upper limit
1 January 2010	70,000	No upper limit

Notes

(1) *Reporting* – All VAT registered businesses are required to submit regular ESLs if they sell goods or services to VAT registered businesses in other EU countries.

(2) *Services* – If the business supplies only services to other EU countries, quarterly ESL returns are required, but monthly returns may be submitted.

(3) *Goods* – Where goods or goods and services are supplied to other EU countries the ESL should be submitted quarterly if the annual value of those sales does not exceed the threshold in the table above. Otherwise the ESL must be submitted monthly.

(4) *Annual ESL* – The trader may ask permission to submit an annual ESL if he uses the annual accounting scheme for VAT and has total taxable sales of no more than the VAT threshold plus £25,500, and annual sales to other EU member states of no more than £11,000.

(5) *Deadlines* – Electronic ESLs must be submitted within 21 days of the end of the quarter or month, paper ESLs must be submitted within 14 days of the end of the quarter or month. Penalties apply for late submission, see **Chapter 17**.

(6) *Further information* – Outline guidance: https://www.gov.uk/vat-how-to-report-your-eu-sales. For detailed guidance see HMRC Notice 725.

13

Other taxes and duties

ANNUAL TAX ON ENVELOPED DWELLINGS (ATED)

(*FA 2013, ss 94–174, Schs 33–35; SI 2016/1244*)

Property value £	2015/16 £	2016/17 £	2017/18 £	2018/19 £	2019/20 £
500,001–1,000,000	Nil	3,500	3,500	3,600	3,650
1,000,0001–2,000,000	7,000	7,000	7,050	7,250	7,400
2,000,001–5,000,000	23,350	23,350	23,550	24,250	24,800
5,000,001–10,000,000	54,450	54,450	54,950	56,550	57,900
10,000,001–20,000,000	109,050	109,050	110,100	113,400	116,100
Over £20,000,000	218,200	218,200	220,350	226,950	232,350

Notes

(1) *Who pays* – The ATED charge is payable annually by non-natural persons (NNP) who hold a beneficial interest in a UK dwelling valued within the above bands. If the NNP owns the property interest for only part of the year, or a relief or exemption applies, (see note 6) the charge is proportionately reduced and a refund can be claimed (*FA 2013, ss 99, 101*).

(2) *Valuations* – For 2018/19 to 2023/24 the value of a property for ATED purposes is its market value on 1 April 2017, or when acquired, if later. For the ATED charged for 2013/14 to 2017/18 the property was valued as at 1 April 2012, or the later acquisition date within that period. HMRC's 'pre-return banding check' service can be used to check which valuation band the property falls into (*FA 2013, s 102*).

(3) *Returns and payments* – ATED is self-assessed by submitting an ATED return and paying the charge, normally by 30 April each year. For dwellings first falling within ATED, returns and payments are due within 30 days if purchased, or 90 days if the dwelling is newly built (*FA 2013, ss 158–161*).

(4) *Reliefs* – There are many reliefs and exemptions from ATED which are similar to but not identical to those for the penal 15% rate of SDLT (see **Chapter 11**). The NNP must make relief declaration return (for 2015/16 onwards) to claim the relevant reliefs from ATED, which can cover an entire property portfolio (*FA 2013, ss 132–150*).

(5) *Gains* – For disposals made before 6 April 2019, where the property has been subject to the ATED, all or part of any gain arising is subject to the ATED-related CGT charge (see **Chapter 8**).

(6) *Further information* – HMRC guidance is available at: http://tinyurl.com/ATEDgd.

MACHINE GAMES DUTY (MGD)

(*FA 2012, s 191, Sch 24; SI 2012/2500*)

Rates

(*FA 2012, Sch 24, para 9*)

Description	Cost to play	Highest prize	Rate
Lower rate – type 1 games	20p or less	£10 or less	5%
Standard rate – type 2 games	21p to £5	more than £10	20%
Higher rate – all other games	More than £5	Any amount	25%

Notes

(1) *Calculated on* – Total net takings from the playing of 'dutiable' machine games in the UK (ie broadly games which offer cash prizes, the value of which exceeds the cost of playing the game). Takings on which MGD is payable are exempt from VAT (*VATA 1994, Sch 9, Group 4, Item 1A*).

(2) *Commencement* – From 1 February 2013 for the standard and lower rates. The higher rate applies from 1 March 2015 (*FA 2012, Sch 24*).

(3) *Games type* – If the machine has games of more than one type, the rate for all games is set at the highest rated game (*FA 2012, Sch 24, para 5*).

(4) *Returns and payments* – MGD accounting periods are normally quarterly. Returns and payments must be made by the 30th day following the end of every accounting period (*SI 2012/2500, regs 12, 13*). Penalties and interest can be charged for errors in returns, failure to register, and failure to make payments on time.

(5) *Registration* – The person who is responsible for premises where dutiable gaming machines are provided for play is required to register for MGD with HMRC, either online or by paper (see VAT Notice 452, para 6.6).

(6) *Further guidance* – Outline guidance: www.gov.uk/machine-games-duty. For detailed guidance see HMRC Notice 452.

INSURANCE PREMIUM TAX (IPT)

(*FA 1994, Pt III, Schs 6A–7A*; *SI 1994/1774*)

Rates of IPT

(*FA 1994, ss 51, 51A*)

Period	Standard Rate %	Higher Rate %
From 1 June 2017	12.0	20.0
1 October 2016 to 31 May 2017	10.0	20.0
1 November 2015 to 30 September 2016	9.5	20.0
4 January 2011 to 31 October 2015	6.0	20.0

Notes

(1) *Effective from* – Insurance premium tax (IPT) is charged on premiums received by insurers under taxable insurance contracts from 1 October 1994.

(2) *Higher rate of IPT* – This applies to insurance sold in certain circumstances relating to motor cars or motorcycles, certain electrical or mechanical domestic appliances and travel insurance (*FA 1994, Sch 6A*).

LANDFILL TAX

(*FA 1996, Pt III, Sch 5*; *FA 2011, s 25; SI 1996/1527*; *SI 2011/1017*)

Rates

(*FA 1996, s 42; SI 2016/376*)

Disposals made or treated as made in year beginning:	Standard rate per tonne £	Lower rate per tonne £	Maximum credit %
1 April 2020	94.15	3.00	TBA
1 April 2019	91.35	2.90	5.3
1 April 2018	88.95	2.80	5.3
1 April 2017	86.10	2.70	5.3
1 April 2016	84.40	2.65	4.2
1 April 2015	82.60	2.60	5.7
1 April 2014	80.00	2.50	5.1

Notes

(1) *Applies to* – Waste disposals by way of landfill at a licensed site in England or Northern Ireland, and at licensed sites in Wales before April 2018, unless specifically exempted. Landfill site operators are taxed on disposals of waste by reference to the weight and type of waste concerned.

(2) *Which rate* – The lower rate of landfill tax relates to inactive (or inert) wastes, as listed in the *Landfill Tax (Qualifying Material) Order 2011, SI 2011/1017*. The standard rate applies to all other taxable waste.

(3) *Tax credits* – Registered landfill site operators can claim a tax credit worth 90% of any qualifying contributions made to approved environmental bodies, subject to a maximum percentage of their landfill tax liability during the contribution year (*Landfill Tax Regulations 1996, SI 1996/1527, reg 31*).

(4) *Scottish landfill* – From 1 April 2015 Scottish landfill tax applies to waste disposal at registered sites in Scotland, see **Chapter 18**.

(5) *Welsh landfill* – From 1 April 2018 Welsh landfill disposal tax applies to waste disposal at registered sites in Wales, see **Chapter 18**.

(6) *Further information* – See www.gov.uk/topic/business-tax/landfill-tax and HMRC Notice LFT1.

AGGREGATES LEVY

(*FA 2001, Pt 2, Schs 4–10; FA 2011, s 24; SI 2002/761*)

Rates

(*FA 2001, s 16*)

Aggregate exploited in period:	Rate per tonne £
1 April 2009–31 March 2020	2.00
1 April 2008–31 March 2009	1.95
1 April 2002–31 March 2008	1.60

Notes

(1) *Charged on* – Aggregates levy is charged on aggregate (broadly rock, sand and gravel) subjected to commercial exploitation.

(2) *How much* – The levy is charged at a rate per tonne, and the amount of levy charged on a part of a tonne of aggregate shall be the proportionately reduced amount (*FA 2001, s 16(4)*).

(3) *Tax credit* – HMRC may pay a tax credit in relation to aggregates levy paid in Northern Ireland under the aggregates levy credit scheme (*FA 2001, ss 30B–30D*).

CLIMATE CHANGE LEVY (CCL)

(*FA 2000 s 30, Sch 6; SI 2001/838*)

Rates

(*FA 2000, Sch 6, para 42; FA 2011, s 23*)

Taxable commodity supplied from:	**Rate at which CCL payable if supply is not a reduced-rate supply**					
	1 April 2021	**1 April 2020**	**1 April 2019**	**1 April 2018**	**1 April 2017**	**1 April 2016**
Electricity	0.775p/kWh	0.811p/kWh	0.847p/kWh	0.583p/kWh	0.568p/kWh	0.559p/kWh
Natural gas	0.465p/kWh	0.406p/kWh	0.339p/kWh	0.203p/kWh	0.198p/kWh	0.195p/kWh
Liquefied petroleum gas	2.175p/kg	2.175p/kg	2.175p/kg	1.304p/kg	1.272p/kg	1.251p/kg
Any other taxable commodity	3.640p/kg	3.174p/kg	2.653p/kg	1.591p/kg	1.551p/kg	1.526p/kg

Notes

(1) *Chargeable on* – The industrial and commercial supply of taxable commodities for lighting, heating and power for consumers in specified business sectors.

(2) *Reduced-rate supplies (FA 2000, Sch 6, para 42(1))* – CCL is charged at 22% (from April 2019) of the full rate for energy intensive industries that have entered into a negotiated energy efficiency Climate Change Agreement and at 7% (from April 2019) for supplies of electricity (*FA 2010, s 18; FA 2016, s 148*).

(3) *Renewable sources* – The exemption from CCL for electricity from renewable sources is removed from 1 August 2018 (*FA 2016, s 144*).

ROAD FUEL DUTY

(*Hydrocarbon Oil Duties Act 1979* (*HODA 1979*); *FA 2011, ss 19, 20; FA 2009, ss 15, 16*; *FA 2010, ss 12, 13*)

Description	**23 March 2011**	**1 January 2011 to 22 March 2011**	**1 October 2010 to 31 December 2010**	**1 April 2010 to 30 September 2010**	**1 September 2009 to 31 March 2010**
Unleaded petrol and bio-ethanol (*HODA 1979, s 6(1A)(a)*)	57.95p	58.95p	58.19p	57.19p	56.19p
Heavy oil and bio-diesel (*HODA 1979, s 6(1A)(c)*)	57.95p	58.95p	58.19p	57.19p	36.19p
Natural road fuel gas (including bio-gas) (*HODA 1979, s 8(3)(a)*)	24.70p per kg	26.15p per kg	25.05p per kg	23.60p per kg	22.16p per kg
Other road fuel gas (eg liquefied petroleum gas) (*HODA 1979, s 8(3)(b)*)	31.61p per kg	33.04p per kg	31.95p per kg	30.53p per kg	27.67p per kg

Notes

(1) *Per litre* – Figures shown in pence per litre (unless otherwise stated).

(2) *Rural relief scheme* – From 1 January 2012, retailers of road fuel in the Scottish Islands and the Scilly Isles can reclaim 5p per litre of duty on unleaded petrol and diesel. This relief is extended to the Scottish Highlands and various other rural districts from 1 April 2015 (*R&C Briefs 40/11, 3 (2015)*).

(3) *Aqua Methanol* – A fuel which is 95% methanol and 5% water used as a greener alternative for petrol and diesel. Duty of 7.9p/litre applies from 1 October 2016.

VEHICLE EXCISE DUTY (VED)

(*Vehicle Excise and Registration Act 1994 (VERA 1994), ss 2, 4, Sch 1; FA 2008, s 17; FA 2009, ss 13, 14; FA 2011, ss 21, 22*)

Older cars – standard rates

(*VERA 1994, Sch 1, para 1B*)

Cars registered on or after 1 March 2001 and before 1 April 2017

VED Band	CO_2 (g/km)	From 1 April:				
		2019	2018 £	2017 £	2016 £	2015 £
A	Up to 100	0	0	0	0	0
B	101 to 110	20	20	20	20	20
C	111 to 120	30	30	30	30	30
D	121 to 130	125	120	115	110	110
E	131 to 140	145	140	135	130	130
F	141 to 150	160	155	150	145	145
G	151 to 165	200	195	190	185	180
H	166 to 175	235	230	220	210	205
I	176 to 185	260	250	240	230	225
J	186 to 200	300	290	280	270	265
K	201 to 225	325	315	305	295	290
L	226 to 255	555	540	520	500	490
M	Over 255	570	555	535	515	505

Newer cars – standard rates

(*F(No 2)A 2015, Pt 5*)

Cars registered on or after 1 April 2017

List price of vehicle	2019/20			2017/18 and 2018/19		
	Petrol or diesel £	Electric £	Alternative fuel £	Petrol or diesel £	Electric £	Alternative fuel £
Up to £40,000	145	0	135	140	0	130
£40,000 and over	455	320	445	450	310	440

Notes

(1) *First year* – There is a different rate of VED due for the first year a car is registered – see below.

(2) *Period of duty* – The above rates apply for 12 month VED. The rate for a six-month VED is 55% of the annual rate, but these are not applicable to vehicles with a standard rate of less than £50 (*VERA 1994, s 4(2)*).

(3) *List price £40,000 or more* – This higher rate applies to cars with a list price of £40,000 or more for five years after the first year of registration.

(4) *Alternative fuels* – For cars that run on alternative fuels (tax class 59).

(5) *Further information* – A full list of VED rates for all vehicles can be found at: www.gov.uk/vehicle-tax-rate-tables.

Cars – First year rates

Cars registered on or after 1 April 2017

(*VERA 1994, Sch 1, para 1B*)

Tax year:	***2019/20* £**	***2019/20* £**	***2018/19* £**	***2018/19* £**	***2017/18* £**
CO_2 emissions	Diesel	Other cars	Diesel	Other cars	All cars
0	0	0	0	0	0
1 to 50	25	10	25	10	10
51 to 75	110	25	105	25	25
76 to 90	130	110	125	105	100
91 to 100	150	130	145	125	120
101 to 110	170	150	165	145	140
111 to 130	210	170	205	165	160
131 to 150	530	210	515	205	200
151 to 170	855	530	830	515	500
170 to 190	1280	855	1240	830	800
191 to 225	1815	1280	1760	1240	1200
226 to 255	2135	1815	2070	1760	1700
Over 255	2135	2135	2070	2070	2000

Notes

(1) *First year rates* – The above rates of vehicle excise duty apply for the first 12 months of duty, with effect from the date of first registration. From the second year onwards, the standard or reduced rate of vehicle excise duty applies, see tables above.

(2) *Six month* duty – VED can be paid for half year periods when the annual VED is more than £50 (*VERA 1994, s 3(2)*).

(3) *Diesel* – These rates apply to diesel cars which don't meet real driving emissions step 2 (RDE2) standard.

Other vehicles

(*VERA 1994, Sch 1, paras 1, 1J, 2*)

Category	**From 1 April**					
	2019	**2018** £	**2017** £	**2016** £	**2015** £	**2014** £
Vans (*Sch 1, para 1J*)	260	250	240	230	225	225
Lower-emissions vans (*Sch 1, para 1J*)	140	140	140	140	140	140
Motor-cycles (*VERA 1994 Sch 1, para 2*)						
Not over 150cc	20	19	18	17	17	17
151 to 400cc	43	42	41	39	38	38
401 to 600cc	66	64	62	60	59	58
Over 600cc	91	88	85	82	81	80
Motor-tricycles						
Not over 150cc	20	19	18	17	17	17
Any other case	91	88	85	82	81	80

Note

The lower rate of VED for lower emission vans applies to models which Euro 4 emissions standards (see *VERA 1994, Sch 1, para 1K*) and were registered on or after 1 March 2003 and before 1 January 2007, or that meet the Euro 5 emissions standards and were registered on or after 1 January 2009 and before 1 January 2011 (*Sch 1, para 1M*).

AIR PASSENGER DUTY (APD)

(*FA 1994, ss 28–30, Sch 5A*; *FA 2010, s 14*)

Band (approximate distance in miles from London to the capital city of the destination country)	**From 1 April 2020**			**From 1 April 2019**			**From 1 April 2018**		
	H £	**S** £	**L** £	**H** £	**S** £	**L** £	**H** £	**S** £	**L** £
Band A (0–2,000)	78	26	13	78	26	13	78	26	13
Band B (over 2,000)	515	176	80	515	172	78	468	156	78

Notes

(1) *Charged on* – Air passenger duty (APD) is chargeable on the carriage of each chargeable passenger on the approximate distance travelled allocated to bands (*FA 1994, s 30(1)*).

(2) *Rates of duty* – The rates of duty (higher: H standard: S and lower: L) depend upon the class of travel. The higher rate (H) applies to passengers in business jets that carry fewer 19 passengers, and have take-off weight of 20 tonnes or more (*FA 2012, s 190, Sch 23*).

(3) *Lower or reduced rate* – Applies to 'Standard class travel' which is:

   (a) in the case of an aircraft on which only one class of travel is available, that class of travel;

   (b) in any other case, the lowest class of travel available on the aircraft (*FA 1994, s 30(10)*).

(4) *Seat space* – Where a seat pitch exceeds 1.016 metres (40 inches), whether the flight has a single class or more than one class, the standard rate S of APD applies (*FA 1994, s 30(11)*; HMRC Notice 550, para 2.6.5).

(5) *Northern Ireland* – The APD for direct long-haul routes (band B) departing from Northern Ireland is nil (*FA 2012, s 190, Sch 23*).

(6) *Child passengers* – No APD is due for children under 16 (*SI 2015/942*).

(7) *Further information* – see https://www.gov.uk/air-passenger-duty.

BANK LEVY

(*FA 2011, s 73, Sch 19*)

Period	Short-term chargeable liabilities	Long-term chargeable equity and liabilities
2021	0.10%	0.05%
2020	0.14%	0.07%
2019	0.15%	0.075%
2018	0.16%	0.080%
2017	0.17%	0.085%
2016	0.18%	0.09%
1 April 2015–31 Dec 2015	0.21%	0.105%
1 Jan 2014–31 March 2015	0.156%	0.078%
1 Jan 2013–31 Dec 2013	0.130%	0.065%
1 Jan 2012–31 Dec 2012	0.088%	0.044%

Notes

(1) *Commencement* – The bank levy applies to periods of account ending on or after 1 January 2011 (*FA 2011, Sch 19, paras 4(8), 5(4)*). Periods falling wholly before 1 January 2011 are ignored for these purposes.

(2) *Chargeable on* – The total chargeable equity and liabilities as reported in the relevant balance sheets of banks and banking groups, building societies and building society groups operating in the UK and UK banks in non-banking groups, at the end of a chargeable period.

(3) *Threshold* – The bank levy is nil if the amount of chargeable equity and liabilities is £20 billion or less. If this limit is exceeded, the first £20 billion (on which no levy is charged) is apportioned between long term equities and liabilities and short term liabilities, in accordance with the proportion of chargeable equity and liabilities of each (*FA 2011, Sch 19, para 6*).

(4) *Payment* – Payment of the bank levy is treated as a payment of corporation tax (*FA 2011, Sch 19, Pt 6*). It is subject to corporation tax payment procedures, including the quarterly instalment payments system (see **Chapter 7: Taxation of companies**).

(5) *Surcharge* – From 1 January 2016 a 8% corporation tax surcharge applies to banking profits above £25 million per year per group (*F(No 2)A 2015, Schs 2, 3*).

(6) *Credits* – For periods ending on and after 1 January 2016, where the bank pays EU single resolution fund levy (SRFL) and UK bank levy, the SRFL can be set as a credit against the bank levy, but it may not reduce the levy below zero (*SI 2016/1212*).

National Insurance Contributions (NIC)

CLASS 1 CONTRIBUTIONS

Primary (employee) contributions

(SSCBA 1992, ss 5(1), 8, 19(4); SI 2001/1004, regs 10, 131; Pension Schemes Act 1993, ss 41, 42A; SI 2006/1009, art 3)

Class 1 NIC rates and thresholds	**2019/20 £**	**2018/19 £**	**2017/18 £**	**2016/17 £**	**2015/16 £**
Lower earnings limit (LEL)	118 per week 512 per month 6,136 per year	116 per week 503 per month 6,032 per year	113 per week 490 per month 5,876 per year	112 per week 486 per month 5,824 per year	112 per week 486 per month 5,824 per year
Primary threshold (PT)	166 per week 720 per month 8,632 per year	162 per week 702 per month 8,424 per year	157 per week 680 per month 8,164 per year	155 per week 672 per month 8,060 per year	155 per week 672 per month 8,060 per year
Upper accrual point (UAP)	Abolished	Abolished	Abolished	Abolished	770 per week 3,337 per month 40,040 per year
Upper earnings limit (UEL)	962 per week 4,167 per month 50,000 per year	892 per week 3,863 per month 46,350 per year	866 per week 3,750 per month 45,000 per year	827 per week 3,583 per month 43,000 per year	815 per week 3,532 per month 42,385 per year
Not contracted out	12% on earnings between PT and UEL 2% on excess over UEL	12% on earnings between PT and UEL 2% on excess over UEL	12% on earnings between PT and UEL 2% on excess over UEL	12% on earnings between PT and UEL 2% on excess over UEL	12% on earnings between PT and UEL 2% on excess over UEL

Class 1 NIC rates and thresholds	2019/20 £	2018/19 £	2017/18 £	2016/17 £	2015/16 £
Contracted out (note 3)	N/A	N/A	N/A	N/A	10.6% on earnings between PT and UAP 12% on earnings between UAP and UEL 2% on excess over UEL
Contracted out rebate – flat rate (note 3)	N/A	N/A	N/A	N/A	1.4%
Reduced rate (note 4)	5.85% on earnings between PT and UEL 2% on excess over UEL	5.85% on earnings between PT and UEL 2% on excess over UEL	5.85% on earnings between PT and UEL 2% on excess over UEL	5.85% on earnings between PT and UEL 2% on excess over UEL	5.85% on earnings between PT and UEL 2% on excess over UEL

Class 1 Primary (employee) contributions (continued)

(*SSCBA 1992, ss 5(1), 8, 19(4)*; *SI 2001/1004, regs 10, 131*; *Pension Schemes Act 1993, ss 41, 42A*; *SI 2006/1009, art 3*)

Class 1 NIC rates and thresholds	2014/15 £	2013/14 £	2012/13 £
Lower earnings limit (LEL)	111 per week 481 per month 5,772 per year	109 per week 473 per month 5,668 per year	107 per week 464 per month 5,564 per year
Primary threshold (PT)	153 per week 663 per month 7,956 per year	149 per week 646 per month 7,755 per year	146 per week 634 per month 7,605 per year
Upper accrual point	770 per week 3,337 per month 40,040 per year	770 per week 3,337 per month 40,040 per year	770 per week 3,337 per month 40,040 per year
Upper earnings limit (UEL)	805 per week 3,489 per month 41,865 per year	797 per week 3,454 per month 41,450 per year	817 per week 3,540 per month 42,475 per year

continued

Class 1 NIC rates and thresholds	**2014/15 £**	**2013/14 £**	**2012/13 £**
Not contracted out	12% on earnings between PT and UEL 2% on excess over UEL	12% on earnings between PT and UEL 2% on excess over UEL	12% on earnings between PT and UEL 2% on excess over UEL
Contracted out	10.6% on earnings between PT and UAP 12% on earnings between UAP and UEL 2% on excess over UEL	10.6% on earnings between PT and UAP 12% on earnings between UAP and UEL 2% on excess over UEL	10.6% on earnings between PT and UAP 12% on earnings between UAP and UEL 2% on excess over UEL
Contracted out rebate – flat rate	1.4%	1.4%	1.4%
Reduced rate (note 4)	5.85% on earnings between PT and UEL 2% on excess over UEL	5.85% on earnings between PT and UEL 2% on excess over UEL	5.85% on earnings between PT and UEL 2% on excess over UEL

Notes

(1) *Nil band* – No Class 1 contributions are payable on earnings between the lower earnings limit and primary threshold, but the employee is treated as having paid such contributions for the purposes of establishing or protecting entitlement to certain state benefits (*SSCBA 1992, s 6A*).

(2) *'Upper Accrual Point' (UAP)* – This is the point from which entitlement to contributory related benefits ceases to accrue.

(3) *Contracting out* – This was abolished for defined contribution (money purchase) pension schemes from 6 April 2012, and for defined benefit (final salary) pension schemes from 6 April 2016 (*FA 2013, s 52*).

(4) *Reduced rate* – This applies to women who were married before 6 April 1977 who have elected to pay a reduced rate of Class 1 contributions.

Class 1 Secondary (employer) contributions

(SSCBA 1992, ss 6(1)(b), 9; SI 2001/1004, reg 10; Pension Schemes Act 1993, ss 41, 42A; SI 2006/1009, arts 2, 3)

Class 1 NIC rates and thresholds	2019/20 £	2018/19 £	2017/18 £	2016/17 £	2015/16 £
Secondary threshold (ST)	166 per week 720 per month 8,632 per year	162 per week 702 per month 8,424 per year	157 per week 680 per month 8,164 per year	156 per week 676 per month 8,112 per year	156 per week 676 per month 8,112 per year
Upper & Apprentice secondary threshold (UST) & (AUST)	962 per week 4,167 per month 50,000 per year	892 per week 3,863 per month 46,350 per year	866 per week 3,750 per month 45,000 per year	827 per week 3,583 per month 43,000 per year	815 per week 3,532 per month 42,385 per year
Not contracted out rate	13.8% on earnings above ST	13.8% on earnings above ST	13.8% on earnings above ST	13.8% on earnings above ST	13.8% on earnings above ST
Contracted out rates Salary related (COSR)	Abolished	Abolished	Abolished	Abolished	10.4%
Contracted out rebate rates Salary related (COSR)	Abolished	Abolished	Abolished	Abolished	3.4%

Class 1 NIC rates and thresholds	2014/15 £	2013/14 £	2012/13 £
Secondary threshold (ST)	153 per week 663 per month 7,956 per year	148 per week 641 per month 7,696 per year	144 per week 624 per month 7,488 per year
Not contracted out rate	13.8% on earnings above ST	13.8% on earnings above ST	13.8% on earnings above ST
Contracted out rates Salary related (COSR)	10.4%	10.4%	10.4%
Contracted out rebate rates Salary related (COSR)	3.4%	3.4%	3.4%

Notes

(1) *Age limits* – Class 1 contributions are not payable in respect of individuals under the age of 16 at the time of payment of the earnings. Employees who have achieved

state pension age (SPA) at the time of payment are not liable to pay primary Class 1 contributions, but employers must continue to pay secondary Class 1 contributions for employees over their SPA (*SSCBA 1992, s 6(3)*); see NIM1001).

(2) *Under 21* – From 6 April 2015 employers' Class 1 NIC is not payable in respect of employees aged under 21 on earnings up to the upper secondary threshold (*SSCBA 1992, s 9A*).

(3) *Apprentices* – From 6 April 2016 employers' Class 1 NIC is not payable in respect of apprentices aged under 25 on earnings up to the Apprentice upper secondary threshold (*SSCBA 1992, s 9B*).

(4) *Disguised remuneration* – Class 1 NIC for employees and employers can arise on 'disguised remuneration' from Employee Benefit Trusts (EBTs), unapproved pension schemes (EFRBS) and other third party intermediaries where such income would not otherwise be within the charge to NIC (see *ITEPA 2003, ss 554A–554Z20*; *Social Security (Contributions) Regulations, SI 2001/1004*).

(5) *Apprenticeship levy* – From 6 April 2017 employers with annual pay costs of £3 million or more must pay 0.5% of their annual pay bill as the Apprenticeship Levy (see **Chapter 3**).

EMPLOYMENT ALLOWANCE

(*NICA 2014, ss 2, 4, 8*)

Tax Year	**Maximum claim per employer or group** £
2019/20	3,000
2018/19	3,000
2017/18	3,000
2016/17	3,000
2015/16	2,000
2014/15	2,000

Notes

(1) *Eligible employers* – Private sector employers, charities and community amateur sports (*NICA 2014, s 8*).

(2) *Excluded employers* – From 6 April 2016 companies where the director is the sole employee. Also public authorities which are not charities and businesses that carry out functions of a public nature such as NHS services (*SI 2016/344*).

(3) *Set against* – Secondary Class 1 NIC liability. NIC on the deemed salary payment under IR35 cannot be set against the allowance (*NICA 2014, s 2*).

(4) *Excluded workers* – The allowance can't be set against Class 1 NIC paid on the wages of domestic workers who work in the employer's own home, unless they are care workers who personally assist the employer or household due to old age, disability, illness or other dependency (*NICA 2014, s 2*).

(5) *How to claim* – Tick a box on the first EPS submitted for the first tax year in which the allowance is claimed. The claim should remain in place for all future years until it is revoked (*NICA 2014, s 4*).

(6) *Further information* – Detailed guidance is found at: tinyurl.com/EAdgd4emps.

(7) *Proposal* – From 6 April 2020 the employment allowance will be restricted to employers with an annual employer NIC liability of less than £100,000 (*Budget, 29 October 2018*).

CLASS 1A CONTRIBUTIONS

(*SSCBA 1992, s 10*)

(1) *Payable by* – Employers (and certain third parties) on taxable benefits provided to employees.

(2) *Charge calculated as* – A percentage of the cash equivalent of the benefits, that percentage is equal to rate of secondary Class 1 NIC for the tax year in question (13.8% for 2019/20).

(3) *Payment due by* – 19 July in the tax year following the tax year for which the benefit was paid (22 July for electronic payments).

(4) *Not payable on* – Benefits which are (see HMRC leaflet CWG5, Pt 2):

- exempt from income tax (*SSCBA 1992, s 10(1)(a)*);
- exempt from Class 1A NIC (*SI 2001/1004, Pt 3*) (see CWG5, pt 5);
- covered by an Extra-Statutory Concession (as listed in *SI 2001/1004, reg 40(7)*);
- included in a PAYE Settlement Agreement (see Class 1B contributions) (*SSCBA 1992, s 10(6)*);
- provided for business use, where any private use is not significant (*ITEPA 2003, s 316*);
- already liable to Class 1 NIC (*SSCBA 1992, s 10(1)(c)*);
- also exempt from Class 1 NIC (*SI 2001/1004, reg 40*).

CLASS 1B CONTRIBUTIONS

(*SSCBA 1992, s 10A*)

- *Payable by* – Employers who enter into a PAYE Settlement Agreement (PSA) with HMRC, which allows the employer to account for tax on certain expense payments and benefits in one payment.
- *Charge applies to* – Items contained within a PSA that would normally attract a liability for Class 1 or Class 1A NICs, and to the total tax payable under the PSA.

- *Calculated as* – A percentage of the total amount chargeable, that percentage is equal to the rate of secondary Class 1 NIC for the tax year in question (13.8% for 2019/20).
- *Payment due by* – 19 October in the tax year following the tax year to which the PSA applies (22 October for electronic payments) (*SI 2003/2682, reg 109(2)*).

CLASS 2 CONTRIBUTIONS

(*SSCBA 1992, ss 11, 12, 117(1), NICA 2015, SI 2001/1004, regs 46(a), 125(c), 152(b)*)

Tax year	Flat rate per week £	Share fishermen per week £	Volunteer development workers per week £	Small earnings exception/small profits threshold £
2019/20	3.00	3.65	5.90	6,365
2018/19	2.95	3.60	5.80	6,205
2017/18	2.85	3.50	5.65	6,025
2016/17	2.80	3.45	5.60	5,965
2015/16	2.80	3.45	5.60	5,965
2014/15	2.75	3.40	5.55	5,885
2013/14	2.70	3.35	5.45	5,725

Notes

(1) *Age limits* – Class 2 NIC are payable by self-employed persons aged between 16 and state pension age (SPA).

(2) *Payments due* – From 2015/16 Class 2 NIC is collected as part of the taxpayer's self-assessment by 31 January following the tax year. For earlier years the contributions were due on 31 July and 31 January, but payments could be made by direct debit for each month in arrears.

(3) *Small profits* – From 2015/16 a Class 2 liability does not arise if the self-employed profits for the year don't exceed the small profits threshold. For earlier years the taxpayer could claim exception from liability to pay Class 2 NICs if profits weren't expected to exceed the small earnings exception limit.

(4) *Voluntary contributions* – Class 2 contributions can be paid voluntarily if a liability does not arise due to low earnings (*SI 2001/1004, reg 46(b)*). Alternatively, an individual may pay Class 3 contributions if entitled to do so (*NIM21044*).

CLASS 3 CONTRIBUTIONS

(*SSCBA 1992, s 13*)

Tax Year	Weekly Rate £
2019/20	15.00
2018/19	14.65
2017/18	14.25
2016/17	14.10
2015/16	14.10
2014/15	13.90
2013/14	13.55

Notes

(1) *Eligibility* – Individuals wishing to pay Class 3 contributions in order to meet the conditions for entitlement to certain benefits must be over the age of 16 and be resident in Great Britain or Northern Ireland in the relevant tax year (*SSCBA 1992, s 1(6)(b)*; *SI 2001/1004, regs 48(1), 145(1)(e)*).

(2) *Earnings factor* – An individual is entitled to pay Class 3 contributions if his or her earnings factor (EF) derived from Class 1, 2 and/or 3 NICs is less than the qualifying earnings factor for the relevant tax year, subject to certain restrictions on the right to pay. A qualifying earnings factor is an amount equal to 52 times that year's lower earnings limit for Class 1 contributions (*SSCBA 1992, s 14*; *SI 1979/676, Sch 1, Pt 2*) (see *NIM25001*).

CLASS 4 CONTRIBUTIONS

(*SSCBA 1992, s 15(3), (3ZA)*)

Tax Year	Main rate %	Additional rate %	Lower profits limit £	Upper profits limit £
2019/20	9	2	8,632	50,000
2018/19	9	2	8,424	46,350
2017/18	9	2	8,164	45,000
2016/17	9	2	8,060	43,000
2015/16	9	2	8,060	42,385
2014/15	9	2	7,956	41,865
2013/14	9	2	7,755	41,450

Notes

(1) *Payable on* – Class 4 NIC are payable on profits from UK trades, professions or vocations, which exceed the lower profits limit and are chargeable to income tax under *ITTOIA 2005, Pt 2, Ch 2*. The additional rate is payable on profits that exceed the upper profits limit.

(2) *Payable by* – Individuals who are aged between 16 and state pension age, at the beginning of the relevant tax year (*SI 2001/1004, regs 91, 93*).

(3) *Annual maximum* – Class 4 NIC are subject to an annual maximum (*SI 2001/1004, reg 100*). The liability for contributions at the main rate is broadly limited to a maximum of 53 times the appropriate weekly amount of Class 2 NIC, plus the maximum amount of Class 4 contributions payable at the main rate, less any Class 2 NIC and any Class 1 NIC paid at the main rate. However, Class 4 NIC remain payable at the additional rate.

(4) *Refund*- An application to HMRC for a refund of Class 4 NIC (if appropriate) can be made online by an individual or by post on form CA5610, see: www.hmrc.gov.uk/forms/ca5610.pdf.

15

Tax credits and state benefits

TAX CREDITS

Child tax credit (CTC)

(Child Tax Credit Regulations 2002, SI 2002/2007, reg 7)

Maximum amounts per year	2019/20 £	2018/19 £	2017/18 £
Family element (note 4)	545	545	545
Child element	2,780	2,780	2,780
Disabled child element	3,355	3,275	3,175
Severely disabled child element	1,360	1,325	1,290

Notes

(1) *Eligibility* – CTC is paid to the main carer for children up to 16 years old, or 18 in full-time education. CTC is separate from, and additional to, Child Benefit.

(2) *Claims* – Tax Credit claims are made provisionally for the coming year based on the previous year's income (2018/19 income forms the basis of 2019/20 claims). A Tax Credits claim must be renewed by 31 July, but estimated figures can be provided, which must be finalised by the following 31 January.

(3) *Disabled or severely disabled* – As to what constitutes disability or severe disability for these purposes, see *SI 2002/2007, reg 8*.

(4) *Family element* – From 6 April 2017 the family element is restricted to families with a child born before 6 April 2017.

(5) *Two child policy* – CTC is not awarded for a third or subsequent child born on or after 6 April 2017. There are exceptions for; multiple births, adopted children, non-parental care arrangements, child conceived by rape and claimant's grandchild.

(6) *Disabled children* – The disabled child elements remain payable even if those children are third or subsequent children (*Parliamentary statement, 20 July 2016*).

(7) *Further information* – Guidance for advisers including access to all the Tax Credits legislation can be found here: www.revenuebenefits.org.uk.

Working Tax Credit (WTC)

(SI 2002/2005, reg 20(1), Sch 2, para 1)

Maximum amounts per year	2019/20 £	2018/19 £	2017/18 £
Basic element (*reg 4*)	1,960	1,960	1,960
Couple and lone parent element (*regs 11, 12*)	2,010	2,010	2,010
30 hour element (*reg 10*)	810	810	810
Disabled worker element (*reg 9*)	3,165	3,090	3,000
Severe disability element (*reg 17*)	1,335	1,330	1,290

Notes

(1) *Eligibility* – To be eligible for WTCs the person must be in qualifying remunerative work, either employed or self-employed as defined *(SI 2015/605).*

(2) *Self-employed* – From 6 April 2015 the claimant must be trading on a commercial basis with a view to a profit, and be registered with HMRC as self-employed (*SI 2015/605*).

(3) *Online tools* – An online tax credits calculator is available: https://www.gov.uk/qualify-tax-credits.

Childcare element

(SI 2002/2005, reg 20(2), (3))

Maximum amounts for weekly costs	2019/20 £	2018/19 £	2017/18 £
Maximum eligible cost for one child	175	175	175
Maximum eligible cost for two or more children	300	300	300
Percentage of eligible costs covered	70%	70%	70%

Notes

(1) *Entitlement* – The childcare element applies where the claimant pays for registered or approved childcare (*SI 2001/2005, regs 13, 14*).

(2) *Employer-supported childcare* – Employees who joined employer-provided childcare support or childcare voucher schemes before 4 October 2018 need to understand how this affects their tax credit entitlement (see **Chapter 2**). An online calculator helps Tax Credit claimants decide whether it would be beneficial to accept the employer-provided childcare vouchers (https://www.gov.uk/childcare-vouchers-better-off-calculator).

INCOME THRESHOLDS AND WITHDRAWAL RATES

(Tax Credits Act 2002, ss 7, 13(2); Tax Credits (Income Thresholds and Determination of Rates) Regulations 2002, SI 2002/2008, regs 3, 7, 8)

Annual Rates and thresholds	**2019/20 £**	**2018/19 £**	**2017/18 £**
Income threshold	6,420	6,420	6,420
Withdrawal (or taper) rate	41%	41%	41%
First threshold for those entitled to CTC only	16,105	16,105	16,105
Income rise disregard	2,500	2,500	2,500
Income fall disregard	2,500	2,500	2,500

Notes

(1) *Withdrawal rate* – Entitlement of a claimant of both WTC and CTC (or WTC only) is reduced at the first withdrawal rate on each £1 by which their income exceeds the first income threshold.

(2) *Income disregards* – Claimants' awards are initially based on their previous year's income. Once they report their current year's income, the award can be finalised.

(3) *Further information* – Detailed guidance concerning Tax Credits can be found at: www.revenuebenefits.org.uk.

UNIVERSAL CREDIT

(Welfare Reform Act 2012, Pt 1; SI 2017/260)

Rates per monthly assessment:	**2019/20 £**	**2018/19 £**	**2017/18 £**
Standard Allowance			
Single claimant under 25	251.77	251.77	251.77
Single claimant 25 and over	317.82	317.82	317.82
Joint claimants, both under 25	395.20	395.20	395.20
Joint claimants, either/both 25 and over	498.89	498.89	498.89
Child Element			
1st child	277.08	277.08	277.08
2nd and subsequent child	231.67	231.67	231.67
Additional amount for disabled child			
Lower rate	126.11	126.11	126.11
Higher rate	392.08	383.86	372.30
Capacity for work			
Limited capability for work	126.11	126.11	126.11
Limited capability for work and work-related activity	336.20	328.32	318.76

continued

Rates per monthly assessment:	2019/20 £	2018/19 £	2017/18 £
Carer element	160.20	156.45	151.89
Childcare costs (maximum)			
One child	646.35	646.35	646.35
Two or more children	1108.04	1108.04	1108.04
Work allowance			
If claim includes housing costs	287.00	198.00	192.00
Claim doesn't include housing support	503.00	409.00	397.00

Notes

(1) *Replaces benefits* – Universal Credit (UC) is a means tested benefit designed to replace the following working age benefits:

- Working and Child Tax Credits;
- Income support;
- Income-related employment and support allowance;
- Income based jobseekers allowance; and
- Housing benefit.

(2) *Rollout* – UC is being rolled out gradually across Great Britain. To check if a postcode area is covered by UC see: http://universalcreditinfo.net/.

(3) *Payment* – UC claims are paid monthly based on the reported income in the monthly assessment period. The above rates are an indication of amounts payable.

(4) *Taper rates* – UC benefits are withdrawn at the rate of 63% (65% before 10 April 2017) above higher and lower work allowances.

(5) *Assessment period* – This starts on the day of the month the claim is first made, and ends on that day minus 1 in the next month (eg, if a UC claim is first received on 4 November, the assessment period for that claimant will run to the 3rd of each month).

(6) *Claims* – Couples living in the same household must make a joint claim, as is the case for Tax Credits.

(7) *Cash basis reporting* – Self-employed claimants must report their net income for the month online every month using a version of a cash basis for trading businesses. A minimum income floor applies after the first 12 months of self-employment.

(8) *Use of RTI* – The Department of Work and Pensions will adjust the amounts paid to UC claimants based on the information received from RTI reports (or self-reported by the claimant) in the assessment period.

(9) *Further information* – Guidance for advisers on UC can be found here: www.revenuebenefits.org.uk/universal-credit/.

SOCIAL SECURITY BENEFIT RATES

(ITEPA 2003, Pts 9, 10)

Benefit (weekly rates unless stated)	April 2019 £	April 2018 £	April 2017 £
Attendance allowance (N)			
• Higher rate	87.65	85.60	83.10
• Lower rate	57.70	57.30	55.65
Bereavement Benefit (note 10)			
• Bereavement Payment lump sum	2000.00	2000.00	2,000.00
• Widowed Parent's Allowance **(T)**	119.90	117.10	113.70
• Bereavement Allowance (Standard rate) **(T)**	–	117.10	113.70
Carer's Allowance (T)	66.15	64.60	62.70
Bereavement support payment (Note 10)			
Standard lump sum	2500.00	2500.00	2500.00
Higher rate lump sum	3500.00	3500.00	3500.00
Standard rate monthly payments	100.00	100.00	100.00
Higher rate monthly payments	350.00	350.00	350.00
Employment and Support Allowance (ESA) (T)			
Personal Allowances			
Single under 25	57.90	57.90	57.90
Single 25 or over	73.10	73.10	73.10
Lone parent under 18	57.90	57.90	57.90
Lone parent 18 and over	73.10	73.10	73.10
Couple			
• Both under 18	57.90	57.90	57.90
• Both under 18 – with child	87.50	87.50	87.50
• Both under 18 (main phase)	73.10	73.10	73.10
• One under 18, or both over 18	114.85	114.85	114.85
• Claimant under 25 partner under 18	57.90	57.90	57.90
Components			
• Work-related activity	29.05	29.05	29.05
• support	37.65	37.65	36.25
Income support (note 8)			
Personal Allowances			
• Single under 25	57.90	57.90	57.90
• Single 25 or over	73.10	73.10	73.10
• Lone parent under 18	57.90	57.90	57.90
• Lone parent 18 or over	73.10	73.10	73.10

continued

Benefit (weekly rates unless stated)	April 2019 £	April 2018 £	April 2017 £
Couple			
• Both under 18	57.90	57.90	57.90
• Both under 18 – higher rate	87.50	87.50	87.50
• One under 18, one under 25	57.90	57.90	57.90
• One under 18, one 25 and over	73.10	73.10	73.10
• Both 18 or over	114.85	114.85	114.85
• Dependent children	66.90	66.90	66.90
Premiums			
Family/lone parent	17.45	17.45	17.45
Pensioner (applies to couples only)	140.40	133.95	128.40
Disability			
• Single	34.35	33.55	32.55
• Couple	48.95	47.80	46.40
Enhanced disability (also for ESA)			
• Single	16.80	16.40	15.90
• Disabled child	26.04	25.48	24.78
• Couple	24.10	23.55	22.85
Severe disability (also for ESA)			
• Single	65.85	64.30	62.45
• Couple (lower rate)	65.85	64.30	62.45
• Couple (higher rate)	131.70	128.60	124.90
Disabled child	64.19	62.86	60.90
Carer (also for ESA claims)	36.85	36.00	34.95
Relevant sum for strikers	40.50	40.50	40.50
Jobseeker's Allowance (JSA) (T)			
Contribution-based JSA – Personal rates			
• Under 25	57.90	57.90	57.90
• 25 or over	73.10	73.10	73.10
Income-based JSA – Personal allowances			
• Under 25	57.90	57.90	57.90
• 25 or over	73.10	73.10	73.10
• Lone parent under 18	57.90	57.90	57.90
• Lone parent 18 or over	73.10	73.10	73.10
Couple			
• Both under 18	57.90	57.90	57.90
• Both under 18 – higher rate	87.50	87.50	87.50
• One under 18, one under 25	57.90	57.90	57.90
• One under 18, one 25 and over	73.10	73.10	73.10
• Both 18 or over	114.85	114.85	114.85
Dependent children	66.90	66.90	66.90
Premiums (see Income Support rates)			

Benefit (weekly rates unless stated)	April 2019 £	April 2018 £	April 2017 £
Maternity Allowance (N)			
• Standard rate	148.68	145.18	140.95
• Maternity Allowance threshold	30.00	30.00	30.00
Personal Independence payment (Note 9)			
• Daily living – enhanced	87.65	85.60	83.10
• Daily living – standard	58.70	57.30	55.65
• Mobility – enhanced	61.20	59.75	58.00
• Mobility – standard	23.20	22.65	22.00
Pension Credit (N)			
Standard minimum guarantee			
• Single	167.25	163.00	159.35
• Couple	255.25	248.80	243.25
Additional amount for severe disability			
• Single	65.85	64.30	62.45
• Couple (one qualifies)	65.85	64.30	62.45
• Couple (both qualify)	131.70	128.60	124.90
Additional amount for carers	36.85	36.00	34.95
Savings credit			
• Threshold – single	144.38	140.67	137.35
• Threshold – couple	229.67	223.82	218.42
• Maximum – single	13.72	13.40	13.20
• Maximum – couple	13.35	14.99	14.90
Amount for claimant and first spouse in polygamous marriage	255.25	248.80	243.25
Additional amount for additional spouse	88.00	85.80	83.90
Severe Disablement Allowance (N)			
Basic rate	79.50	77.65	75.40
Age-related addition			
• Higher rate	11.90	11.60	11.25
• Middle rate	6.60	6.45	6.25
• Lower rate	6.60	6.45	6.25
Widow's Benefit (T)			
Widowed Mother's Allowance	119.90	117.10	113.70
Widow's Pension (Standard rate)	119.90	117.10	113.70

Notes

(1) *Eligibility* – The above list represents a selection of state benefit rates. More comprehensive guidance of who is entitled to which benefit can be found at: www.entitledto.co.uk.

(2) *Commencement* – The benefit rates for 2019/20 apply from 8 April 2019.

(3) *Uprating of benefits* – The annual uprating of benefits takes place for state pensions and most other benefits in the first full week of the tax year.

(4) *Taxable or not* – In the table above, (**T**) indicates a taxable benefit and (**N**) indicates a non-taxable benefit. Only those UK social security benefits that are specified in Table A at *ITEPA 2003, s 660(1)* are taxable as social security income under *ITEPA 2003, Pt 10*. Some other social security benefits, specified at *ITEPA 2003, s 577*, are taxable as pension income under *ITEPA 2003, Pt 9*.

(5) *Foreign benefits* – Certain foreign social security payments are exempt from UK tax (see *ITEPA 2003, Pt 10, Ch 7*).

(6) *Statutory payments* – Details of statutory sick pay, maternity pay, paternity pay and adoption pay are given in **Chapter 16**.

(7) *ESA* – Replaced Incapacity Benefit and Income Support paid on incapacity grounds for claims starting from 27 October 2008. Existing recipients of Incapacity Benefit or Income Support continue to receive that benefit until they are moved to ESA (EIM76180).

(8) *Income support* – For further information on taxable and non-taxable parts of income support, see EIM76190.

(9) *Personal Independence Payment (PIP)* – Replaced Disability Living Allowance for people aged 16 to 64 from 8 April 2013. For further guidance, see: www.gov.uk/pip.

(10) *Bereavement payment* – Applies for deaths before 6 April 2017. For later deaths bereavement support payments apply at the higher rate for those with children, or the lower rate for those without children. The monthly payments continue for 18 months.

NON-TAXABLE SOCIAL SECURITY BENEFITS

(*ITEPA 2003, Pt 10*)

- Attendance Allowance
- Bereavement Payment
- Child Benefit (but see HICBC in **Chapter 1**)
- Child Tax Credit
- Cold Weather Payments
- Council Tax Benefit
- Constant Attendance Allowance (see Industrial Injuries Benefits)
- Disability Living Allowance
- Employment and Support Allowance (income related)
- Exceptionally Severe Disablement Allowance (see Industrial Injuries Benefits)
- Guardian's Allowance
- Housing Benefit
- Income Support (certain payments)

- Industrial Injuries Benefits (ie industrial injuries pension, reduced earnings allowance, retirement allowance, constant attendance allowance and exceptionally severe disablement allowance)
- Maternity Allowance
- Payments to reduce under-occupation by housing benefit claimants ('bedroom tax')
- Pensioner's Christmas Bonus
- Severe Disablement Allowance
- Social Fund Payments
- State Pension credit
- Universal credit
- War Widow's pension
- Winter Fuel payment
- Working Tax Credit
- Young person's bridging allowance

(Sources – *ITEPA 2003, s 677 (Table B);* EIM76100; tinyurl.com/txntxstbn)

Notes

(1) *Industrial injuries benefits* – The above excludes industrial death benefit, which is taxable (*ITEPA 2003, ss 577(1), 677(2)*).

(2) *Payments out of the social fund* – Payments are made to people on low incomes to help with maternity expenses, funeral costs, financial crises and as community care grants. The fund also makes interest-free loans.

(3) *War Widow's pension* – Where a pension or allowance is not paid or only a reduced amount is paid because the claimant gets a different benefit (eg widowed mother's allowance or widow's pension), the amount of that other benefit that equals the amount of pension withheld, is exempt from income tax (*ITEPA 2003, s 640*; see EIM76103).

With regard to wounds and disability pensions for service with the forces, see EIM74302. For allowances payable to civilians in respect of war injuries, see EIM74700.

(4) *Foreign benefits* – Certain foreign social security payments are exempt from UK tax (see *ITEPA 2003, Pt 10, Ch 7*).

CHILD BENEFIT AND GUARDIAN'S ALLOWANCE

(*Child Benefit (Rates) Regulations 2006, SI 2006/965*)

Weekly rates	First child rate £	Additional children rate £	Guardian's allowance £
2019/20	20.70	13.70	17.60
2018/19	20.70	13.70	17.20
2017/18	20.70	13.70	16.70
2016/17	20.70	13.70	16.55
2015/16	20.70	13.70	16.55
2014/15	20.50	13.55	16.35

Notes

(1) *Payment* – Child benefit is not income related and is automatically paid to the claimant (usually the mother) after a single claim, until the child is no longer eligible, or until the claimant elects not to receive the benefit.

(2) *Not taxable* – Child benefit is not taxable, and it does not form part of the recipient's taxable income. However, child benefit can be clawed-back from high earners, see **Chapter 1: High Income Child Benefit Charge.**

(3) *Election not to receive* – The child benefit claimant may elect not to receive child benefit, but will retain an entitlement to the benefit (see **Chapter 1**)

(4) *NI credits* – A person who claims child benefit for a child under 12 years and who does not earn above the LEL will automatically receive national insurance credits, which can help make up qualifying years for the State pension.

(5) *Guardian's allowance* – This is a tax-free payment for people who are bringing up children whose parents have died.

(6) *Further information* – For child benefit and guardian's allowance, see www.gov.uk/browse/benefits/child.

STATE PENSION

(*Pensions Act 2011*)

Weekly rates	New state pension £	Basic single person: category A £	Spouse's pension: category B £	Non-contributory: category C or D £
2019/20	168.60	129.20	77.45	77.45
2018/19	164.35	125.95	75.50	75.50
2017/18	159.55	122.30	73.30	73.30
2016/17	155.65	119.30	71.50	71.50
2015/16	N/A	115.95	69.50	69.50
2014/15	N/A	113.10	67.80	67.80
2013/14	N/A	110.15	66.00	66.00

Notes

(1) *Payable from* – An individual is eligible to draw the state retirement pension when he or she reaches state pension age (SPA). This varies for men and women, and is gradually increasing to 68, see calculator at: www.gov.uk/state-pension-age.

(2) *Deferment* – An individual who qualifies for the state pension may choose to defer claiming the pension. Where the claim is deferred for 12 months or more, that pensioner may opt to receive either the pension foregone as a lump sum or as a higher pension.

(3) *Taxable* – The state pension is taxable, as is any state pension lump sum received due to deferment (*F(No 2)A 2005, ss 7–10*; see EIM74650).

(4) *Qualifying years* – An individual must have 35 qualifying years to receive the full state pension if they reach SPA on or after 6 April 2016. A qualifying year is when the person has paid sufficient NI contributions, or received NI credits, in a tax year.

(5) *Age bonus* – A person who qualifies for the old state pension receives an additional payment of 25p per week from age 80.

(6) *Pension forecast* – An individual can request a forecast of their state pension through their personal tax account online or by completing DWP form BR19: www.gov.uk/check-state-pension.

(7) *New state pension* – Individuals who reach SPA on or after 6 April 2016 receive the new flat-rate state pension. This replaces pension credit, the old state pension and second state pension (see: www.gov.uk/new-state-pension).

16

Statutory payments

NATIONAL MINIMUM WAGE (NMW)

(*NMWA 1998, s 2; SI 1999/584, Pt 2*)

Hourly rate from	Living wage £/hr	Adult £/hr	Youth development £/hr	Under 18 £/hr	Apprentice £/hr	Accommodation daily off-set £/day
1 April 2019	8.21	7.70	6.15	4.35	3.90	7.55
1 April 2018	7.83	7.38	5.90	4.20	3.70	7.00
1 April 2017	7.50	7.05	5.60	4.05	3.50	6.40
1 October 2016	7.20	6.95	5.55	4.00	3.40	6.00
1 April 2016	7.20	6.70	5.30	3.87	3.30	5.35
1 October 2015	N/A	6.70	5.30	3.87	3.30	5.35
1 October 2014	N/A	6.50	5.13	3.79	2.73	5.08

Notes

(1) *Living Wage* – Payable to employees aged 25 and over for pay periods starting on and after 1 April 2016 (*SI 2016/68*).

(2) *Adult rate* – Applies to workers aged 21 or over, and from 1 April 2016 to workers who have reached age 21 but not 25 (*SI 1999/584, reg 11*).

(3) *Development rate* – Applies to workers who have reached the age of 18, but not 21 (*SI 1999/584, reg 13(1)*).

(4) *Apprentice rate* – Applies to apprentices who are either aged under 19, or in the first year of their apprenticeship (*SI 1999/584, reg 13(3)*).

(5) *Under 18 rate* – Applies from school leaving age, which varies in the different countries within the UK.

(6) *Accommodation off-set* – The maximum daily rate of accommodation charge permitted to be set against wages by the employer. If the charge for accommodation

is greater, the difference is deducted from the employees pay as calculated for NMW. If accommodation is provided for free the off-set rate is added to the worker's pay to calculate the deemed amount for NMW.

(7) *Penalties* – Where an employer fails to pay correct NMW, it must pay the back wages at the correct level, plus a penalty of 100% of the underpayment capped at £20,000 (from 7 March 2014). The employer will also be 'named and shamed' for failing to pay correct NMW where underpaid amount is £100 or more for entire payroll. Tax penalties may be due on any unpaid tax and NICs (*SI 2014/547*).

(8) *Records* – Employers are required to keep records for three years to prove correct NMW has been paid.

(9) *Further information* – Guidance for employers, see: www.gov.uk/national-minimum-wage.

STATUTORY SICK PAY (SSP)

(*SI 1995/512; SI 1995/513*)

Tax year	Weekly earnings threshold £	Weekly rate £
2019/20	118	94.25
2018/19	116	92.05
2017/18	113	89.35
2016/17	112	88.45
2015/16	112	88.45
2014/15	111	87.55
2013/14	109	86.70

Notes

(1) *No SSP* – If the weekly earnings do not exceed the earnings threshold, no SSP is payable.

(2) *No recovery* – SSP cannot be recovered by employers for periods beginning on or after 6 April 2014.

(3) *Treatment* – Employers can pay up to £500 for recommended medical treatment for employees to help them back to work (see **Chapter 2**).

(4) *Further information* – For guidance on SSP see: www.gov.uk/employers-sick-pay.

STATUTORY MATERNITY PAY (SMP)

(*SI 1994/1882*)

Tax year	Weekly earnings threshold £	Weekly flat rate £
2019/20	118	148.68
2018/19	116	145.18
2017/18	113	140.98
2016/17	112	139.58
2015/16	112	139.58
2014/15	111	138.18
2013/14	109	136.78

Notes

(1) *Rates* – SMP is paid at 90% of average weekly earnings for the first six weeks and at the lower of the flat rate above and 90% of average weekly earnings for the next 33 weeks.

(2) *No SMP* – If weekly earnings do not exceed the weekly earnings threshold, no SMP is payable.

(3) *Recovery of SMP* – Employers can recover SMP from HMRC at 92% of the amount paid if their total Class 1 NIC liability for the previous tax year was more than £45,000.The recovery amount is set a 103% if the total Class 1 NIC liability for the employer was no more than £45,000 in the previous tax year. Recovery is achieved by showing the recoverable amounts on the EPS for each pay period.

(4) *Shared parental pay* – For babies due on and after 5 April 2015 working parents can share parental leave and pay. A maximum of 37 weeks of SMP can be shared or 35 weeks for factory workers. All shared pay is paid at the lower flat rate unless the employer chooses to pay a contractually higher amount.

(5) *Further information* – For guidance for employers on SMP see: www.gov.uk/employers-maternity-pay-leave.

STATUTORY ADOPTION PAY (SAP)

(*SI 2002/2818*)

Tax year	Weekly earnings threshold £	Weekly flat rate £
2019/20	118	148.68
2018/19	116	145.18
2017/18	113	140.98
2016/17	112	139.58
2015/16	112	139.58
2014/15	111	138.18
2013/14	109	136.78

Notes

(1) *Rates* – SAP is paid at the lower of the flat rate above and 90% of average weekly earnings for up to 39 weeks.

(2) *No SAP* – If weekly earnings do not exceed the weekly earnings threshold, no SAP is payable.

(3) *Recovery of SAP* – Employers can recover SAP from HMRC at the rate of 92% of SAP paid out, or at the rate of 103% of the SAP paid, if the employer's total Class 1 NIC liability was no more than £45,000 in the previous tax year. Recovery is achieved by showing the recoverable amounts on the EPS for each pay period.

(4) *Further information* – For guidance for employers on SAP see: www.gov.uk/employers-adoption-pay-leave.

STATUTORY PATERNITY PAY (SPP)

(*SSCBA 1992, Pt 12ZA; SI 2011/678; SI 2010/1060*)

Tax year	Weekly earnings threshold £	Weekly flat rate £
2019/20	118	148.68
2018/19	116	145.18
2017/18	113	140.98
2016/17	112	139.58
2015/16	112	139.58
2014/15	111	138.18
2013/14	109	136.78

Notes

(1) *SPP Rates* – Statutory Paternity Pay (SPP) is paid at the lower of the flat rate above and 90% of average weekly earnings for up to two weeks.

(2) *No SPP* – If the employee's weekly earnings do not exceed the weekly earnings threshold no SPP is payable.

(3) *Recovery of SPP* – Employers can recover SPP from HMRC at the rate of 92% of such payments, or at the rate of 103%, if the total Class 1 NIC liability for the previous year was no more than £45,000. Recovery is achieved by showing the recoverable amounts on the EPS for each pay period.

(4) *Further information* – For guidance on paternity pay see: www.gov.uk/employers-paternity-pay-leave.

17

HMRC penalties, interest and powers

STRUCTURE OF PENALTIES

HMRC may impose penalties on taxpayers in the following circumstances:

- Late payment of tax or duty;
- Late filing of returns;
- Failure to notify chargeability to tax;
- Errors on returns and documents;
- Failure to keep or retain records;
- VAT and excise wrong-doing; and
- Failure to submit returns online.

Notes

(1) *Scope* – The structure of tax penalties is now generally the same across all the taxes administered by HMRC, but there are different regimes for late filing and late payment of VAT and PAYE.

(2) *Effective from* – This penalty regime came into force for income tax, CGT, CT, VAT and direct tax claims not included in a return, from 1 April 2009, and for failure to pay CIS or PAYE from 6 April 2010.

(3) *Other taxes* – The new penalty regime came into effect for IPT, SDLT, aggregates levy, climate change levy and landfill tax from 1 April 2010 or 1 April 2012. Record keeping requirements apply to bank payroll tax from 8 April 2010, and excise duties from 1 April 2011.

(4) *GAAR penalty* – For arrangements entered into on or 15 September 2016 a penalty of 60% of the counteracted tax can apply when an arrangement is counteracted by application of the general anti-abuse rule (GAAR) (*FA 2016, s 158*).

UK matters

The amount of penalty that can be imposed is determined according to the behaviour of the taxpayer, the degree of disclosure the taxpayer has made to HMRC, and whether that disclosure was prompted or unprompted (the *quality* of the disclosure). The penalty is charged as a percentage of the potential lost revenue (PLR), as set out on the following grid.

Behaviour of taxpayer:	Unprompted disclosure Max. Penalty	Unprompted disclosure Min. Penalty	Prompted disclosure Max. Penalty	Prompted disclosure Min. Penalty
Reasonable care taken	0%	0%	0%	0%
Careless	30%	0%	30%	15%
Deliberate but not concealed	70%	20%	70%	35%
Deliberate and concealed	100%	30%	100%	50%

Notes

(1) *Applicable to* – this grid applies to penalties imposed for the following:

- Errors in returns and documents (*FA 2007, s 97, Sch 24*);
- Failures to notify (*FA 2008, s 123, Sch 41*);
- Late submission (see **Late filing**, *FA 2009, s 106, Sch 55*); and
- Under-assessment by HMRC (*FA 2007, Sch 24, paras 2, 4C*).

(2) *Commencement* – The penalty provisions generally apply to assessments for tax periods commencing from 1 April 2008, where the filing date is on or after 1 April 2009 (*SI 2008/568, art 2(b)*).

(3) *Potential lost revenue (PLR)* – This is the amount of tax which is payable as a result of correcting the error, or notifying HMR of the liability. Where inflated losses have been claimed, but not yet utilised, the PLR is 10% of the unused loss, (*FA 2007, Sch 24, paras 5–8*).

(4) *Failure to notify* – If HMRC become aware of the failure to notify less than 12 months after the tax first becomes unpaid due to the failure, the penalty for careless behaviour ranges from 0% to 30% for unprompted disclosure, and from 10% to 30% for prompted disclosure. Otherwise, the penalty ranges stated above apply (*FA 2008, Sch 41, para 13(3)*).

(5) *Error by another person* – A penalty can also apply to an error in a taxpayer's document which is attributable to another person (*FA 2007, Sch 24, para 1A*).

(6) *Late returns: Penalty aggregation* – The penalty regime for late returns applies both fixed and tax-geared penalties (see **Late filing** below). A taxpayer may become liable to more than one category of penalty in respect of the same return, etc (*FA 2009, Sch 55, para 1(3)*). However, where more than one tax-geared penalty arises, the aggregate must not exceed a statutory maximum (*FA 2009, Sch 55, para 17(3)*).

(7) *Reasonable excuse* – No penalty arises if there is a 'reasonable excuse' throughout the period of default for a failure to notify (*FA 2008, Sch 41, para 20*). Similar rules apply to late returns (*FA 2009, Sch 55, para 23*).

(8) *Errors: Under-assessment* – A penalty can be charged on a person if an HMRC assessment understates the tax payable, and the person fails to take reasonable steps to notify HMRC of the under-assessment within 30 days from the date of the assessment (*FA 2007, Sch 24, para 2*).

(9) *Special reductions* – HMRC may reduce a penalty for errors because of 'special circumstances' (*FA 2007, Sch 24, para 11*). Similar rules apply to a failure to notify (*FA 2008, Sch 41, para 14*) and late returns (*FA 2009, Sch 55, para 16*).

(10) *Enablers of avoidance* – Individuals and entities who enable the use of tax avoidance arrangements, which are shown to fail, by court judgment or agreement with HMRC, can be subject to a penalty of 100% of the fee charged for the advice or scheme (*F(No 2)A 2017, Sch 16 para 5*).

(11) *Further information* – See HMRC's compliance factsheets: tinyurl.com/y8dp55u5, and overview of penalties: tinyurl.com/PovtAA.

Offshore matters

Classification of territories

Territories are classified in accordance with the penalty regime for errors (*FA 2007, Sch 24, para 21A, FA 2015, Sch 20 para 2*).

There are different levels of penalty for failure to notify which apply only for income tax and CGT (see tables below). If HMRC become aware of the failure to notify less than 12 months after the tax first becomes unpaid due to the failure, the minimum penalty for a non-deliberate action is reduced for an unprompted disclosure.

CATEGORY 1 TERRITORY

Behaviour leading to error:	**Unprompted disclosure**		**Prompted disclosure**	
	Maximum penalty	**Minimum penalty**	**Maximum penalty**	**Minimum penalty**
Careless	30%	0%	30%	15%
Deliberate, not concealed	70%	20%	70%	35%
Deliberate and concealed	100%	30%	100%	50%

Reason behind the failure to notify or disclose	**Unprompted disclosure**		**Prompted disclosure**	
	Maximum penalty	**Minimum penalty**	**Maximum penalty**	**Minimum penalty**
Non-deliberate failure within 12 months of tax due	30%	0%	30%	10%
Non-deliberate failure over 12 months of tax due	30%	10%	30%	20%
Deliberate but not concealed within 12 months of tax due	70%	20%	70%	35%
Deliberate but not concealed over 12 months of tax due	70%	20%	70%	35%
Deliberate and concealed	100%	30%	100%	50%

Notes

(1) *Category 1 information* – This is information involving:

(a) A UK domestic matter; or

(b) An offshore matter, where the territory is in Category 1 or the tax at stake is income tax or CGT (or IHT from April 2017).

(2) *Failure to notify* – The penalties for failure to notify only relate to matters connected with income tax or CGT from 2016/17, and for IHT for transfers from 1 April 2017.

(3) *Which countries* – A list of Category 1 and Category 3 territories is available at: tinyurl.com/OSTRCT.

CATEGORY 2 TERRITORY

(*FA 2007, Sch 24, para 10*)

Behaviour behind inaccuracy or error	**Unprompted disclosure**		**Prompted disclosure**	
	Maximum penalty	**Minimum penalty**	**Maximum penalty**	**Minimum penalty**
Careless	45%	0%	45%	22.5%
Deliberate but not concealed	105%	30%	105%	52.5%
Deliberate and concealed	150%	45%	150%	75%

Reason behind the failure to notify or disclose	**Unprompted disclosure**		**Prompted disclosure**	
	Maximum penalty	**Minimum penalty**	**Maximum penalty**	**Minimum penalty**
Non-deliberate failure within 12 months of tax due	45%	0%	45%	15%
Non-deliberate failure over 12 months of tax due	45%	15%	45%	30%
Deliberate but not concealed	105%	30%	105%	52.5%
Deliberate and concealed	150%	45%	150%	75%

Notes

(1) *Category 2 information* – This is information involving an offshore matter, in a *Category 2* territory, which would enable or assist HMRC to assess an income tax or CGT liability.

(2) *Which countries* – All countries which are not Category 1 or 3 are Category 2.

(3) *Failure to notify* – The penalties for failure to notify only relate to matters connected with income tax or CGT from 2016/17, and for IHT for transfers from 1 April 2017.

(4) *Further information* – See HMRC Compliance Handbook CH11660 and HMRC factsheets CC/FS17 and CC/FS17a.

CATEGORY 3 TERRITORY

(*FA 2007, Sch 24, para 10*)

Behaviour behind the inaccuracy or error	**Unprompted disclosure**		**Prompted disclosure**	
	Maximum penalty	**Minimum penalty**	**Maximum penalty**	**Minimum penalty**
Careless	60%	0%	60%	30%
Deliberate but not concealed	140%	40%	140%	70%
Deliberate and concealed	200%	60%	200%	100%

Reason behind the failure to notify or disclose	**Unprompted disclosure**		**Prompted disclosure**	
	Maximum penalty	**Minimum penalty**	**Maximum penalty**	**Minimum penalty**
Non-deliberate failure within 12 months of tax due	60%	0%	60%	20%
Non-deliberate failure over 12 months of tax due	60%	20%	60%	40%
Deliberate but not concealed	140%	40%	140%	70%
Deliberate and concealed	200%	60%	200%	100%

Notes

(1) *Category 3 information* – This is information involving an offshore matter, in a Category 3 territory, which would enable or assist HMRC to assess an income tax or CGT liability.

(2) *Failure to notify* – The penalties for failure to notify only relate to matters connected with income tax or CGT from 2016/17, and for IHT for transfers from 1 April 2017.

(3) *Further information* – See HMRC Compliance Handbook CH116700.

LATE FILING OR LATE PAYMENT

Late filing

(*FA 2009, s 106, Sch 55*)

Period	**Penalty**	**Notes**
Up to 3 months late	£100	Automatic fixed penalty
More than 3 months late	£10 per day	Maximum of 90 days ie £900. Payable only if HMRC give notice of the penalty, and the notice specifies the date from which the penalty is payable.

Period	Penalty	Notes
More than 6 months late	Greater of: • 5% of tax liability; and • £300	'Tax liability' is any tax which would have been shown in the return in question.
More than 12 months late, except where taxpayer withholds information deliberately (see below).	Greater of: • 5% of tax liability; and • £300	
12 months + late and information withheld deliberately **but not** concealed	Greater of: • Relevant % of tax liability; and • £300	See **Structure of penalties** above
12 months + late and information withheld deliberately **and** concealed	Greater of: • Relevant % of tax liability; and • £300	See **Structure of penalties** above

Notes

(1) *Applies to* – Income Tax, CGT, ATED, SDRT, Bank Payroll Tax and Registered Pensions Schemes. There are slightly different penalty models for other taxes.

(2) *Effective from* – For returns due for 2010/11 and later tax years (*FA 2009, s 106, Sch 55; SI 2011/702*).

(3) *Further information* – See HMRC's Compliance Handbook at CH61000.

Late payment

(*FA 2009, s 107, Sch 56)*

Length of delay	Penalty
30 days	5% of the unpaid tax
6 months	5% of the unpaid tax (additional)
12 months	5% of the unpaid tax (additional)

Notes

(1) *Applies to* – Income tax, CGT, PAYE, NIC, Student Loan deductions, CIS, ATED, MGD, Bank Payroll Tax and Registered Pension Schemes. For income tax under self-assessment these penalties only apply to late balancing payments (ie based on tax returns for individuals or trustees etc).

(2) *Effective from* – In relation to 2010/11 and later tax years (*SI 2011/702, art 3*).

(3) *Assessments and appeals* – HMRC must assess the late payment penalty, and notify the person liable as to the period to which the penalty relates. The penalty is payable within 30 days from the day on which the penalty notice is issued. There is a right of

appeal against both the imposition of a penalty, and the amount involved (*FA 2009, Sch 56, paras 11, 13*).

(4) *Reduction and suspension* – HMRC may reduce a late payment penalty in 'special circumstances', which does not include inability to pay (*FA 2009, Sch 56, para 9*). In addition, a defence of 'reasonable excuse' may be available (*Sch 56, para 16*).

(5) *Payments on account* – The maximum penalty for fraudulent or negligent claims by taxpayers to reduce payments on account is the difference between the correct amount payable on account and the amount of any payment on account made by him (*TMA 1970, s 59A(6)*).

(6) *Further information* – See HMRC's Compliance Handbook at CH150500.

FAILURE PENALTIES

Failure to keep or retain tax records

(*TMA 1970, s 12B; FA 2003, Sch 10; FA 2008, s 115, Sch 37*)

(1) *Maximum penalty* – For failing to keep and preserve records: £3,000 per tax year or accounting period (*TMA 1970, s 12B(5); FA 1998, Sch 18, para 23*).

(2) *Applies to* – Direct taxes and VAT from 1 April 2009 (*SI 2009/402*) and for all other taxes and duties generally from 1 April 2010 (*SI 2010/815*).

Failures relating to offshore tax evasion

(1) *Criminal offences* – The *Criminal Finances Act 2017* introduced these offences:

- a criminal offence for individual offshore tax evaders;
- a corporate criminal offence for failure to prevent tax evasion.

(2) *Enabling off-shore tax evasion* – Tax Advisers can be subject to a penalty as enablers of offshore tax evasion from 1 January 2017. The person enabled by the adviser must be liable to a civil tax penalty or have committed a criminal tax offence, both in relation to offshore matters. The penalty for the enabler is the higher of £3,000 and 100% of the PLR (*SI 2016/1249*).

(3) *Requirement to correct* – Where an offshore inaccuracy or omission existed at 6 April 2017, and the correction was not made before 30 September 2018, the taxpayer may be subject to a penalty of between 100% and 200% of the PLR (*F(No 2)A 2017, Sch 18 para 15(2)*). For further information see tinyurl.com/RTCTDOA.

CORPORATION TAX PENALTIES

(*FA 1998, Sch 18*; *FA 2007, s 97, Sch 24*; *FA 2008, s 113, Sch 36, s 123, Sch 41*)

Offence	Maximum penalty
Failure to notify chargeability (*FA 2008, s 123, Sch 41, paras 1, 6, 6A; SI 2009/511*)	
Deliberate and concealed act or failure	100% of potential lost revenue
Deliberate but not concealed act or failure	70% of potential lost revenue
Any other case	30% of potential lost revenue
Failure to deliver a return (*FA 1998, Sch 18, paras 17, 18*)	
Up to 3 months after filing date	£100 third successive failure: £500
More than 3 months after filing date	A further £100 plus third successive failure: £1000
At least 18 months but less than 24 months after end of return period	10% of tax unpaid at 18 months after end of return period
24 months or more after end of return period	A further 10% of tax unpaid at 18 months after end of return period
Errors in returns etc (*FA 2007, s 97, Sch 24, para 4; SI 2008/568*)	
Reasonable care taken	No penalty liability
Careless inaccuracy	30% of potential lost revenue
Deliberate but not concealed inaccuracy	70% of potential lost revenue
Deliberate and concealed inaccuracy	100% of potential lost revenue
Quarterly instalment payments	
Deliberate or reckless failure to pay the correct amount on an instalment date; Fraudulent or negligent claim for repayment (under *reg 6(2)* of the instalment regulations) (*TMA 1970, s 59E(4); SI 1998/3175, reg 13*)	Up to twice the amount of interest charged on any unpaid amount in respect of the company's total liability for the accounting period

Notes

(1) *Failure to notify* – These provisions took effect from 1 April 2010. For earlier periods penalties were charged under *FA 1998, Sch 18, para 2(3)*, up to a maximum of 100% of tax payable for the accounting period and remaining unpaid 12 months after the end of the period.

(2) *Failure to make returns etc* – A fixed and tax related penalty regime applies for the late filing of corporation tax returns from 6 October 2011 (*FA 2009, s 106, Sch 55; SI 2011/2391*).

(3) *Failure to deliver a return* – The above flat rate penalties do not apply if the return period is one for which the company must deliver accounts under the *Companies Act 2006*, and the return is filed by the date allowed by Companies House (*FA 1998, Sch 18, para 19*). This has no effect on the tax geared penalties which may arise.

(4) *Information notices and inspections* – See **HMRC Powers** below.

VAT PENALTIES

Default surcharge

(*VATA 1994, ss 59–59B, 71*; VAT Notice 700/50)

Number of defaults during rolling 12 month period	Surcharge where turnover less than £150,000 (VAT Notice 700/50, para 4.2)	Surcharge if turnover is £150,000 or more
1st	No surcharge, but if default within 12 months will enter surcharge default period. Help letter issued	No surcharge, but enter a surcharge period. Surcharge Liability Notice issued.
2nd	No surcharge but enter a surcharge period	2% (no surcharge issued if charge is under £400)
3rd	2% (no surcharge issued if charge is under £400)	5% (no surcharge issued if charge is under £400)
4th	5% (no surcharge issued if charge is under £400)	greater of 10% or £30
5th	greater of 10% or £30	greater of 15% or £30
6th	greater of 15% or £30	greater of 15% or £30

Notes

(1) *Applies to* – Failure to submit a return or pay amount of VAT payable on time, or pay the amount due under the payment on account scheme on time. The surcharge is calculated as a percentage of the unpaid VAT in default.

(2) *Reasonable excuse* – A surcharge liability does not arise if HMRC or the Tax Tribunal are satisfied that there is a reasonable excuse for the return or VAT payment being late (*VATA 1994, s 59(7)*). As to circumstances which cannot constitute a 'reasonable excuse' for these purposes, see *VATA 1994, s 71(1)*.

(3) *Payments on account* – Surcharges can apply to late payments on account; see *VATA 1994, s 59A* and VAT Notice 700/50, para 4.4.

(4) *Further information* – For further information on default surcharges, and on VAT penalties see www.gov.uk/vat-returns/surcharges-and-penalties.

Unauthorised issue of VAT invoice

(*FA 2008, Sch 41, paras 2, 6*)

- *General* – A penalty is payable by a person who makes an unauthorised issue of a VAT invoice, ie where an 'unauthorised person' (eg a person not registered under *VATA 1994*) issues an invoice showing an amount of VAT or a VAT inclusive amount).
- *Commencement* – The provisions apply to any unauthorised issue of an invoice taking place from 1 April 2010 (*SI 2009/511, art 3*).
- *Level of penalty* – The same penalties apply as for failure to notify (see **UK matters** above), except that the lower penalties for non-deliberate behaviour do not apply.

- *Special reductions and reasonable excuse* – HMRC may reduce a penalty in 'special circumstances' and penalties do not arise if HMRC or the tribunal are satisfied that there is a 'reasonable excuse' for the act or failure (*FA 2008, Sch 41, paras 14, 20*).

Incorrect certificates as to zero-rating etc

(*VATA 1994, s 62*)

- *General* – The penalty is charged in respect of incorrect certificates within *VATA 1994, s 62(1)*, or in respect of acquisitions of goods from other member states within the fiscal warehousing regime; see *s 62(1A)*.
- *Person liable* – The person giving or preparing the certificate is liable to the penalty.
- *Level of penalty* – The penalty is equal to the difference between the VAT chargeable if the certificate had been correct and any VAT actually charged, or (in respect of acquisitions from other member states within the fiscal warehousing regime) the amount of VAT actually chargeable on the acquisition.

Breach of walking possession agreements

(*VATA 1994, s 68*)

- *General* – A penalty can be imposed for the breach of an undertaking contained in a walking possession agreement (NB a penalty under *VATA 1994, s 68* does not extend to Scotland).
- *Amount of penalty* – The person in default is liable to a penalty equal to 50% of VAT due or any amount recoverable as if it were VAT due.

Breaches of regulatory provisions

(*VATA 1994, s 69;* VCP11100 et seq)

Failures in the two year period	**Prescribed rate**	**Late payment or late submission of return**
First failure	£5 per day	1/6th of 1% of VAT due
Second failure	£10 per day	1/3rd of 1% of VAT due
Any other case	£15 per day	1/2 of 1% of VAT due

Notes

(1) *Who it applies to* – A penalty for a failure to comply with any regulatory requirement is determined according to the number of occasions in the previous two years on which the person has failed to comply with that requirement.

(2) *Amount of penalty* – Greater of £50 and the prescribed daily rate for up to 100 days.

(3) *Late payments or late filing* – Where the breach is a late payment failure or the late filing of a VAT return, the prescribed penalty rate is the greater of the penalty in note 2, and the amounts shown in the table above (*VATA 1994, s 69(5)*).

(4) *Double penalties* – A late payment or filing penalty cannot be assessed if a default surcharge is to be assessed for the same failure (VCP11134).

Failure to preserve records

(VATA 1994, ss 69(2), 69B, Sch 11, para 6A(1), (6))

Failure to keep records:	**Penalty**
Under requirement imposed by VATA *Sch 11, para 6(3)*	£500
As required by HMRC direction	£200 per day up to 30 days
As required by HMRC to preserve records for up to 6 years	£500

Notes

(1) *General failure* – HMRC may require records to be preserved for a period specified in writing, but not exceeding 6 years (*VATA 1994, Sch 11, para 6(3)*).

(2) *Amount of penalty* – As shown in table above, unless there is a reasonable excuse for the failure.

(3) *Breach of direction* – Penalties as shown in table above unless HMRC or the tribunal is satisfied that there is a reasonable excuse for the failure.

Evasion of import VAT (and other relevant duties)

(*FA 2003, ss 24(2)(d), 25*)

- *General* – A penalty can be imposed where a person engages in conduct to evade import VAT, or by which he contravenes a legislative duty, obligation, requirement or condition in relation to import VAT.
- *Penalty* – The penalty for evasion involving dishonesty is an amount equal to the import VAT evaded or sought to be evaded.
- *Other relevant duties* – The same penalty provisions that apply to import VAT apply to other relevant duties.

Contravention of relevant rules

(*FA 2003, ss 26, 27, 29; SI 2003/3113*)

- *General* – A penalty can arise for contravening a 'relevant rule' (see *FA 2003, s 26(8)*; *SI 2003/3113*, *reg 3, Sch*).
- *Penalty* – A penalty of up to £2,500 (or other amount prescribed by Treasury Order) can be imposed, unless HMRC or the tribunal are satisfied that there is a reasonable excuse for the failure, or unless the penalty is reduced or cancelled by HMRC or the tribunal.

Failure to file VAT returns online

(*SI 1995/2518, reg 25A*)

Annual VAT exclusive turnover	Penalty	Annual VAT exclusive turnover	Penalty
Over £22.8m	£400	£100,001 to £5.6m	£200
£5.6 m to £22.8m	£300	£100,000 and under	£100

Notes

(1) *Commencement* – VAT traders can be liable to penalties in relation to returns made for prescribed accounting periods ending on or after 31 March 2011 (*SI 1995/2518, reg 25A(15)*).

(2) *Online submission* – All VAT registered traders are required to submit VAT returns through the HMRC online form (the portal) from 1 April 2012, unless they qualify for exemption (see note 4).

(3) *Penalties* – Are charged for paper VAT returns submitted for VAT periods ending on or after 31 March 2013, unless the taxpayer qualifies for exemption, or the person has a reasonable excuse for failing to file online.

(4) *Exemptions* – Businesses run by individuals who have a religious conscience objection to the use of computers, and those who find it impossible or impractical to use computers due to age, disability or location, can apply to HMRC for an exemption to online filing. In those cases, arrangements can be made with HMRC to submit the VAT figures by phone.

(5) *MTD* – Most VAT registered traders will be required to submitted VAT returns via MTD-compatible software for periods beginning on and after 1 April 2019 (see **Chapter 6**). There penalties for not submitting via MTD software are to be revised from 2021, but in the meantime the above penalty structure will apply.

EC SALES LIST (ESL) PENALTIES

(*VATA 1994, ss 65, 66*)

Defaults	Inaccuracy in return	Late or non-submission (up to 100 days)
First default	–	£5 per day
Second default	–	£10 per day
Any other case	£100 (see note 1)	£15 per day

Notes

(1) *Inaccuracies* – The error must be a material inaccuracy included on statement submitted within two years after a penalty notice has been issued by HMRC. A penalty will only be imposed where the third ESL containing an inaccuracy has been submitted (see VCP11044).

(2) *Late filing* – Penalties are only charged if HMRC has served a default notice and the ELS is not submitted within 14 days. The penalty is the greater of: £50 and up to 100 days of the daily penalties.

SDLT PENALTIES

(*FA 2003, Schs 10, 11; FA 2007, Sch 24*)

Offence	Penalty
Failure to deliver a return by the filing date (*FA 2003, Sch 10, paras 3, 4*)	Up to 3 months late – £100 Over 3 months late – £200 Over 12 months – tax related penalty not exceeding the tax chargeable

Notes

(1) *New filing date* – From 1 March 2019 the SDLT return and payment will have to be made within 14 days of the completion date (see **Chapter 11**).

(2) *Errors* – For penalties relating to errors or mistakes in SDLT and SDRT returns, see **Structure of penalties** above.

Stamp duty penalties – late stamping

(*SA 1891, s 15B*)

Document late by:	Penalty
Up to 12 months	10% of duty, capped at £300
12 to 24 months	20% of duty
More than 24 months	30% of duty

Notes

(1) *Effective for* – Instruments submitted for stamping from 1 October 2014.

(2) *Interest* – In addition to the above penalty for late filing, if the stamp duty was not paid on time, interest will also be due on the late payment at the official rate (see below).

(3) *Further information* – See https://www.gov.uk/stamp-duty-penalties-appeals-and-interest.

INTEREST RATES

Income tax, NICs, CGT and stamp duties

(*SA 1891, s 15A*; *FA 1999, s 110*; *FA 2003, ss 87, 89*; *SI 1986/1711, regs 13, 14*)

Period from	Rate payable %	Repayment Rate %
21 August 2018	3.25	0.50
21 Nov 2017 to 20 Aug 2018	3.00	0.50
23 Aug 2016 to 20 Nov 2017	2.75	0.50
29 Sept 2009 to 22 Aug 2016	3.0	0.50
24 Mar 2009 to 28 Sept 2009	2.5	0.00
27 Jan 2009 to 23 Mar 2009	3.5	0.00

Notes

(1) *Interest payable* – The interest regime in *FA 2009, ss 101–103* ('Late payment interest on sums to be paid by HMRC', 'Repayment interest on sums to be paid by HMRC' and 'Rates of interest') applies with effect from 31 October 2011, for the purposes of self-assessment payments and repayments (*SI 2011/701*).

(2) *Unified rates* – From 29 September 2009, the rates of interest charged and paid by HMRC for all the main taxes and duties are aligned (*SI 2009/2032*).

(3) *Stamp duty* – Interest on unpaid stamp duty applies from the end of 30 days after the date on which the document was executed until the duty is paid. The interest is rounded down to the nearest multiple of £5, and no interest is payable (or repayable) on amounts of less than £25.

(4) *SDLT* – Interest on unpaid SDLT runs from the end of 30 days after the 'relevant date' (generally the effective date of the transaction) until the tax is paid. The relevant dates for repayment of overpaid SDLT are from the date on which the payment is lodged with HMRC until the date when the repayment order is issued.

(5) *SDRT* – Interest on SDRT is charged from the 'accountable date' to the date of payment. If SDRT is overpaid then any repayment of SDRT will be made with interest from the date that it was paid. However, no interest is added to SDRT repayments under £25.

(6) *Earlier years* – Interest rates on late payments and repayments for earlier years can be found here: tinyurl.com/HMINTRS.

VAT, APD, IPT, customs duties, etc

Period from	Statutory interest %	Default interest %
21 August 2018	0.5	3.25
21 Nov 2017 to 20 Aug 2018	0.5	3.00

continued

Period from	Statutory interest %	Default interest %
23 Aug 2016 to 20 Nov 2017	0.5	2.75
29 Sept 2009 to 22 Aug 2016	0.5	3.00
24 Mar 2009 to 28 Sept 2009	0.0	2.5
27 Jan 2009 to 23 Mar 2009	0.0	3.50
6 Jan 2009 to 26 Jan 2009	1.0	4.50

Notes

(1) *Default interest* – This is charged where due on any amount of VAT which has been underdeclared or overclaimed, from the time the amount should have been paid to the time it is assessed (VAT Notice 700/43, para 1.2).

(2) *Payment of interest* – If all the VAT liable to interest is not paid within 30 days of a notification from HMRC, further interest is chargeable. Interest continues to be charged on a monthly basis until all the VAT liable to interest is paid (VAT Notice 700/43, para 2.8).

(3) *Statutory interest* – This is paid by HMRC, where errors have been made or if the mistake meant that the recipient had to wait an unreasonable time before receiving payment of an amount related to VAT.

(4) *Claiming interest* – A separate claim must be made for any interest from HMRC, as it is not paid automatically. The claim must be made not more than four years after the end of the applicable period to which it relates (*VATA 1994, s 78(11)*).

(5) *Further information* – For rates in earlier periods see: https://tinyurl.com/dfstint.

Companies – general

(*TMA 1970, ss 87, 87A, 109; SI 1998/3175, reg 7*)

Description	Interest runs from
Corporation tax	Due and payable date
Corporation tax payable in instalments	Date instalment is due to be paid
Overdue income tax deducted from certain payments	14 days after end of return period
Overdue tax on loans to participators of close companies	Due and payable date

Notes

(1) *Historical interest rates* – The rates of interest charged on underpaid quarterly instalments are found here: tinyurl.com/HMINTRS.

(2) *Surrender of tax refund within a group* – A group company which is due a tax refund for an accounting period may surrender it to another group member, if both companies give notice to HMRC. The effect is that the recipient company is generally treated as having paid the tax when the surrendering company paid it (or on the due and payable date for the surrendering company, if paid earlier) (*CTA 2010, ss 963, 964*).

Corporation tax not paid by instalments (CTSA)

From	Under-paid %	Over-paid %
21 August 2018	3.25	0.50
21 Nov 2017 to 20 Aug 2018	3.00	0.50
23 Aug 2016 to 20 Nov 2017	2.75	0.50
29 Sept 2009 to 22 Aug 2016	3.0	0.50
24 Mar 2009 to 28 Sept 2009	2.5	0.00
27 Jan 2009 to 23 Mar 2009	3.5	0.00
6 Jan 2009 to 26 Jan 2009	4.5	1.00

Corporation tax paid by instalments (Periods ending from 1 July 1999)

From	Under-paid %	Over-paid or early paid not by instalments %
13 August 2018	1.75	0.50
13 Nov 2017 to 12 Aug 2018	1.50	0.50
15 Aug 2016 to 12 Nov 2017	1.25	0.50
21 Sept 2009 to 14 Aug 2016	1.50	0.50
16 Mar 2009 to 20 Sept 2009	1.50	0.25
16 Feb 2009 to 15 Mar 2009	2.00	0.75
19 Jan 2009 to 15 Feb 2009	2.50	1.25
15 Dec 2008 to 18 Jan 2009	3.00	1.75

Corporation tax pay and file

From	Under-paid %	Over-paid %
21 August 2018	3.25	0.50
21 Nov 2017 to 20 Aug 2018	3.00	0.50
23 Aug 2016 to 21 Nov 2017	2.75	0.50
29 Sep 2009 to 22 Aug 2016	3.00	0.50
24 Mar 2009 to 28 Sept 2009	1.75	0.00
27 Jan 2009 to 23 Mar 2009	2.75	0.00

Corporation tax pre-pay and file

From	Under-paid %	Over-paid %
21 August 2018	3.25	0.50
21 Nov 2017 to 20 Aug 2018	3.00	0.50
23 Aug 2016 to 20 Nov 2017	2.75	0.50
29 Sept 2009 to 22 Aug 2016	3.00	0.50

continued

From	Under-paid %	Over-paid %
24 Mar 2009 to 28 Sept 2009	2.00	2.00
27 Jan 2009 to 23 Mar 2009	2.75	2.75
6 Jan 2009 to 26 Jan 2009	3.50	3.50

IHT

(*IHTA 1984, s 233*)

Interest period	Interest rate (%)	Interest on repayments (%)	Days
21 Aug 2018 to date	3.25	0.50	–
21 Nov 2017 to 20 Aug 2018	3.00	0.50	273
23 Aug 2016 to 20 Nov 2017	2.75	0.50	456
29 Sept 2009 to 22 Aug 2016	3.0	0.50	2520
24 Mar 2009 to 28 Sept 2009	0	0	189
27 Jan 2009 to 23 Mar 2009	1.0	1.0	56

Note

Earlier years – Interest rates for IHT for earlier years can be found here: https://tinyurl.com/IHTinsrts.

Interest on IHT paid in yearly instalments

(*IHTA 1984, ss 227, 234*)

Month of death	Due date	Interest starts from
January	31 July	1 August
February	31 August	1 September
March	30 September	1 October
April	31 October	1 November
May	30 November	1 December
June	31 December	1 January
July	31 January	1 February
August	28/29 February	1 March
September	31 March	1 April
October	30 April	1 May
November	31 May	1 June
December	30 June	1 July

Note

For IHT payable by ten equal yearly instalments, the first instalment is due six months from the end of the month in which the individual died. The second instalment is due on the same day 12 months after the first payment, and subsequent instalments are due on the same day each year. The preceding table shows how to work out the due date. Interest commences from the following day.

Discovery assessments

(TMA 1970, ss 29, 34, 36, FA 1998, Sch 18, para 46)

	Time limit for assessment to be raised on:	
Circumstances	***Individual***	***Company***
Loss of tax but no careless or deliberate behaviour by taxpayer	4 years from the end of the tax year (*TMA 1970, s 34*)	4 years from the end of the accounting period (6 years for periods ending before 1 April 2010) (*FA 1998, Sch 18, para 46(1)*)
Loss of tax due to careless behaviour of taxpayer or agent	6 years from the end of the tax year (*TMA 1970, s 36(1), (1B)*)	6 years from the end of the accounting period (*FA 1998, Sch 18, para 46(2), (2B)*)
Loss of tax due to deliberate behaviour by taxpayer or agent	20 years from the end of the tax year (*TMA 1970, s 36(1A), (1B)*)	20 years from end of the accounting period (*FA 1998, Sch 18, para 46(2A)(a), (2B)*)
Fraudulent or negligent conduct by taxpayer or in case of a company: someone acting on behalf of the company.	For periods before 6 April 2009: 20 years after 31 January following the tax year (*TMA 1970, s 36(1)*)	For periods ending on or before: 31 March 2010: 21 years after the end of the accounting period (*SI 2009/403*).

Notes

(1) *Scope* – Separate 'discovery' assessment provisions and time limits apply in certain circumstances, such as:

- Failure to provide information about a tax avoidance scheme (*TMA 1970, s 118(2); FA 1998, Sch 18, para 46(1), (2A)(b), (c)*);
- Failure to notify liability to tax (*TMA 1970, ss 34, 36(1A), (1B), 118(2)*); and
- Discovery assessment on personal representatives of a deceased person in respect of years/periods up to the date of death (*TMA 1970, s 40(1), (2)*).

(2) *Further information* – See HMRC's Compliance Handbook for tables of assessment time limits for income tax, capital gains tax (CH56100) and for corporation tax purposes (CH56200).

Data-gathering

(*FA 2011, Sch 23, Pt 4, paras 30, 31, 32*)

Offence	Penalty
Failure to comply with a data-holder notice	
• Initial penalty	• £300 fixed
• Continued failure	• Up to £60 per day on which the failure continues
• Continued failure for more than 30 days after £300 penalty imposed	• Up to £1000 per day if approved by First-tier tribunal
Concealing, destroying, disposing of documents required by data-holder notice	£300 fixed
Carelessly or deliberately providing inaccurate data or information when complying with a data-holder notice.	Up to £3,000

Notes

(1) *Data notice* – An HMRC officer may require a 'relevant data-holder' to provide 'relevant data'. Penalties can apply from 1 April 2012 to a failure by the data-holder to comply with a data-holder notice relevant to any period (ie before, on or after that date) (*FA 2011, Sch 23, para 65*).

(2) *Right of appeal* – Against the liability to, or amount of, the penalties listed in the table above (*FA 2011, Sch 23, para 36*).

(3) *Reasonable excuse* – The £300 fixed penalty, and the penalties of up to £60 per day, do not apply if there is a 'reasonable excuse' for the failure (*FA 2011, Sch 23, para 34*).

Information and inspection

(*FA 2008, s 113, Sch 36, paras 5, 39, 40, 40A, 50*)

Offence	Penalty
Failure to comply with an information notice	
• Initial failure	• £300 fixed
• Continued failure after £300 penalty imposed	• Up to £60 per day on which failure or obstruction continues
• Where notice is 'identity unknown' notice and failure continues for more than 30 days	• Up to £1000 per day if approved by First-tier tribunal
• Continued failure where significant tax is at risk	• Tax related penalty of amount to be decided by the Upper Tribunal
Concealing, destroying, disposing of documents required by information notice	£300 fixed

Offence	Penalty
Deliberately obstructing an inspection approved by the tribunal	£300 fixed
• Continued deliberate obstruction	£60 per day while obstruction continues
Carelessly or deliberately providing inaccurate information or documents	Up to £3,000 for each inaccuracy

Notes

(1) *Applies to* – Information notices issued or inspections carried out from 1 April 2009 for direct tax and VAT purposes (*SI 2009/404, art 2*), and for other taxes and duties generally from 1 April 2010 (*FA 2009, s 96, Sch 48; SI 2009/3054*).

(2) *Reasonable excuse* – Penalties for the above offences do not arise if there is a 'reasonable excuse' for the failure or obstruction (*FA 2008, Sch 36, para 45*).

Anti-avoidance Notices

(*FA 2014, ss 204–229, Sch 32*)

HMRC power to issue:	Right of appeal?
Accelerated Payment Notice (APN) when there is an open enquiry or appeal relating to taxpayer's affairs, HMRC think the taxpayer has achieved a tax advantage and he has: • used a DOTAS disclosed scheme; or • received a Follower Notice; or • received a GAAR counteraction notice.	No, but taxpayer or agent can make representations to HMRC within 90 days of issue of APN.
Follower Notice (FN) when there is an open enquiry into taxpayer's affairs or open appeal and: • taxpayer has obtained a tax advantage from use of particular tax arrangements; and • HMRC believe there is a final judicial ruling relevant to those arrangements; and • FN has not been issued to that taxpayer for those tax arrangements which has not been withdrawn.	No, but can make representations to HMRC within 90 days of issue of FN that conditions for issue have not been met.
GAAR counteraction notice after the issue has been considered by the GAAR advisory panel and an opinion has been given.	Yes.

Notes:

(1) *APN tax due* – Within 90 days of the issue of the APN or within 30 days of HMRC decision regarding representations, if later. Taxpayer can ask for time to pay. Note the tax amount demanded by the APN doesn't have to be proved to be due by a Court or Tribunal.

(2) *Penalties* – Where APN tax is paid late: 5% of tax due, when 5 months late: further 5% of tax due, when 11 months late further 5% of tax due. If the APN is withdrawn any tax and the penalties paid in respect of the APN will be repaid.

(3) *Interest* – No interest is charged for late payment of APN tax, but interest is charged if underlying tax liability is found to be due and is paid late.

(4) *FN action* – When FN is received taxpayer must either amend their own tax return as requested on FN and pay tax due, or carry on fighting the case and risk receiving an APN. If no action is taken a penalty of up to 50% of the tax due may be imposed.

(5) *Further information* – Detailed guidance on Follower Notices and Accelerated Payments: tinyurl.com/fnapns and HMRC Factsheets: CC/FS24, CC/FS25a, and CC/FS26.

Tax agents: dishonest conduct

(*FA 2012, s 223, Sch 38*)

HMRC power	Right of appeal?
Obtain working papers from tax agent voluntarily or under a file access notice. Penalties apply if the notice is not complied with.	No appeal against file access notice, but can appeal against the penalties
Issue a Conduct Notice which includes evidence of the dishonest conduct	Yes, within 30 days.
Charge civil penalties of between £5,000 and £50,000, plus interest on late paid penalties (*SI 2013/280*)	Yes, against the amount of the penalty but not against the imposition of the penalty.
Disclose details of the agent's dishonest conduct to the agent's professional body	No appeal.
'Name and shame' by publishing details of the tax agent on the HMRC website, where the agent has been charged a penalty of more than £5,000	No appeal.

Notes

(1) *Who these powers apply to* – A tax agent is an individual who, in the course of business, assists other persons (ie clients) with their tax affairs. These terms are defined widely (*FA 2012, Sch 38, para 2*).

(2) *What is dishonest conduct* – An individual engages in dishonest conduct if, in the course of acting as a tax agent, the individual does something dishonest with a view to bringing about a loss of tax revenue (*FA 2012, Sch 38, para 3*).

(3) *Commencement* – The powers listed above came into force on 1 April 2013 (*SI 2013/279*).

(4) *Further information* – For a summary of the dishonest conduct powers see https://www.gov.uk/dishonest-conduct-by-tax-agents. Technical guidance is found in the HMRC Compliance Handbook at paras CH180000-186220. A factsheet is available at: www.hmrc.gov.uk/agents/strategy/tafs.pdf.

DISCLOSURE OF TAX AVOIDANCE SCHEMES

(*FA 2004, Pt 7; SSAA 1992, s 132A; VATA 1994, Sch 11A*)

DOTAS form	Tax avoidance scheme form for:
AAG1	Notification by scheme promoter
AAG2	Notification by scheme user where offshore promoter does not notify
AAG3	Notification by scheme user where no promoter, or promoted by lawyer unable to make full notification
AAG4	Notification of scheme reference number by scheme user
AAG4(SDLT)	Notification of SDLT scheme reference number
AAG4(IHT)	Disclosure of IHT scheme reference number
AAG4(ATED)	Notification of ATED scheme reference number
AAG4(PRN)	Report of promoter reference number
AAG5	Continuation sheet
AAG6	Notification of scheme reference number
AAG7	Employers providing a scheme reference number to an employee
AAG8	Disclosure of details about employees in relation to avoidance schemes

Notes

(1) *What is notifiable* – A tax arrangement is broadly notifiable if it falls within a description ('hallmark') prescribed by regulations, and it enables (or might be expected to enable) any person to obtain a tax or NIC advantage, and it is such that the main benefit (or one of them) that might be expected to arise from the arrangement is the obtaining of that advantage (*FA 2004, s 306(1)*).

(2) *Who discloses* – The scheme 'promoter' (or in certain circumstances the scheme user, or someone who designs and implements their own 'in-house' scheme) must generally disclose the relevant scheme within a prescribed period, normally five days beginning with one of certain trigger events (*SI 2004/1864, reg 4*).

(3) *DOTAS number* – Following disclosure HMRC will issue a scheme reference number which users of the scheme must include on their returns or form AAG4. A promoter must also provide HMRC with periodic lists of persons to whom they become liable to issue a scheme reference number. The DOTAS number **does not** indicate the scheme has been approved by HMRC.

(4) *Penalties* – May be applied for failure to disclose a scheme, other compliance failures and failure by a scheme user to report a scheme reference number to HMRC. No penalty generally arises if there is a 'reasonable excuse' for the compliance failure.

(5) *Notifications* – Disclosures using the forms listed above can generally be made online, see: www.hmrc.gov.uk/aiu/forms-tax-schemes.htm. Paper forms should be submitted to:

HMRC Counter-Avoidance
DOTAS Taskforce S0483
Newcastle
NE98 1ZZ

(6) *Further information* – HMRC guidance can be found at: tinyurl.com/DOTASOV. Email enquiries about DOTAS: tinyurl.com/DOTASQ. Specific questions may be sent to the Anti-Avoidance Group: aag@hmrc.gov.uk.

Disclosure of tax avoidance schemes (VAT)

(*VATA 1994, Sch 11A, paras 10, 11*; *VAT (Disclosure of Avoidance Schemes) Regulations 2004, SI 2004/1929*; *Value Added Tax (Disclosure of Avoidance Schemes) (Designations) Order 2004, SI 2004/1933*; VAT Notice 700/8).

(1) *Failure to disclose* – A penalty can apply to the failure to disclose the following (within the statutory time limit in *SI 2004/1929, reg 2;* see VAT Notice 700/8, section 5):

- The use of a designated avoidance scheme, unless the taxable person has already notified HMRC; or
- A notifiable scheme that is not a designated scheme.

(2) *Amount of penalty* – The penalties for failing to comply with the notification requirements (unless there is a reasonable excuse for the failure) are as follows:

- Notifiable scheme that is not a designated scheme – £5,000; or
- Designated scheme – 15% of the VAT saving.

(3) *Making a notification* – Guidance on how to make notifications for VAT purposes is contained in VAT Notice 700/8 ('Disclosure of VAT avoidance schemes'). Notifications should be posted or emailed to the addresses given in the VAT Notice 700/8. Notifications should be posted to:

VAT Avoidance Disclosures Unit, Anti Avoidance Group (Intelligence):
HM Revenue & Customs
CTIAA Intelligence S0528
PO Box 194
Bootle
L69 9AA

or emailed to: vat.avoidance.disclosures.bst@hmrc.gsi.gov.uk.

(4) *Further information* – Detailed guidance on the disclosure of VAT avoidance schemes is contained in VAT Notice 700/8.

HMRC CLEARANCES

Non-Statutory Clearances

(a) *All taxpayers* – HMRC's non-statutory clearance service is available to businesses, individuals and their advisers.

(b) *What is covered* – The tax consequences of transactions for which there is material uncertainty and:

- that uncertainty arises due to interpretation of legislation within the last four Finance Acts; or
- if the point relates to legislation older than the last four Finance Acts there is material uncertainty around the tax outcome of a transaction.

(c) *When to make an application* – Clearance applications can be made both pre-transaction (where evidence is supplied that the transaction is genuinely contemplated) and post-transaction. But HMRC expect the taxpayer (or their tax adviser) to have first fully considered all the HMRC relevant guidance and/or contacted the HMRC helpline, if there is one.

(d) *Not suitable* – HMRC will not accept clearance applications that:

- ask whether the General Anti-Abuse rule (GAAR) applies;
- concern employment contracts (although applications may ask for confirmation on the tax treatment of salary sacrifice arrangements put in place);
- ask HMRC for tax or NICs planning advice;
- are minor variations of previous applications in respect of the same person and the same transaction;
- concern arrangements primarily to gain a tax or NICs advantage rather than being primarily commercially motivated;
- relate to a period for which HMRC have already opened an enquiry;
- relate to a period for which the 'enquiry window' has closed or the tax return is final;
- include questions not involving interpretations of tax law or its application (eg asset valuations or transfer pricing);
- concern tax consequences of executing trust deeds or settlements, and whether the 'settlements' anti-avoidance provisions apply (*ITTOIA 2005, Pt 5, Ch 5*).

(e) *Contents of application* – HMRC publish three checklists (Annexes A, B & C) which list the information required in support a clearance application. HMRC they ask that the numbering of the questions be adhered to in the clearance application. The checklists in should be used as follows:

A – for all transactions other than business investment relief and BRP;

B – for business investment relief for non-domiciled persons; and

C – for BPR for inheritance tax.

Those checklists can be downloaded here: tinyurl.com/nrpowa9.

(f) *Send it to* – Clearance applications from large business should be submitted to the Client Relationship Manager (CRM) assigned to that business. Those from other applicants should be sent to the address on the appropriate checklist.

(g) *Further information* – See HMRC's Other Non-Statutory Clearance Guidance Manual (ONSCG).

Valuation checks for capital gains

(a) *Checking service* – Any taxpayer can request a check of a valuation of assets or shares from HMRC in order to compute capital gains tax, or corporation tax on chargeable gains.

(b) *When to apply* – This service can be used after a disposal, or after a deemed disposal to support a claim that an asset has become of negligible value. But the application should be made well before the related tax return is submitted. HMRC states it will take at least two months to check a valuation. If HMRC have agreed a valuation, it will not challenge the subsequent use of it in a tax return.

(c) *Contents of application* – Form CG34 must be completed for each valuation which HMRC are asked to check, and submitted together with the information listed on the form. Copies of Form CG34 can be downloaded from: tinyurl.com/FMCG35.

(d) *Where to send it* – Completed forms CG34 plus related documents should be submitted by post to the appropriate HMRC office shown on the form.

Statutory Clearances

Clearance applications may be submitted to HMRC by letter, fax or email, including in respect of the following:

Clearance category	Statutory reference
Demergers*	*CTA 2010, s 1091*
Demergers: Chargeable payments*	*CTA 2010, s 1092*
Purchase of own shares*	*CTA 2010, s 1044*
EIS shares: acquisition by new company*	*ITA 2007, s 247(1)(f)*
Employee share schemes	*ITEPA 2003, Schs 2, 3 & 4*
Transactions in securities*	*ITA 2007, s 701; CTA 2010, s 748*
Share exchanges*	*TCGA 1992, s 138(1)*
Share exchanges: continuity of SEIS relief*	*ITA 2007, s 257HB(1)(f)*
Reconstructions involving the transfer of a business*	*TCGA 1992, s 139(5)*
Transfer or division of a UK business between EU member states*	*TCGA 1992, s 140B*
Transfer or division of non-UK business by a UK company to a company resident in another EU member state	*TCGA 1992, s 140D*
Company reorganisations involving intangible assets*	*CTA 2009, s 831*
Loan relationships: transfers*	*CTA 2009, s 427*
Loan relationships: mergers*	*CTA 2009, s 437*
Derivative contracts: transfers*	*CTA 2009, s 677*
Derivative contracts: mergers*	*CTA 2009, s 686*
Targeted Anti Avoidance Rule 3 (Capital Gains)*	*TCGA 1992, ss 184G–184H*

Clearance category	Statutory reference
Company migrations	*TMA 1970, s 109B*
Insurance companies: Transfer of long-term business	*FA 2012, s 133*
Insurance companies: Transitional rules	*FA 2012, Sch 17, para 18*
Assignment of lease at undervalue*	*ITTOIA 2005, s 300; CTA 2009, s 237*
Transactions in land*	*ITA 2007, s 770; CTA 2010, s 831, CTA 2009, s 237, ITTOIA 2005, s 300*
Offshore funds:	*SI 2009/3001, reg 54(2)*
(a) Reporting fund status	*SI 2009/3001, reg 78*
(b) Equivalence and genuine diversity of ownership requirements	
Stamp Duty Adjudication	*SA 1891, s 12A*

* See note (2) below.

(1) *Submission of applications* – A list of HMRC contact details in respect of each category of statutory clearance application can be found here: tinyurl.com/SCCNTAD.

(2) *Clearance applications* under more than one of the provisions marked * above may be submitted to HMRC as a single application, by email or letter, as follows:

HMRC Clearance and Counteraction Team
BAI Clearance
HMRC
BX9 1JL

Email: reconstructions@hmrc.gsi.gov.uk

Mark the application 'Market sensitive' or 'Non-market sensitive'.

For general enquiries to the unit: Tel 03000 589 004

Scottish and Welsh Taxes

SCOTTISH INCOME TAX (SIT)

(ITA 2007, ss 18, 19; FA 2004, ss 192, 192A; SI 2015/1810)

Non-savings and non-dividend income £	**Effective rates for band** %	**Tax in band** £	**Cumulative tax** £
2019/20			
0–2,049	19	389.31	389.31
2,050–12,444	20	2,079.00	2,468.31
12,445–30,930	21	3,882.06	6,350.37
30,931–150,000	41	48,818.70	55,169.07
Over 150,000	46	–	–
2018/19			
0–2,000	19	380.00	380.00
2,001–12,150	20	2,030.00	2,410.00
12,151–31,580	21	4,080.30	6,490.30
31,581–150,000	41	48,552.20	55,042.50
Over 150,000	46	–	–
2017/18			
0–31,500	20	6,300.00	6,300.00
31,501–150,000	40	47,400.00	53,700.00
Over 150,000	45	–	–
2016/17 (SRIT)			
0–32,000	20	6,400.00	6,400.00
32,001–150,000	40	47,200.00	53,600.00
Over 150,000	45	–	–

Notes

(1) *Scottish income tax (SIT)* – This applies from 6 April 2017 to 'other income' (see note 3) received by Scottish taxpayers, and all revenues from SIT flow to the Scottish Government.

(2) *Proposed* – The SIT rates and bands for 2019/20 were presented to the Scottish Parliament on 12 December 2018 (*Scottish Budget: 2019–20*).

(3) *SIT rates and bands apply to* – Income which is not savings income or dividend income, so broadly earned income, pensions, income from self-employed trades and property businesses. The tax bands which used to determine the rates of CGT

or the personal savings allowance are those which apply in the rest of the UK (see **Chapter 1**).

(4) *Pension relief* – Tax relief at source is deducted at 20% for all Scottish taxpayers on pension contributions from 6 April 2018, and that tax is reclaimed by the pension fund. Scottish taxpayers with a higher marginal tax rate (21% or above) must claim additional tax relief by contacting HMRC or through their SA tax return (*FA 2004, s 192*).

(5) *Marriage allowance* – This transferred portion of personal allowance can only be received by taxpayers who are taxed at rates no higher than the basic rate (20%) or the Scottish intermediate rate (21%). Thus Scottish taxpayers can continue to qualify for the marriage allowance from 6 April 2018 onwards even if they are taxed at 21%, see **Chapter 1** (*ITA 2007, s 55B(2)*).

(6) *SIT also affects* – The following income tax charges and reliefs are affected by the rate of SIT paid by Scottish taxpayers:

   (a) lump sum payments of the state retirement pension;

   (b) deficiency relief in respect of a life insurance policy (*ITTOIA 2005, s 539*);

   (c) annual allowance charge under *FA 2004, s 227* (see **Chapter 5**);

   (d) tax relief on Gift Aid donations.

(7) *Adminstered by* – SIT is collected through PAYE and self-assessment, adminstered by HMRC not by Revenue Scotland.

(8) *Scottish rate of income tax (SRIT)* – Applied for 2016/17 only. SRIT replaced 10% points of income tax in each rate band applicable to such 'other income' (see note 3) received by Scottish taxpayers, and the revenues from SRIT flowed to the Scottish Government. As the SRIT was set at 10% for 2016/17 there was no effect on taxpayers for 2016/17.

(9) *Further information* – Guidance on Scottish taxpayer status: http://tinyurl.com/GSTPS, guidance on scope of SRIT: https://www.gov.uk/scottish-rate-income-tax.

LAND AND BUILDINGS TRANSACTION TAX

LBTT on freehold property in Scotland

(*Land and Buildings Transaction Tax (Scotland) Act 2013*)

Wholly residential property

Purchase price	**Main Rate %**	**ADS + main rate %**	**ADS + main rate %**
Sales completed from:	1 April 2015	1 April 2016	25 January 2019
Up to £145,000	0	3	4
£145,001–£250,000	2	5	6
£250,001–£325,000	5	8	9
£325,001–£750,000	10	13	14
Over £750,000	12	15	16

Notes

(1) *Applies to* – Transactions involving property located in Scotland from 1 April 2015. There are transitional rules for contracts entered into on or before 1 May 2012 to determine if SDLT or LBTT applies.

(2) *First-time buyers* – From 30 June 2018 where all the purchasers have never owned an interest in a residential property, LBTT on the first £175,000 is charged at 0% with no upper limit on the value of the property (*SSI 2018/221*).

(3) *Additional Dwelling Supplement (ADS)* – Applies to the whole purchase price where an additional residential property is purchased for more than £40,000. The ADS may apply to mixed-use properties where the non-residential rates apply. The conditions for which the ADS applies are not identical to those for which the SDLT supplement applies (see **Chapter 11**).

(4) *Calculation of duty* – The LBTT is calculated as a percentage of the amount of relevant consideration which lies within each appropriate band.

(5) *Payable by* – The purchaser is liable to pay the LBTT within 30 calendar days of the effective date of the transaction (normally the settlement date). Registers of Scotland will not register the buyer's title to the property until the LBTT return has been submitted and the tax has been paid.

(6) *Mixed use property* – Where the property acquired in a single transaction consists of both residential and non-residential property, the LBTT rates for non-residential property apply to the whole transaction (see below).

(7) *No penal rate* – There is no higher rate of LBTT equivalent to the penal 15% rate of SDLT which may apply where a residential property is purchased by non-natural person (see **Chapter 11**), but the ATED can apply to Scottish properties (see **Chapter 13**).

(8) *Proposed* – The increase in the ADS rate is to take effect from 25 January 2019, but it won't apply if the contract for a transaction was entered into prior to 12 December 2018 (*Scottish Budget: 2019–20*).

(9) *Further information* – See Revenue Scotland: www.revenue.scot/land-buildings-transaction-tax.

Non-residential

Purchase price or lease premium From 1 April 2015	**Rate %**	**Purchase price or lease premium** From 25 Jan 2019	**Rate %**	**Leases NPV of rents** From 1 April 2015	**Rate %**
Up to £150,000	0	Up to £150,000	0	£150,000	0
£150,001 to £350,000	3	£150,001 to £250,000	1	over £150,000	1
Over £350,000	4.5	Over £250,000	5		

Notes

(1) *Calculation* – Where the chargeable consideration includes rent, LBTT is payable on the lease premium and on the 'net present value' (NPV) of the rent payable. The LBTT chargeable on a lease is generally subject to a three-yearly regular review on

assignation or termination of the lease. Online LBTT calculators are available on the Revenue Scotland website in respect of both new leases and freehold transactions: (https://www.revenue.scot/land-buildings-transaction-tax/tax-calculators).

(2) *Annual rent* – Where the annual rent for the lease of non-residential property amounts to £1,000 or more, the 0% LBTT band is unavailable in respect of any lease premium (*LBTT(S)A 2013, Sch 9*).

(3) *Licence to occupy* – Such licences for retail shops are subject to LBTT.

(4) *Residential leases* – No LBTT is charged on a residential lease unless the term exceeds 175 years.

(5) *Exemptions* – There are a large number of exemptions and reliefs from LBTT such as for transactions with no chargeable consideration, sale and leaseback arrangements, incorporation of LLPs, for charities and crofting community right to buy (*LBTT(S)A 2013, Schs 3–16*).

(6) *Proposed* – The change in LBTT rates and bands are to take effect from 25 January 2019, but they won't apply if the contract for a transaction was entered into prior to 12 December 2018 (*Scottish Budget: 2019–20*).

SCOTTISH LANDFILL TAX (SLfT)

(*Landfill Tax (Scotland) Act 2014; SSI 2018/87*)

Disposals made or treated as made in year beginning:	Standard rate per tonne £	Lower rate per tonne £	Maximum credit %
1 April 2020	95.00	3.00	5.6
1 April 2019	91.35	2.90	5.6
1 April 2018	88.95	2.80	5.6
1 April 2017	86.10	2.70	5.6
1 April 2016	84.40	2.65	5.6
1 April 2015	82.60	2.60	5.1

Notes

(1) *Commencement* – Scottish landfill tax applies to disposals of waste in licensed sites in Scotland made on and after 1 April 2015.

(2) *Applies to* – Waste disposals by way of landfill at a licensed site, unless specifically exempted. Landfill site operators are taxed on disposals of waste by reference to the weight and type of waste concerned. Unlike Landfill tax, SLfT also applies to illegal disposals of waste.

(3) *Which rate* – The lower rate of landfill tax relates to inactive (or inert) wastes, as listed in the the *Scottish Landfill Tax (Qualifying Material) Order 2015, SSI 2015/45*. The standard rate applies to all other taxable waste.

(4) *Further information* – see Revenue Scotland www.revenue.scot/scottish-landfill-tax.

(5) *Proposals* – Rates for periods from 1 April 2019 onwards are proposed (*Scottish Budget: 2019/20*).

WELSH RATE OF INCOME TAX (WRIT)

(*ITA 2007, s 6B; SI 2018/1327*)

Rates of income tax payable by Welsh taxpayer on:			2019/20
Savings income:	**Dividend income:**	**Other income: (see note 2)**	**WRIT = 10%**
Savings rates	Dividend rates	Up to £37,500	10% + WRIT
see **Chapter 1**	see **Chapter 1**	£37,501–150,000	30% + WRIT
		Over £150,000	35% + WRIT

Notes

(1) *Commencement* – Welsh rate of income tax (WRIT) replaces 10% points of income tax in each rate band applicable to 'other income' (see note 2) received by Welsh taxpayers on and after 6 April 2019.

(2) *Applies to* – WRIT applies to income which is not savings or dividends. It will also affect:

- (a) the 'marriage allowance' which is 10% of the personal allowance transferred between married couples on election (see **Chapter 1**);
- (b) income tax relief at source on pension contributions, and the income tax reclaimed by the pension fund;
- (c) deficiency relief in respect of a life insurance policy (*ITTOIA 2005, s 539*);
- (d) tax on state pension lump sum;
- (e) tax relief on Gift Aid donations, but not the basic rate tax reclaimed by the charity under *ITA 2007, s 520*.

(3) *Adminstered by* – WRIT is collected through PAYE and self-assessment, adminstered by HMRC not by the Welsh Revenue Authority.

(5) *Further information* – Guidance on Welsh taxpayer status: tinyurl.com/Wlshtpg.

LAND TRANSACTION TAX

LTT on freehold property in Wales

(*SI 2018/128, SI 2018/126, SI 2018/125*)

Wholly residential property purchase price	Main Rate %	Higher rates %	Non-residential & mixed property purchase price	Rate %
Up to £180,000	0	3.0	Up to £150,000	0
£180,001–£250,000	3.5	6.5	£150,001 to £250,000	1
£250,001–£400,000	5.0	8.0	£250,000–£1m	5
£400,001–£750,000	7.5	10.5	Over £1m	6
£750,001–£1,500,000	10.0	13.0		
Over £1,500,000	12.0	15.0		

Notes

(1) *Applies to* – Transactions involving property located in Wales from 1 April 2018.

(2) *Higher Rates* – Where an individual or connected individuals purchase an additional residential property, or a company purchases any residential property, for £40,000 or more, the higher rates of LTT apply to the whole purchase price. The conditions under which the LTT higher rates apply are not identical to those under which the SDLT supplement applies (see **Chapter 11**).

(3) *Calculation of duty* – The LTT is calculated as a percentage of the amount of relevant consideration which lies within each appropriate band, see https://beta.gov.wales/land-transaction-tax-calculator.

(4) *Payable by* – The purchaser is liable to pay the LTT within 30 calendar days of the effective date of the transaction.

(5) *Administered by* – Welsh Revenue Authority (WRA) https://beta.gov.wales/welsh-revenue-authority.

Non-residential lease rentals

(*SI 2018/133*)

NPV of rents threshold	Rate %
Up to £150,000	0
£150,000 to £2m	1
Over £2m	2

Notes

(1) *Applies to* – Leases of commercial property located in Wales entered into on or after 1 April 2018.

(2) *Specified rent* – If the annual rent is more than £9,000 (inc VAT), the 0–£150,000 band is removed for the lease premium, so that the first amount £250,000 of the premium falls within the 1% band.

(3) *Calculation of duty* – Use WRA calculator to work out the duty due: https://beta.gov.wales/land-transaction-tax-calculator.

WELSH LANDFILL DISPOSALS TAX (LDT)

(*Landfill Disposals Tax (Wales) Act 2017*)

Disposals made or treated as made in year beginning:	Standard rate per tonne £	Lower rate per tonne £	Unauthorised disposals per tonne £
1 April 2019	92.10	2.90	137.55
1 April 2018	88.95	2.80	133.45

Notes

(1) *Commencement* – Landfill disposals tax applies to disposals of waste in licensed sites in Wales made on and after 1 April 2018.

(2) *Applies to* – Waste disposals by way of landfill at a licensed site, unless specifically exempted. Landfill site operators are taxed on disposals of waste by reference to the weight and type of waste concerned.

(3) *Further information* – see http://tinyurl.com/WLftgd.

DISTRIBUTION OF INTESTATE ESTATES

Prior rights of surviving spouse or civil partner in Scotland: threshold limits

(Succession (Scotland) Act 1964, ss 8, 9; Prior Rights of Surviving Spouse And Civil Partner (Scotland) Order 2011, SSI 2011/436)

Prior rights	**From 1 February 2013 £**	**1 June 2005 to 31 Jan 2013 £**
Interest of spouse in dwelling house where surviving spouse or civil partner lived	473,000	300,000
Entitlement to furniture and plenishings in that dwelling house	29,000	24,000
Entitlement out of the estate:		
If the deceased left children	50,000	42,000
If there are no children	89,000	75,000

Notes

(1) *General* – The prior rights of a surviving spouse or civil partner take precedence over all other rights of succession in a fully or partially intestate estate.

(2) *Further information* – For a table of prior rights for previous periods, see HMRC's Inheritance Tax Manual at IHTM12212.

Scotland – Legal rights*

Survivors	**Surviving spouse or civil partner**	**Children (Legitim)**	**Dead's part**
Spouse or civil partner and children	One-third	One-third	One-third
Spouse or civil partner but no children	One-half	None	One-half
Children but no spouse or civil partner	None	One-half	One-half
No spouse, civil partner or children	None	None	Whole moveable estate

* *Source* – HMRC's Inheritance Tax Manual at IHTM12221.

Notes

(1) *General* – Legal rights apply whether the estate is testate or intestate, and can be claimed only from the moveable estate of the deceased person. A surviving spouse or civil partner is entitled to both prior rights and legal rights.

(2) *Dead's part* – The balance of the estate which the deceased was free to dispose of by will, or which passes under the laws of intestacy, is called the dead's part.

(3) *Further guidance* – See HMRC's Inheritance Tax Manual at IHTM12141-12156, and the Scottish Parliament briefing: http://tinyurl.com/IntSctEst.

Remainder of estate

(*Succession (Scotland) Act 1964, s 2*)

After the prior and legal rights have been satisfied, the rest of the estate broadly devolves in the following order of succession:

- children;
- parents and brothers or sisters (and children) – one-half each;
- brother and sisters (and children) if no surviving parents;
- parents if no surviving brothers or sisters;
- spouse or civil partner;
- uncles and aunts;
- grandparents;
- brothers or sisters of grandparents;
- other ancestors (eg great grandparents);
- The Crown.

19

International issues

DIVERTED PROFITS TAX (DPT)

(*FA 2015, Pt 3*)

Period	Main rate	Special rate
From 1 April 2015	25%	55%

Notes

(1) *Objective* – To counteract contrived arrangements by international groups of companies to avoid paying corporation tax on profits generated by activities carried on in the UK.

(2) *Applies to* – Taxable diverted profits arising on and after 1 April 2015. Profits of accounting periods that straddle that date are apportioned (*FA 2015, ss 88–91*).

(3) *Payable by* – UK resident companies that enter into transactions which lack economic substance, and non-resident companies carrying on a trade through a permanent establishment in the UK with UK-related sales revenue of at least £10 million or UK-related expenses of at least £1 million for the accounting period. There are exceptions for small and medium sized companies, and provisions to catch companies that avoid a UK taxable presence (*FA 2015, ss 86, 87*).

(4) *Paid when* – HMRC issue a charging notice to the company specifying the amount of taxable diverted profits (*FA 2015, ss 79(1), 95*).

(5) *Special rate* – This applies to diverted ring fence profits from the oil and gas industry (*FA 2015, s 79(3)*).

(6) *Requirement to notify* – A company which is potentially liable to pay DPT must notify HMRC in writing within three months of the end of the accounting period to which the DPT charge relates. There is no requirement to notify if it is reasonable to conclude no charge to DPT will arise in the period, or HMRC has confirmed the company does not have to notify (*FA 2015, s 92*).

(7) *Off-set* – The DPT is not a deduction for income tax or corporation tax purposes, but the DPT paid may be given as a credit against certain UK or foreign taxes in defined circumstances (*FA 2015, s 100*).

(8) *Further information* – HMRC technical note: tinyurl.com/ppxyusp and HMRC Compliance Manual CH155481.

FOREIGN EXCHANGE RATES

Average for the year to 31 December 2017		Country/Currency		Average for the year to 31 March 2018	
Sterling value of Currency Unit £	Currency Units per £1	Country	Unit of Currency	Sterling value of Currency Unit £	Currency Units per £1
0.8725	1.14615	European Community	Euro	0.8793	1.137292
0.2123	4.7113	Abu Dhabi	Dirham	0.2063	4.8472
0.0065	153.8706	Albania	Lek	0.0066	151.8556
0.0071	141.8388	Algeria	Dinar	0.0068	147.293
0.0047	212.7512	Angola	Readj Kwanza	0.0044	228.3987
0.2888	3.462775	Antigua	E Caribbean Dollar	0.2807	3.562625
0.0474	21.10178	Argentina	Peso	0.0438	22.83511
0.0016	618.4244	Armenia	Dram	0.0016	635.0502
0.4355	2.296008	Aruba	Florin	0.4233	2.362217
0.5976	1.6733	Australia	Dollar	0.5879	1.701108
0.4528	2.208425	Azerbaijan	New Manat	0.4472	2.236083
0.7796	1.282692	Bahamas	Dollar	0.7578	1.319675
2.0672	0.48375	Bahrain	Dinar	2.0093	0.497683
0.0096	103.9334	Bangladesh	Taka	0.0092	108.2459
0.3898	2.565383	Barbados	Dollar	0.3789	2.63935
0.3883	2.575008	Belarus	Rouble	0.3795	2.635217
0.3896	2.5669	Belize	Dollar	0.3789	2.638883
0.0013	751.841	Benin	CFA Franc	0.0013	746.0235
0.7796	1.282692	Bermuda	Dollar (US)	0.7578	1.319675
0.0119	83.8606	Bhutan	Ngultrum	0.0117	85.16727
0.1127	8.871158	Bolivia	Boliviano	0.1097	9.118975

continued

Average for the year to 31 December 2017		Country/Currency		Average for the year to 31 March 2018	
Sterling value of Currency Unit £	Currency Units per £1	Country	Unit of Currency	Sterling value of Currency Unit £	Currency Units per £1
0.4461	2.24175	Bosnia-Herzegovinia	Marka	0.4496	2.2244
0.0754	13.26578	Botswana	Pula	0.0749	13.34494
0.2444	4.091392	Brazil	Real	0.2368	4.223092
0.5624	1.778117	Brunei	Dollar	0.5572	1.794625
0.446	2.241908	Bulgaria	Lev	0.4495	2.224542
0.0013	751.841	Burkina Faso	CFA Franc	0.0013	746.0235
0.0005	2206.899	Burundi	Franc	0.0004	2294.578
0.0002	5190.532	Cambodia	Riel	0.0002	5336.462
0.0013	751.841	Cameroon Republic	CFA Franc	0.0013	746.0235
0.6012	1.663342	Canada	Dollar	0.591	1.692158
0.0079	126.7711	Cape Verde Islands	Escudo	0.0079	125.8519
0.9509	1.051642	Cayman Islands	Dollar	0.9241	1.082142
0.0013	751.841	Central African	CFA Franc	0.0013	746.0235
0.0013	751.841	Chad	CFA Franc	0.0013	746.0235
0.0012	833.3212	Chile	Peso	0.0012	839.9378
0.115	8.694692	China	Yuan	0.1137	8.7935
0.0003	3780.096	Colombia	Peso	0.0003	3868.971
0.0018	563.8801	Comoros	Franc	0.0018	559.5168
0.0013	751.841	Congo (Brazaville)	CFA Franc	0.0013	746.0235
0.0005	1837.751	Congo (DemRep)	Congo Fr	0.0005	2010.992
0.0014	726.8113	Costa Rica	Colon	0.0013	752.4613
0.0013	751.841	Cote d'Ivoire	CFA Franc	0.0013	746.0235
0.1169	8.554467	Croatia	Kuna	0.1179	8.478242
0.7796	1.282692	Cuba	Peso	0.7578	1.319675

Average for the year to 31 December 2017		Country/Currency		Average for the year to 31 March 2018	
Sterling value of Currency Unit £	**Currency Units per £1**	**Country**	**Unit of Currency**	**Sterling value of Currency Unit £**	**Currency Units per £1**
0.033	30.30255	Czech Republic	Koruna	0.0338	29.61736
0.1173	8.526183	Denmark	Krone	0.1182	8.463283
0.0044	227.9536	Djibouti	Franc	0.0043	234.5269
0.2888	3.462775	Dominica	E Caribbean Dollar	0.2807	3.562625
0.0165	60.62481	Dominican Republic	Peso	0.0159	63.08064
0.2123	4.7113	Dubai	Dirham	0.2063	4.8472
0.7796	1.282692	Ecuador	Dollar	0.7578	1.319675
0.0434	23.02096	Egypt	Pound	0.0424	23.55929
0.0891	11.21861	El Salvador	Colon	0.0866	11.54444
0.0013	751.841	Equatorial Guinea	CFA Franc	0.0013	746.0235
0.052	19.23639	Eritrea	Nakfa	0.0505	19.79056
0.0329	30.40442	Ethiopia	Birr	0.0304	32.89525
0.3786	2.641267	Fiji Islands	Dollar	0.371	2.695158
0.0073	136.7713	Fr. Polynesia	CFP Franc	0.0074	135.7138
0.0013	751.841	Gabon	CFA Franc	0.0013	746.0235
0.0171	58.40342	Gambia	Dalasi	0.0163	61.42258
0.3095	3.230683	Georgia	Lari	0.3065	3.262392
0.1751	5.711967	Ghana	Cedi	0.1685	5.93355
0.2888	3.462775	Grenada	E Caribbean Dollar	0.2807	3.562625
0.1059	9.4389	Guatemala	Quetzal	0.1034	9.67145
0.0013	751.841	Guinea Bissau	CFA Franc	0.0013	746.0235

continued

Average for the year to 31 December 2017		Country/Currency		Average for the year to 31 March 2018	
Sterling value of Currency Unit £	**Currency Units per £1**	**Country**	**Unit of Currency**	**Sterling value of Currency Unit £**	**Currency Units per £1**
0.0001	11730	Guinea Republic	Franc	0.0001	11950.68
0.0038	266.3023	Guyana	Dollar	0.0037	273.9248
0.0119	83.77875	Haiti	Gourde	0.0118	85.08042
0.0332	30.10485	Honduras	Lempira	0.0323	30.98735
0.1001	9.989125	Hong Kong	Dollar	0.0971	10.29557
0.0028	353.9522	Hungary	Forint	0.0028	351.9797
0.0072	138.3089	Iceland	Krona	0.0072	138.9647
0.0119	83.8606	India	Rupee	0.0117	85.16727
0.0001	17144.69	Indonesia	Rupiah	0.0001	17681.33
0.0007	1516.902	Iraq	Dinar	0.0006	1561.088
0.215	4.650458	Israel	Shekel	0.2138	4.676292
0.0061	164.7465	Jamaica	Dollar	0.0059	168.3024
0.007	143.8376	Japan	Yen	0.0068	146.2893
1.0995	0.909492	Jordan	Dinar	1.0688	0.935658
0.0024	418.3503	Kazakhstan	Tenge	0.0023	429.5978
0.0075	132.6116	Kenya	Schilling	0.0073	136.0633
2.5677	0.389458	Kuwait	Dinar	2.5062	0.399008
0.0113	88.31848	Kyrgyz Republic	Som	0.011	90.69014
0.0001	10584.88	Lao People's Dem Rep	Kip	0.0001	10924.06
0.0005	1936.11	Lebanon	Pound	0.0005	1993.56
0.0588	17.01156	Lesotho	Loti	0.0588	17.00989
0.7796	1.282692	Liberia	Dollar (US)	0.7578	1.319675
0.5583	1.791	Libya	Dinar	0.5507	1.815833

Average for the year to 31 December 2017		Country/Currency		Average for the year to 31 March 2018	
Sterling value of Currency Unit £	Currency Units per £1	Country	Unit of Currency	Sterling value of Currency Unit £	Currency Units per £1
0.0972	10.28686	Macao	Pataca	0.0943	10.60368
0.0142	70.57449	Macedonia	Denar	0.0143	70.02866
0.0002	4014.999	Madagascar	Malagasy Ariary	0.0002	4119.578
0.0011	930.329	Malawi	Kwacha	0.001	957.419
0.1805	5.540642	Malaysia	Ringgit	0.1807	5.533767
0.0505	19.79605	Maldive Islands	Rufiyaa	0.0491	20.36688
0.0013	751.841	Mali Republic	CFA Franc	0.0013	746.0235
0.0022	459.3181	Mauritania	Ouguiya	0.0021	470.8156
0.0225	44.45937	Mauritius	Rupee	0.0223	44.8052
0.0411	24.30927	Mexico	Mexican Peso	0.0411	24.35593
0.0418	23.91861	Moldova	Leu	0.0425	23.55028
0.0003	3134.001	Mongolia	Tugrik	0.0003	3200.468
0.2888	3.462775	Montserrat	E Caribbean Dollar	0.2807	3.562625
0.08	12.49882	Morocco	Dirham	0.0795	12.57965
0.0121	82.46754	Mozambique	Metical	0.0123	81.16754
0.0006	1750.151	Myanmar	Kyat	0.0006	1793.33
0.0075	134.178	Nepal	Rupee	0.0073	136.2688
0.0073	136.7713	New Caledonia	CFP Franc	0.0074	135.7138
0.5558	1.799358	New Zealand	Dollar	0.5431	1.841325
0.026	38.41891	Nicaragua	Gold Cordoba	0.025	40.02141
0.0013	751.841	Niger Republic	CFA Franc	0.0013	746.0235
0.0024	422.0334	Nigeria	Naira	0.0022	449.3709

continued

Average for the year to 31 December 2017		Country/Currency		Average for the year to 31 March 2018	
Sterling value of Currency Unit £	**Currency Units per £1**	**Country**	**Unit of Currency**	**Sterling value of Currency Unit £**	**Currency Units per £1**
0.0943	10.60359	Norway	Norwegian Krone	0.0931	10.74359
2.0253	0.493758	Oman	Rial	1.9686	0.507983
0.0074	134.7409	Pakistan	Rupee	0.0071	140.5867
0.7796	1.282692	Panama	Balboa	0.7578	1.319675
0.2448	4.084467	Papua New Guinea	Kina	0.2369	4.220958
0.0001	7229.707	Paraguay	Guarani	0.0001	7398.515
0.2384	4.1948	Peru	New Sol	0.2332	4.287767
0.0155	64.70133	Philippines	Peso	0.0149	66.97383
0.2042	4.896733	Poland	Zloty	0.2082	4.803675
0.2139	4.674633	Qatar	Riyal	0.2079	4.809233
0.1912	5.2299	Romania	New Leu	0.1912	5.230075
0.0134	74.80083	Russia	Rouble	0.0131	76.26167
0.0009	1072.779	Rwanda	Franc	0.0009	1114.912
0	28151.88	Saotome & Principe	Dobra	0	27909.51
0.2079	4.810008	Saudi Arabia	Riyal	0.2021	4.94855
0.0013	751.841	Senegal	CFA Franc	0.0013	746.0235
0.0072	139.5633	Serbia	Dinar	0.0073	137.005
0.0575	17.40575	Seychelles	Rupee	0.0555	18.00575
0.0001	9467.216	Sierra Leone	Leone	0.0001	10019.49
0.5626	1.777417	Singapore	Dollar	0.5574	1.793925
0.1003	9.966892	Soloman Islands	Dollar	0.0976	10.24402
0.0013	747.5013	Somali Republic	Schilling	0.0013	774.1179
0.0588	17.01156	South Africa	Rand	0.0588	17.00989
0.0007	1456.988	South Korea	Won	0.0007	1468.298

Average for the year to 31 December 2017		Country/Currency		Average for the year to 31 March 2018	
Sterling value of Currency Unit £	**Currency Units per £1**	**Country**	**Unit of Currency**	**Sterling value of Currency Unit £**	**Currency Units per £1**
0.0051	195.3017	Sri Lanka	Rupee	0.0049	202.2708
0.2888	3.462775	St Kitts & Nevis	E Caribbean Dollar	0.2807	3.562625
0.2888	3.462775	St Lucia	E Caribbean Dollar	0.2807	3.562625
0.2888	3.462775	St Vincent	E Caribbean Dollar	0.2807	3.562625
0.1177	8.493742	Sudan Republic	Pound	0.0982	10.18029
0.1042	9.594867	Surinam	Dollar	0.1013	9.870767
0.0588	17.01156	Swaziland	Lilangeni	0.0588	17.00989
0.0908	11.01259	Sweden	Krona	0.0906	11.03676
0.7917	1.263125	Switzerland	Franc	0.7807	1.280883
0.0255	39.18284	Taiwan	Dollar	0.0252	39.66451
0.0003	2865.612	Tanzania	Schilling	0.0003	2959.31
0.0229	43.75608	Thailand	Baht	0.0228	43.85441
0.0013	751.841	Togo Republic	CFA Franc	0.0013	746.0235
0.5976	1.6733	Tonga Islands	Pa'anga (AUS)	0.5879	1.701108
0.1154	8.662525	Trinidad/Tobago	Dollar	0.1121	8.9183
0.3262	3.065167	Tunisia	Dinar	0.313	3.194825
0.2154	4.643	Turkey	Turkish Lira	0.2074	4.82165
0.2225	4.493717	Turkmenistan	New Manat	0.2162	4.624408
0.2123	4.7113	UAE	Dirham	0.2063	4.8472
0.0002	4621.574	Uganda	Schilling	0.0002	4771.053

continued

Average for the year to 31 December 2017		Country/Currency		Average for the year to 31 March 2018	
Sterling value of Currency Unit £	**Currency Units per £1**	**Country**	**Unit of Currency**	**Sterling value of Currency Unit £**	**Currency Units per £1**
0.0295	33.94875	Ukraine	Hryvnia	0.0284	35.26375
0.0272	36.79754	Uruguay	Peso	0.0264	37.83171
0.7796	1.282692	USA	Dollar	0.7578	1.319675
0.0002	6171.073	Uzbekistan	Sum	0.0001	7987.389
0.0071	140.8467	Vanuatu	Vatu	0.007	143.8267
0.077	12.97888	Venezuela	Bolivar Fuerte	0.0003	2921.779
0	29144.09	Vietnam	Dong	0	29988.88
0.0073	136.7713	Wallis & Futuna Islands	CFP Franc	0.0074	135.7138
0.3109	3.216367	Western Samoa	Tala	0.303	3.300658
0.0031	320.9799	Yemen (Rep of)	Rial	0.003	330.2591
0.0821	12.18463	Zambia	Kwacha	0.0798	12.5313
0.0022	464.2023	Zimbabwe	Dollar	0.0021	477.5865

Note

This table is reproduced from information provided by HMRC (tinyurl.com/ExrYrASpt) and is Crown copyright.

Table of spot rates on 31 December 2017 and 31 March 2018					
31 December 2017		**Country/Currency**		**31 March 2018**	
Sterling value of Currency Unit £	**Currency Units per £1**	**Country**	**Unit of currency**	**Sterling value of Currency Unit £**	**Currency Units per £1**
0.5782	1.7295	Australia	AUD Dollar	0.5468	1.8288
0.59	1.6949	Canada	CAD Dollar	0.5529	1.8086
0.1192	8.3876	Denmark	DKK Krone	0.1176	8.5022
0.8876	1.1266	European Community	EUR Euro	0.8767	1.1406
0.0946	10.57	Hong Kong	HKD Dollar	0.0909	11
0.0066	152.38	Japan	JPY Yen	0.0067	149.18
0.0904	11.06	Norway	NOK Krone	0.0908	11.01
0.0597	16.74	South Africa	ZAR Rand	0.0602	16.62
0.0903	11.07	Sweden	SEK Krona	0.0852	11.74
0.7586	1.3183	Switzerland	CHF Franc	0.7444	1.3433
0.7392	1.3528	USA	USD Dollar	0.7129	1.4028

Notes

(1) This table is reproduced from information provided by HMRC (tinyurl.com/ExrYrASpt) and is Crown copyright.

RECOGNISED STOCK EXCHANGES

(*ITA 2007, s 1005*; *CTA 2010, s 1137*)

A 'recognised stock exchange' is one which is either:

- A recognised investment exchange designated as a recognised stock exchange by an order of the Commissioners for HMRC; or
- Any designated market outside the UK.

A recognised stock exchange within *ITA 2007, s 1005* is also treated as such for corporation tax purposes (*CTA 2010, s 1137(1)*).

Stock exchanges designated as recognised stock exchanges

Stock exchange	Date of recognition
The Athens Stock Exchange	14 June 1993
The Australian Stock Exchange (and any of its stock exchange subsidiaries)	22 September 1988
National Stock Exchange of Australia	19 June 2014
Bahamas International Securities Exchange (BISX)	19 April 2010
The Bermuda Stock Exchange	4 December 2007
The Bond Exchange of South Africa	16 April 2008
The Cayman Islands Stock Exchange	4 March 2004
The Colombo Stock Exchange	21 February 1972
The Copenhagen Stock Exchange	22 October 1970
The Cyprus Stock Exchange	22 June 2009
European Wholesale Securities market	18 January 2013
Euronext London	4 February 2015
Global Board of Trade	30 July 2013
Gibraltar (GSX Ltd)	16 August 2016
GXG Official List	16 May 2013
GXG Main Quote	23 September 2013
The Helsinki Stock Exchange	22 October 1970
The Iceland Stock Exchange	31 March 2006
NEX Exchange Ltd	25 April 2013
The Johannesburg Stock Exchange	22 October 1970
The Korea Stock Exchange	10 October 1994
The Kuala Lumpur Stock Exchange	10 October 1994
The London International Financial Futures and Options Exchange Administration and Management (LIFFE A&M)	26 September 2011
The London Stock Exchange	19 July 2007
The Malta Stock Exchange	29 December 2005
The Mexico Stock Exchange	10 October 1994
The MICEX Stock Exchange	5 January 2011
NASDAQ OMX Tallinn (except its First North market)	5 May 2010
NASDAQ OMX Vilnius (except securities quoted solely on its First North market)	12 March 2012
The New Zealand Stock Exchange	22 September 1988
The Plus-listed Market	19 July 2007
The Rio De Janeiro Stock Exchange	17 August 1995
The Sao Paulo Stock Exchange	11 December 1995
The Singapore Stock Exchange	30 June 1977
Singapore Exchange Securities	7 October 2014
The Stockholm Stock Exchange	16 July 1985

Stock exchange	Date of recognition
The Stock Exchange of Mauritius	31 January 2011
The Stock Exchange of Thailand	10 October 1994
The Swiss Stock Exchange	12 May 1997
The Warsaw Stock Exchange	25 February 2010

Recognised stock exchange countries

The following are countries where any stock exchange in that country that is a stock exchange within the law of that country is a recognised stock exchange.

Stock exchange	Date of recognition
Austria	22 October 1970
Belgium	22 October 1970
Canada	22 October 1970
France	22 October 1970
Germany	5 August 1971
Guernsey	10 December 2013 (note 2)
Hong Kong	26 February 1971
Ireland (Republic of)	22 October 1970
Italy	3 May 1972
Japan	22 October 1970
Luxembourg	21 February 1972
Netherlands	22 October 1970
Norway	22 October 1970
Portugal	21 February 1972
Spain	5 August 1971
USA	See note 1

Notes

(1) *USA* – A stock exchange in the USA is a recognised stock exchange for UK tax purposes if it meets the following criteria:

> 'Any exchange registered with the Securities and Exchange Commission of the United States (SEC) as a national securities exchange under Section 6 of the Securities Exchange Act of 1934 is a recognised stock exchange for UK tax purposes.'

(2) *Channel Islands* – The Channel Islands Stock Exchange restructured on 20 December 2013 with the business of the exchange being transferred to The Channel Islands Securities Exchange Authority Limited.

Alternative finance investment bonds

(*ITA 2007 s 564G*)

The following is a list of recognised stock exchanges designated solely for the purposes of *ITA 2007, s 564G* (alternative finance arrangements: investment bonds). The date of recognition in all cases is 1 April 2007:

- Abu Dhabi Securities Market
- Bahrain Stock Exchange
- Dubai Financial Market
- NASDAQ Dubai (formerly Dubai International Financial Exchange)
- Labuan International Financial Exchange
- Saudi Stock Exchange (Tadawul)
- Surabaya Stock Exchange

Recognised futures exchanges

(*TCGA 1992, s 288(6)*)

Tax year of recognition	Exchange
1985/86	ICE Futures (formerly: International Petroleum Exchange London) The London Metal Exchange (IME) The London Rubber Market The London Gold Market The London Silver Market
1986/87	The Chicago Mercantile Exchange The Philadelphia Board of Trade The New York Mercantile Exchange
1987/88	The Chicago Board of Trade The Montreal Exchange The Mid America Commodity Exchange The Hong Kong Futures Exchange The New York Board of Trade (NYBOT)
1988/89	The Commodity Exchange, Inc (COMEX) The Citrus Associates of the New York Cotton Exchange, Inc The New York Cotton Exchange The Sydney Futures Exchange Ltd
1991/92	London International Financial Futures and Options Exchange (LIFFE) OM London OM Stockholm AB
2015/16	Eurex Deutschland

Notes

(1) Recognised futures exchange means the London International Financial Futures Exchange and any other futures exchange which is designated (for the purposes of *TCGA 1992*) by order of the Board.

(2) The above exchanges are accepted as recognised futures exchanges for the tax year of recognition onwards (CG56120).

Recognised investment exchanges

(*ITEPA 2003, s 702*)

Date of recognition	Exchange
22 November 2001	ICE Futures Europe
11 July 2013	Cboe Europe Limited (formerly BATS trading)
2 June 2014	Euronext London Limited
19 July 2007	NEX Exchange (formerly ICAP Securities & Derivatives Exchange Limited)
22 November 2001	London Stock Exchange plc
22 November 2001	The London Metal Exchange Limited

Recognised overseas investment exchanges

(*ITEPA 2003, s 702*)

Date of recognition	Exchange
30 January 2002	Australian Securities Exchange Limited
23 November 2001	Chicago Board of Trade (CBOT)
23 November 2001	EUREX [Switzerland]
23 November 2001	National Association of Securities Dealers Automated Quotations (NASDAQ)
23 November 2001	New York Mercantile Exchange Inc. [NYMEX Inc.]
23 November 2001	SIX Swiss Exchange AG
23 November 2001	The Chicago Mercantile Exchange [CME]

Notes for recognised investment and overseas investment exchanges

(1) Source: The Financial Services Register: (www.fsa.gov.uk/register/exchanges.do).

(2) The definition of 'readily convertible asset' (*ITEPA 2003, s 702*) includes an asset capable of being sold or otherwise realised on a recognised investment exchange, within the meaning of the *Financial Services and Markets Act 2000*. The Financial Conduct Authority recognises and supervises a number of recognised overseas investment exchanges.

DOUBLE TAXATION AGREEMENTS

(*TIOPA 2010, Pt 2, Ch 1*)

Countries with a Double Taxation Agreement with the UK

Country	Authority	Coverage
Albania	SI 2013/3145	C
Algeria	SI 1984/362 SI 2015/1888	ATP C
Antigua & Barbuda	SRO 1947/2865 Amended by SI 1968/1096	C
Argentina	SI 1997/1777 Amended by Protocol of 3 January 1996	C
Armenia	SI 2011/2722	C
Australia	SI 2003/3199	C
Austria	SI 1970/1947 Amended by Protocols SI 1979/117, SI 1994/768 and SI 2010/2688	C
Azerbaijan	SI 1995/762	C
Bahrain	SI 2012/3075	C
Bangladesh	SI 1980/708	C
Barbados	SI 2012/3076	C
Belarus	SI 1974/1269 replaced by: SI 2018/778	C C
Belgium	SI 1987/2053 Amended by Protocol SI 2010/2979	C
Belize	SRO 1947/2866 Amended by Protocols SI 1968/573 and SI 1973/2097	C
Bolivia	SI 1995/2707	C
Bosnia-Herzegovina	SI 1981/1815	C
Botswana	SI 2006/1925	C
Brazil	SI 1968/572	S, ATP
British Virgin Islands	SI 2009/3013	IT
Brunei Darussalam	SI 1950/1977 Amended by Protocols SI 1968/306 and SI 1973/2098 brought into effect by SI 2013/3146	C
Bulgaria	SI 1987/2054 SI 2015/1890	C
Cameroon	SI 1982/1841	ATP
Canada	SI 1980/709 Amended by Protocols SI 1980/1528, SI 1985/1996 and SI 2003/2619 SI 2015/2011	C
Cayman Islands	SI 2010/2973	IT

Country	Authority	Coverage
Chile	SI 2003/3200	C
China	SI 1981/1119 (not superseded)	ATP
	SI 2011/2724	C
	Amended by Protocol, SI 2013/3142	
Colombia	SI 2018/377	C
Croatia	SI 1981/1815	C
	SI 2015/1889	
Cyprus	SI 1975/425	C
	Replaced by: SI 2018/839	
Czech Republic	SI 1991/2876	C
Denmark	SI 1980/1960	C
	Amended by Protocols SI 1991/2877 and SI 1996/3165	
Egypt	SI 1980/1091	C
Estonia	SI 1994/3207	C
Ethiopia	SI 2011/2725	ATP C
Falkland Islands	SI 1997/2985	C
Faroes	SI 2007/3469	C
Fiji	SI 1976/1342	C
Finland	SI 1970/153	C
	Amended by Protocols SI 1973/1327, SI 1980/710, SI 1985/1997, 1991/2878 and 1996/3166	
France	SI 2009/226	C
	SI 2012/458	B
Gambia	SI 1980/1963	C
Georgia	SI 2004/3325	C
	Amended by Protocol SI 2010/2972	
Germany	SI 2010/2975	C
	SI 2012/459	B
	Amended by Protocol SI 2014/1874	
Ghana	SI 1993/1800	C
Greece	SI 1954/142	C
Grenada	SI 1949/361	C
	Amended by Protocol SI 1968/1867	
Guernsey	SI 1952/1215	C
	Amended by Protocol SI 1994/3209, Supplementary Arrangement SI 2009/3011 SI 2015/2008, SI 2016/750	
Guyana	SI 1992/3207	C
Hong Kong	SI 2010/2974 including Protocol	C
Hungary	SI 2011/2726	C
Iceland	SI 1991/2879	C
India	SI 1993/1801 plus Protocol SI 2013/3147	C

continued

Country	Authority	Coverage
Indonesia	SI 1994/769	C
Iran	SI 1960/2419	ATP
Ireland	SI 1976/2151 Amended by Protocols SI 1976/2152, SI 1995/764 and SI 1998/3151	C
Isle of Man	SI 1955/1205 Amended by Supplementary Arrangements SI 1991/2880, SI 1994/3208, SI 2009/228 and SI 2016/749 and exchange of letters in 2013	C
Israel	SI 1963/616 Amended by Protocol – SI 1971/391	C
Italy	SI 1990/2590	C
Ivory Coast	SI 1987/169	C
Jamaica	SI 1973/1329	C
Japan	SI 2006/1924	C
Jersey	SI 1952/1216 Amended by Arrangements SI 1994/3210 and SI 2009/3012, SI 2015/2009 and SI 2016/752	C
Jordan	SI 2001/3924	C
Kazakhstan	SI 1994/3211 Amended by Protocol SI 1998/2567	C
Kenya	SI 1977/1299	C
Kiribati	SI 1950/750 Amended by Arrangements SI 1968/309 and SI 1974/1271	C
Korea (Republic of)	SI 1996/3168	C
Kosovo	SI 2015/2007	C
Kuwait	SI 1999/2036	C
Latvia	SI 1996/3167	C
Lebanon	SI 1964/278	S, ATP
Lesotho	SI 1997/2986 SI 2018/376	C
Libya	SI 2010/243	C
Liechtenstein	SI 2012/3077	C
Lithuania	SI 2001/3925 Amended by Protocol SI 2002/2847	C
Luxembourg	SI 1968/1100 Amended by Protocols SI 1980/567, SI 1984/364 and SI 2010/237	C
Macedonia	SI 2007/2127	C
Malawi	SI 1956/619 Amended by Protocols SI 1964/1401, SI 1968/1101 and SI 1979/302	C
Malaysia	SI 1997/2987, SI 2010/2971	C

Country	Authority	Coverage
Malta	SI 1995/763	C
Mauritius	SI 1981/1121 replaced by SI 2018/840	C
Mexico	SI 1994/3212 Amended by Protocol SI 2010/2686	C
Moldova	SI 2008/1795	C
Mongolia	SI 1996/2598	C
Montenegro	SI 1981/1815	C
Montserrat	SRO 1947/2869 Amended by Protocol SI 1968/576 SI 2011/1083	C
Morocco	SI 1991/2881	C
Myanmar (Burma)	SI 1952/751 including Protocol	C
Namibia	SI 1962/2352 Extended by SI 1962/2788 – Amended by Protocol SI 1967/1489 as extended by SI 1967/1490	C
Netherlands	SI 2009/227 amended by Protocol SI 2013/3143 SI 2015/344 Bank Levy double taxation	C
New Zealand	SI 1984/365 Amended by Protocols SI 2004/1274, SI 2008/1973	C
Nigeria	SI 1987/2057	C
Norway	SI 2013/3144	C
Oman	SI 1998/2568 Amended by Protocol SI 2010/2687	C
Pakistan	SI 1987/2058	C
Panama	SI 2013/3149	C
Papua New Guinea	SI 1991/2882	C
Philippines	SI 1978/184	C
Poland	SI 2006/3323	C
Portugal	SI 1969/599	C
Qatar	SI 2010/241, SI 2011/1684	C
Romania	SI 1977/57	C
Russia	SI 1994/3213	C
St. Christopher (St. Kitts) and Nevis	SRO 1947/2872	C
Saudi Arabia	SI 1994/767 (not superseded) SI 2008/1770 including Protocol	ATP C
Senegal	SI 2015/1892	C
Serbia	SI 1981/1815	C

continued

Country	Authority	Coverage
Sierra Leone	SRO 1947/2873 Amended by Protocol SI 1968/1104	C
Singapore	SI 1997/2988 Amended by Protocols SI 2010/2685 and SI 2012/3078	C
Slovak Republic	SI 1991/2876	C
Slovenia	SI 2008/1796	C
Solomon Islands	SI 1950/748 Amended by Arrangements SI 1968/574 and SI 1974/1270	C
South Africa	SI 2002/3138 Amended by Protocol SI 2011/2441	C
Spain	SI 2013/3152	C
Sri Lanka	SI 1980/713	C
Sudan	SI 1977/1719	C
Swaziland	SI 1969/380	C
Sweden	SI 2015/1891	C
Switzerland	SI 1978/1408 Amended by Protocols SI 1982/714, SI 1994/3215, SI 2007/3465, SI 2010/2689 and exchange of letters from 19 December 2012. SI 2018/627	C
Taiwan	SI 2002/3137	C
Tajikistan	SI 2014/3275	ATP C
Thailand	SI 1981/1546	C
Trinidad and Tobago	SI 1983/1903	C
Tunisia	SI 1984/133	C
Turkey	SI 1988/932	C
Turkmenistan	SI 1986/224 SI 2016/1217	ATP C
Tuvalu	SI 1950/750 Amended by SI 1968/309 and SI 1974/1271	C
UAE	SI 2016/754	C
Uganda	SI 1993/1802	C
Ukraine	SI 1993/1803	C
Uruguay	SI 2016/753	C
USA	SI 2002/2848 including Protocol and Exchange of Notes	C
Uzbekistan	SI 1994/770 replaced by: SI 2018/628	C
Venezuela	SI 1996/2599	C

Country	Authority	Coverage
Vietnam	SI 1994/3216	C
Zaire	SI 1977/1298	S, ATP
Zambia	SI 2014/1876	C
Zimbabwe	SI 1982/1842	C

Notes

(1) Key to coverage of agreements:

ATP Air Transport Profits

B Bank Levy

C Comprehensive

S Shipping Profits

IT Income taxes only

(2) *Multilateral Instrument (MLI)* – This was signed on 7 July 2017 and will have effect for UK tax treaties from:

- 1 January 2019 for taxes withheld at source;
- 1 April 2019 for corporation tax; and
- 6 April 2019 for income tax and capital gains tax.

The date which individual UK tax treaties are modified by the MLI depends on the date the treaty partner deposits their own instruments of ratification, acceptance or approval.

(3) *Further information* – Full collection of Double Taxation Treaties: www.gov.uk/government/collections/tax-treaties, MLI: tinyurl.com/y79h46tr, and HMRC's Double Taxation Relief Manual DT2140 et seq.

DTAs signed but not in force

(1) *Brazil* – An agreement to avoid the double taxation of the salaries of members of the crew of aircraft operated in international traffic was signed in Brasilia on 2 September 2010.

(2) *Belgium* – Second Protocol to the Double Taxation Convention was signed on 14 March 2014.

(3) *Anguilla* – Exchange of letters were signed on 20 December 2013.

(4) *Ukraine* – Protocol to Double Taxation Convention signed on 9 October 2017.

(5) *Switzerland* – Protocol to Double Taxation Convention signed on 30 November 2017.

(6) *Austria* – Double Taxation Agreement signed 23 October 2018.

(7) *Kyrgyzstan* – Double Taxation Relief and International Tax Enforcement.

Double Taxation Conventions (DTCs): Inheritance Tax

(*IHTA 1984, s 158*; IHTM 27161 et seq)

Country	Authority
France	SI 1963/1319
India	SI 1956/998
Ireland	SI 1978/1107
Italy	SI 1968/304
Netherlands	SI 1980/706 Amended by Protocol SI 1996/730
Pakistan	SI 1957/1522
South Africa	SI 1979/576
Sweden	SI 1981/840 Amended by Protocol SI 1989/986
Switzerland	SI 1994/3214 including Protocol
USA	SI 1979/1454

Note

The UK Government may enter into a DTC with the Government of any territory outside the UK. Where the deceased was domiciled in a DTC territory or owned property situate in one of those territories, the terms of the relevant DTC should be considered in relation to IHT and any tax imposed by the laws of that territory which is of a similar character or is chargeable by reference to death or gifts made *inter vivos* (*IHTA 1984, s 158;* IHTM27161).

Tax Information Exchange Agreements (TIEAs)

TIEAs in force

An updated list of TIEAs in force is available at: tinyurl.com/TIEAIF.

Country	Authority	Scope
Anguilla	SI 2010/2677 SI 2014/1357	B NR
Antigua and Barbuda	SI 2011/1075	B
Aruba	SI 2011/2435	R
Bahamas	SI 2010/2684	B
Bermuda	SI 2018/518	B
Belize	SI 2011/1685	B
British Virgin Islands	SI 2005/1457 SI 2009/3013	R B
Cayman Islands	Agreement effective 16 April 2005	NR
Curaçao, Sint Maarten and BES Islands	SI 2011/2433	B
Dominica	SI 2011/1686	B

Country	Authority	Scope
Gibraltar	SI 2006/1453	R
	SI 2010/2680	B
Grenada	SI 2011/1687	B
Guernsey	SI 2009/3011	B
Isle of Man	SI 2005/1263	R
	SI 2009/228	B
Jersey	SI 2009/3012	B
Liberia	SI 2011/2434	B
Liechtenstein	SI 2010/2678	B
Montserrat	SI 2005/1459	R
Monaco	SI 2015/804	B
Netherlands Antilles	SI 2005/1460	B
San Marino	SI 2011/1688	B
St Christopher (St Kitts) and Nevis	SI 2011/1077	B
St Lucia	SI 2011/1076	B
St Vincent and the Grenadines	SI 2011/1078	B
Turks and Caicos Islands	SI 2010/2679	B
		NR
Uruguay	SI 2014/1358	B

Notes

Key to scope of TIEAs:

B Bilateral agreements for co-operation in tax matters through exchange of information

NR Non-reciprocal Agreements relating to the EU Directive on taxation of savings income in the form of interest payments

R Reciprocal Agreements relating to the EU Directive on taxation of savings income in the form of interest payments

TIEAs signed/not in force

Country	Signed
Turks & Caicos Islands	26 November 2013
British Virgin Islands	28 November 2013
Guernsey	22 October 2013
Jersey	22 October 2013
Marshall Islands	17 September and 26 October 2012
Brazil	2012

Index